Hillel Schmid, PhD
Editor

Organizational and Structural Dilemmas in Nonprofit Human Service Organizations

Organizational and Structural Dilemmas in Nonprofit Human Service Organizations has been co-published simultaneously as *Administration in Social Work,* Volume 28, Numbers 3/4 2004.

Pre-publication REVIEWS, COMMENTARIES, EVALUATIONS . . .

"**A** RICH AND ECLECTIC OVERVIEW OF CONTEMPORARY ISSUES. . . . Readers will find useful analyses of congregations as providers of social services and nonprofits as providers of welfare to work services among the many topics. This book gives a good sense of the very wide range of issues facing human services organizations and of the scholarship that attempts to understand those issues. The collection is almost as diverse as the nonprofit human services sector it portrays."

Elizabeth T. Boris, PhD
Director
Center on Nonprofits and Philanthropy
Urban Institute
Washington, DC

The Haworth Social Work Practice Press
An Imprint of The Haworth Press, Inc.

New York • London • Victoria (AU)
www.HaworthPress.com

Organizational and Structural Dilemmas in Nonprofit Human Service Organizations

Organizational and Structural Dilemmas in Nonprofit Human Service Organizations has been co-published simultaneously as *Administration in Social Work*, Volume 28, Numbers 3/4 2004.

The *Administration in Social Work* Monographic "Separates"

Below is a list of "separates," which in serials librarianship means a special issue simultaneously published as a special journal issue or double-issue *and* as a "separate" hardbound monograph. (This is a format which we also call a "DocuSerial.")

"Separates" are published because specialized libraries or professionals may wish to purchase a specific thematic issue by itself in a format which can be separately cataloged and shelved, as opposed to purchasing the journal on an on-going basis. Faculty members may also more easily consider a "separate" for classroom adoption.

"Separates" are carefully classified separately with the major book jobbers so that the journal tie-in can be noted on new book order slips to avoid duplicate purchasing.

You may wish to visit Haworth's website at . . .

http://www.HaworthPress.com

. . . to search our online catalog for complete tables of contents of these separates and related publications.

You may also call 1-800-HAWORTH (outside US/Canada: 607-722-5857), or Fax 1-800-895-0582 (outside US/Canada: 607-771-0012), or e-mail at:

docdelivery@haworthpress.com

Organizational and Structural Dilemmas in Nonprofit Human Service Organizations, edited by Hillel Schmid, PhD (Vol. 28, No. 3/4, 2004). *Organizational and Structural Dilemmas in Non-Profit Human Service Organizations explores the common pitfalls that plague nonprofit human service organizations and cause them to fail in their missions. In this book, leading scholars analyze and evaluate the inherent difficulties that impede effectiveness in these organizations and offer solutions for repairing or preventing any permanent damage. This wide-ranging body of knowledge, research findings, and information will help you set successful long-term strategies for your organization, despite changes in laws, programs, and public sentiment.*

Social Services in the Workplace: Repositioning Occupational Social Work in the New Millennium, edited by Michàl E. Mor Barak, PhD, and David Bargal, PhD (Vol. 23, No. 3/4, 2000). *This volume will help social workers meet the challenges that the changes in the world of work today present. These challenges present new opportunities for you as a social work professional in general and for the field of occupational social work in particular. Through this unique book, you will discover the need for an increase in the provision of social work services to individuals who are employed, in need of employment, or in transitional situations, to their families, and to work organizations and, more importantly, ideas on how they can meet this challenge.*

Human Services Integration, edited by Michael J. Austin, PhD (Vol. 21, No. 3/4, 1997). *Addresses the multiple meanings of service integration and represents an important effort to take a look at some lessons learned.*

Organizational Change and Development in Human Service Organizations, edited by David Bargal, PhD, and Hillel Schmid, PhD (Vol. 16, No. 3/4, 1993). *Describes and analyzes recent research on organizational change and development in the social and human services to help readers better understand the process of change and the role of the environment in creating change.*

Community Organization and Social Administration: Advances, Trends, and Emerging Principles, edited by Terry Mizrahi, PhD, and John Morrison, DSW (Supp. #04, 1993). *"A blend of research and practical significance in the critical area of societal organization for today and tomorrow." (Journal of the American Association of Psychiatric Administrators)*

Efficiency and the Social Services, edited by Robert Pruger, DSW (Vol. 15, No. 1/2, 1991). *"A timely reminder that social work, in an era of decreased spending, cannot afford to ignore the economic realities of making scarce resources reach as far as possible." (The Indian Journal of Social Work)*

Administrative Leadership in the Social Services: The Next Challenge, edited by Yeheskel Hasenfeld, PhD (Vol. 13, No. 3/4, 1990). *"This excellent book makes an outstanding contribution to knowledge and should win an appreciative audience in several academic disciplines and professional practice fields." (Barry Checkoway, PhD, Associate Professor, School of Social Work, University of Michigan)*

Alternative Social Agencies: Administrative Strategies, edited by Felice Davidson Perlmutter, PhD (Vol. 12, No. 2, 1989). *"This is an excellent book. . . . Anyone who practices, teaches, or studies social work can benefit from what this book provides." (Administration in Social Work)*

Managing for Service Effectiveness in Social Welfare Organizations, edited by Rino J. Patti, DSW, John Poertner, DSW, and Charles A. Rapp, PhD (Vol. 11, No. 3/4, 1988). *"Exceptionally helpful to both managers and those who teach management to graduate social work students." (Journal of Teaching in Social Work)*

Practice Issues in Social Welfare Administration, Policy and Planning, edited by Milton M. Lebowitz, PhD (Vol. 6, No. 2/3, 1982). *"Rich with ideas that can stimulate social work leaders to press for solutions. . . . Highly recommended to all educators in macro practice and to practitioners in policy and planning positions." (Journal of Education for Social Work)*

Applying Computers in Social Service and Mental Health Agencies: A Guide to Selecting Equipment, Procedures, and Strategies, edited by Simon Slavin, EdD, ACSW (Vol. 5, No. 3/4, 1982). *"If your agency is thinking about computerizing, don't take another step until you read this book! . . . An invaluable overview of issues and strategies arising from any consideration of computer use in social agencies. . . . A very useful book for administrators to have on their shelves." (The Social Worker)*

Guide to Ethical Decisions and Actions for Social Service Administrators: A Handbook for Managerial Personnel, by Charles S. Levy (Supp #01, 1982). *"A very useful tool for adminisrators and teachers of administration, who will find its reminders and cautions helpful and necessary . . . to improve the ethical awareness that should inform their practice." (The Jewish Social Work Forum)*

Published by

The Haworth Social Work Practice Press, 10 Alice Street, Binghamton, NY 13904-1580 USA

The Haworth Social Work Practice Press is an imprint of The Haworth Press, Inc., 10 Alice Street, Binghamton, NY 13904-1580 USA.

Organizational and Structural Dilemmas in Nonprofit Human Service Organizations has been co-published simultaneously as *Administration in Social Work,* Volume 28, Numbers 3/4 2004.

The development, preparation, and publication of this work has been undertaken with great care. However, the publisher, employees, editors, and agents of The Haworth Press and all imprints of The Haworth Press, Inc., including The Haworth Medical Press® and The Pharmaceutical Products Press®, are not responsible for any errors contained herein or for consequences that may ensue from use of materials or information contained in this work. Opinions expressed by the author(s) are not necessarily those of The Haworth Press, Inc.

Cover design by Kerry E. Mack

Library of Congress Cataloging-in-Publication Data

Organizational and structural dilemmas in nonprofit human service organizations / Hillel Schmid, editor.
    p. cm.
    "Co-published simultaneously as Administration in Social Work, Volume 28, Numbers 3/4 2004."
    Includes bibliographical references and index.
    ISBN 0-7890-2550-7 (cloth : alk. paper)–ISBN 0-7890-2551-5 (pbk.: alk. paper)
    1. Social service. 2. Nonprofit organizations. 3. Non-governmental organizations. I. Schmid, Hillel. II. Administration in social work.
HV40 .0693 2004
361.7′63′0684–dc22   2004001421

Organizational
and Structural Dilemmas
in Nonprofit
Human Service Organizations

Hillel Schmid, PhD
Editor

Organizational and Structural Dilemmas in Nonprofit Human Service Organizations has been co-published simultaneously as *Administration in Social Work*, Volume 28, Numbers 3/4 2004.

The Haworth Social Work Practice Press
An Imprint of The Haworth Press, Inc.

New York • London • Victoria (AU)
www.HaworthPress.com

Indexing, Abstracting & Website/Internet Coverage

This section provides you with a list of major indexing & abstracting services. That is to say, each service began covering this periodical during the year noted in the right column. Most Websites which are listed below have indicated that they will either post, disseminate, compile, archive, cite or alert their own Website users with research-based content from this work. (This list is as current as the copyright date of this publication.)

(continued)

(continued)

Special Bibliographic Notes related to special journal issues (separates) and indexing/abstracting:

- indexing/abstracting services in this list will also cover material in any "separate" that is co-published simultaneously with Haworth's special thematic journal issue or DocuSerial. Indexing/abstracting usually covers material at the article/chapter level.
- monographic co-editions are intended for either non-subscribers or libraries which intend to purchase a second copy for their circulating collections.
- monographic co-editions are reported to all jobbers/wholesalers/approval plans. The source journal is listed as the "series" to assist the prevention of duplicate purchasing in the same manner utilized for books-in-series.
- to facilitate user/access services all indexing/abstracting services are encouraged to utilize the co-indexing entry note indicated at the bottom of the first page of each article/chapter/contribution.
- this is intended to assist a library user of any reference tool (whether print, electronic, online, or CD-ROM) to locate the monographic version if the library has purchased this version but not a subscription to the source journal.
- individual articles/chapters in any Haworth publication are also available through the Haworth Document Delivery Service (HDDS).

Organizational and Structural Dilemmas in Nonprofit Human Service Organizations

CONTENTS

ABOUT THE EDITOR

Hillel Schmid, PhD, is a senior faculty member at the Hebrew University of Jerusalem. Professor Schmid's field of expertise is the policy and management of nonprofit organizations providing human, social and community services. His research interests include: (a) organization-environment relations and strategies of adaptation to changing environments; (b) the managerial and administrative processes in nonprofit organizations; (c) organizational strategy and structure in human service organizations; (d) executive leadership in non- and for-profit organizations providing human services; (e) organizational change and organizational development.

Professor Schmid's most important studies are in the fields of community-centers and neighborhood self-management, the implications of the Long-Term Care Insurance Law on the organizational behavior of for-profit and nonprofit organizations delivering home care services to the frail elderly and organizational and structural patterns in nonprofit organizations providing services to children, the finding of which have been published in professional journals. His book "Community Centers: Trends and Changes" was published (in Hebrew) in 1997, and his book "Neighborhood Self-Management/Experiments in Civil Society" was published by Plenum/Kluwer in 2001. Professor Schmid has also published articles, research studies, and monographs on the topic of the management of social welfare and community organizations in the professional literature both locally in Israel and abroad. He currently serves as the associate editor in *Nonprofit Management* and *Leadership and Administration in Social Work*, leading journals in the area of management of nonprofit organizations. Professor Schmid is a member of various international professional associations and regularly presents his research findings at conferences in the U.S., the UK and Europe.

Professor Schmid was the founder and director of the first graduate MA program in Management of Community and Nonprofit Organizations and Public Policy at the Paul Baerwald School of Social Work. In 1999/2000, Professor Schmid was awarded the Rector's Prize for excellence in his research and instruction and for his active involvement in the academic livelihood and the Hebrew University of Jerusalem. Professor Schmid currently serves as the Centraid-L. Jaques Ménard Chair in Social Work for the Study of Volunteer and Nonprofit Organizations and as of October 2003 serves as a Dean of the Paul Baerwald School of Social Work.

The Role of Nonprofit Human Service Organizations in Providing Social Services: A Prefatory Essay

Hillel Schmid, PhD

SUMMARY. The essay presents the recent developments in nonprofit human service organizations that belong to the "third sector." The author describes and analyzes the changing context of human services, in which a new division of labor has emerged between the government and nongovernmental organizations, including nonprofit and for-profit service providers. "Demand and supply" theories are presented, in order to explain the mission, goals, and roles of nonprofit human service providers and their contribution to the state economy. Finally, the author explores the extent to which these organizations actualize their ideology in a society characterized by growing inequality, and by widening social and economic gaps between "haves" and "have nots." *[Article copies available for a fee from The Haworth Document Delivery Service: 1-800-HAWORTH. E-mail address: <docdelivery@ haworthpress.com> Website: <http://www.HaworthPress.com> © 2004 by The Haworth Press, Inc. All rights reserved.]*

KEYWORDS. Nonprofit human service organizations, government failure theory, contract failure theory, third-party government theory,

---

Hillel Schmid is affiliated with the School of Social Work, The Hebrew University of Jerusalem, Mt. Scopus, Jerusalem 91905 Israel (E-mail: mshsmid@mscc.huji.ac.il).

[Haworth co-indexing entry note]: "The Role of Nonprofit Human Service Organizations in Providing Social Services: A Prefatory Essay." Schmid, Hillel. Co-published simultaneously in *Administration in Social Work* (The Haworth Social Work Practice Press, an imprint of The Haworth Press, Inc.) Vol. 28, No. 3/4, 2004, pp. 1-21; and: *Organizational and Structural Dilemmas in Nonprofit Human Service Organizations* (ed: Hillel Schmid) The Haworth Social Work Practice Press, an imprint of The Haworth Press, Inc., 2004, pp. 1-21. Single or multiple copies of this article are available for a fee from The Haworth Document Delivery Service [1-800-HAWORTH, 9:00 a.m. - 5:00 p.m. (EST). E-mail address: docdelivery@ haworthpress.com].

1

entrepreneurship theory, trustworthiness, disguised nonprofits, shadow government

Over the past decade, there has been growing research interest in nonprofit organizations that are part of the "third sector," even though the suitability of that term has been questioned (Kramer, 2000). Recent studies have explored the role and functioning of nonprofit service providers in modern societies from various perspectives. Theoretical and empirical investigations have dealt with the activities of these organizations, as well as with their contribution toward building a civil society, their role vis-a-vis the government, their relations with for-profit organizations, and their efforts to improve service quality for the benefit of their clients (Eisenberg, 2000; Hammack, 2001). Research institutions and academic and nonacademic programs have been established in the United States, England, and several countries in Western Europe, as well as in Japan, Australia, Israel, and third world countries. Furthermore, professional journals have published research and scholarly articles on social, political, economic, technological, and other issues that relate to the functioning of these organizations and their role in providing social, human, and other services (DiMaggio, Weiss, & Clotfelter, 2002; DiMaggio & Anheier, 1990).

What are the causes for the tremendous growth and expansion of nonprofit organizations, and the increase in the scope of their activities? Why has there been heightened public and research interest in this topic, when voluntary nonprofit organizations existed way before professionals became concerned with them? Is it because of the government's policy of encouraging their establishment, or is it because of social entrepreneurs who seek to establish organizations which will promote ideas that they cannot implement through the governmental system or through market mechanisms? Or has the government's role in providing social, educational, and health services declined to the point where there is a vacuum that social entrepreneurs are attempting to fill in order to promote post-modernist ideologies? These entrepreneurs seek to contribute toward developing civil society on the one hand, while caring for the well-being of needy and at-risk populations on the other. There are those who claim that governments have failed to provide services to all citizens, and others who claim that governments have neglected their responsibility for the well-being of their citizens. These questions concern many social scientists, especially in light of the rapid changes in the task environments of governmental agencies, and the impact of the changes on their functioning and on their ability to promote the well-being of their citizens (Ben-Ner, 1986).

THE CHANGING CONTEXTS OF NONPROFIT
HUMAN SERVICE ORGANIZATIONS

Nonprofit human service organizations have witnessed major changes over the past two decades.

First, governments in the Western world as well as in other countries have shown an increasing tendency to diminish their role in the provision of social services. This trend can be attributed to several motives, some of which are ideological while others are utilitarian and economic. The ideology that has led to the change in government policy is based on the concept of self reliance, which entails a redefinition of the rights and obligations of citizens toward the state. Even though the state has obligations to its citizens, liberal ideology emphasizes that citizens are obligated to contribute their share to the state. Moreover, according to this ideology, citizens cannot rely only on government services or on sources of government funding to support them. Rather, they need to develop independent sources of income that will enable them to purchase the services they need. In the worst case, the state will serve as a safety net for the weakest strata of society that cannot cope and solve their own problems or satisfy their own needs. From the utilitarian perspective, many countries have found that the burden of providing universal services is heavy, and creates deficits that can be avoided if the state allocates its resources more carefully and creates a new division of labor vis-a-vis other authorities that promote the well-being of citizens. It has also been argued that by transferring some of the traditional roles of the government to nonprofit or for-profit organizations, it will be possible to economize and achieve greater efficiency, in addition to reducing bureaucracy and administrative red-tape in provision of services. As a result, the organizations will be better able to respond to the needs of clients and to encourage innovative programs and new service technologies. In addition, transferring some traditional governmental functions to nongovernmental provider organizations undoubtedly serves some inherent interests of the government, such as: (1) creating a political climate that enables and justifies cuts in government programs; (2) laying the groundwork to charge clients directly for some expenses for services (health, welfare, education, housing, etc.); (3) protecting the government against public responses to budget cuts, and increasing the potential that nongovernmental organizations will serve as institutional intermediaries between the government and citizens. These inherent functions shift the accountability and responsibility for reporting about the availability accessibility, and quality of services from the government to nongovernmental organizations, thereby relieving the government of direct responsibility for the well-being of its citizens.

This trend intensified during the 1980s and 1990s, partially due to a significant decline in the political and public legitimation of the welfare state (Mishra, 1990). Among other causes, this decline can be attributed to pressure and economic crises, as well as to rising unemployment. The blame for these problems has largely been placed on the welfare state itself and on the beneficiaries of services, whom the opponents of the welfare state claim do not contribute anything to society. According to that perspective, the welfare state encourages parasitic behavior, so that citizens demand assistance and support from the state instead of relying on their own resources or trying to solve their own problems.

The continuous decline of the welfare state and the entry of nongovernmental organizations into the arena of service delivery (Austin, 2003) have also been accompanied by demographic processes such as aging of the population and a substantial increase in life expectancy, as well as by economic processes, such as the transition from a production economy to a service economy, and from an "old economy" to a "new economy." As a result of these transitions, many workers have joined the ranks of the unemployed and increased the burden of the government, which has had to deal with social pathologies such as crime, mental illness, addiction (to drugs and alcohol), family violence, and other non-normative behavior. The information revolution has also widened gaps between populations with higher education, who benefit from the new opportunities offered by the knowledge economy, and populations without appropriate education, who are pushed to the margins of society. For educated populations, international markets have taken the place of local markets. The international markets offer abundant professional opportunities, and give workers much greater mobility than in the past. By contrast, uneducated populations cannot compete in the new markets and have much less opportunity for employment and personal advancement. Hence, they become a burden to the state. All of these trends even increase the social gaps and inequality between different population groups, separating the "haves" from the "have nots" while the state ignores the problems of the needy. These trends have intensified under many governments in the Western world, whose declared policy encourages processes of new public management, decentralization, and devolution (Gronbjerg & Salamon, 2002). These processes aim to relieve the state of direct responsibility for service delivery, by transferring that function to peripheral units that maintain close ties with the client populations and provide solutions to their needs. The decentralization process has been political and administrative. On the political level, formal powers have been granted to the local authorities and community service organizations. With regard to administrative decentralization, local authorities and neighborhoods manage their affairs independently, and their autonomy has been strengthened with regard to decision-making and control of financial resources (Berger, Neuhaus, &

Novak, 1996; Schmid, 2001a). The practical manifestations of this process have been policies of contracting out social services (Cordes, Henig, & Twombly, 2001; Schmid, 2003; Smith & Lipsky, 1993; Taylor, 2002), privatization of government services, and incentives for voluntary nonprofit organizations and for-profit organizations to enter domains of service provision that were controlled almost exclusively by governmental agencies in the past (Austin, 2003; Tuckman, 1998).

NONPROFIT HUMAN SERVICE ORGANIZATIONS AND THEIR CONTRIBUTION TO THE STATE ECONOMY

Over the past decade, Professor Lester M. Salamon and his colleagues at Johns Hopkins University have engaged in efforts to define and categorize the different types of nonprofit organizations that belong to the third sector and to evaluate their contribution to the national economy. Their seminal work has been published in several publications that have made a lasting imprint on theory and research dealing with the role and functions of nonprofit organizations (Salamon, 2003; Salamon & Anheier, 1992, 1997; Salamon, Anheier, List, Toepler, & Sokolowski, 1999). According to their definition, nonprofit organizations include "thousands of private community groups, health clinics, schools, day care centers, environmental organizations, social clubs, development organizations, cultural institutions, professional associations, consumer groups, and similar entities that comprise what is increasingly coming to be known as the private or civil society sector" (Salamon et al., 1999, p. xvii).

According to Salamon and Anheier (1992), these organizations meet the following criteria:

a. formal or institutionalized to some extent;
b. private–institutionally separate from the government;
c. nonprofit distributing–not returning profits generated to their owners;
d. self-governing–equipped to control their own activities;
e. voluntary–involving some meaningful degree of voluntary participation.

They are legally defined as tax-exempt organizations, namely those that are eligible for exemption under either section 501(c)(3) or 401(c)(4) of the tax code (Hopkins, 1992).

In the domain of human services, nonprofit organizations include those that provide individual and family services (social counseling, welfare, or referral), job training (training, work experience, vocational or rehabilitative courses for the unemployed, underemployed, and physically challenged), day care (children and infants, and residential care (children, elderly, etc.)). There are also many faith-based organizations that are particularly involved in low-income communities, and that provide a variety of human services from housing to drug counseling, emergency food distribution, and employment assistance (Cnaan, 2002).

Following a survey of third sector organizations in 11 countries, Salamon et al. (1999) found that the nonprofit sector is an 11 trillion dollar industry that employs nearly 19 million full-time equivalent paid workers, and 10.6 million full-time equivalent volunteer workers, not including religious congregations. In the U.S., the estimation was that the total spending from all sources and by all types of entities amounted to 8% of the Gross Domestic Product. By comparison, the proportion of spending among third sector organizations in France, England, and Israel was estimated at 3.7%, 7%, and 12% of the GNP, respectively. The proportion of Full-Time Equivalent workers (FTEs) in third sector organizations was found to be about 8% in the United States, 4.5% in France, 6.2% in England, and 9.5% in Israel. With regard to provision of health and social services, it was found that third sector organizations comprise 59.8% of the market in the United States, 55.2% in France, 17.4% in England, and 84% in Israel (Salamon et al., 1999).

As for funding sources, Salamon et al. (1999) found that in the United States, 49% of the organizations' average revenue derives from fees, 43% from the public sector, and 11% from private philanthropy. With regard to funding of human services, private donations and other forms of philanthropic support accounted for 13% of the 74 billion dollars in total social services expenditures, whereas private fees and service charges (paid by individuals, employers, or insurance companies) accounted for almost 43%, followed by direct public spending (37%). Salamon et al. (1999) also found that the nonprofit sector dominates individual and family services (80%) and vocational rehabilitation agencies (70%), while it accounts for more than half of residential care facilities (55%) but less than a third of day care agencies (31%). By comparison, it should be mentioned that in France, third sector organizations derive 58% of their revenue from public, governmental, and municipal funding, while 7.5% derives from private sources and another 35% from sale of services. In England, third sector organizations derive 47% of their revenue from public funding, while 9% derives from private sources and 45% derives from sale of services. In Israel, revenue from public funding is 55%, compared with 5% from private sources and 26% from sale of services. Analysis of the data indicates that the nonprofit sector is larger in more developed countries than in developing and transitional economies. Western Europe emerges as the region with the most highly developed voluntary and nonprofit sector (Salamon et al., 1999, p. 12).

Government social welfare spending and the size of the nonprofit sector are positively correlated. Putnam (2000) found that across American states and across Organization for Economic Cooperation (OECD) nations, there is a positive correlation between size of government (or welfare) spending and various measures of social capital (voluntary group membership, social trust, etc.). In contrast to the nonprofit sector, the overall financial profile of the for-profit human service sector is unknown. According to Gronbjerg (2001), it is presumed to involve primary reliance on fees and service charges. Nonetheless, in an attempt to estimate the size of both sectors in social services, Frumkin (2002) calculated that from 1977 to 1997 the number of nonprofit social service providers (including individual and family services, job training and vocational rehabilitation, day care for children, and residential care) increased by 125%, while the number of for-profit providers increased by 202%. The respective increases in revenue amounted to 705% for nonprofits and 827% for for-profits. Moreover, during that period, there was an increase of 202% in the number of for-profit organizations that provided individual and family services, job training and vocational rehabilitation, day care for children, and residential care for the elderly (Frumkin, 2002, p. 68).

Using revenues as a measure of market share, the prominence of for-profit organizations varies by social service sector. In 1997, for-profit firms had 60% of all revenues in nursing and residential care, as well as a surprising 48% in emergency and other relief services (food, shelter, clothing, medical relief, resettlement, etc.), 40% in child care, 18% in vocational rehabilitation, and only 2% of individual and family services (U.S. Census Bureau, 1997). There are some notable examples of large corporations in the human services, including firms such as Kinder-Care, which operates over 1,250 learning centers that serve over 120,000 children between the ages of six weeks and 12 years, with a revenue of over 250 million dollars in 2002. In the field of correction services, privately owned and managed prisons have become a big industry. Correction corporations of America is responsible for 54,000 inmates in 60 facilities (37 are company-owned) in 21 states, and their revenue amounted to over 700 million dollars in 2002 (Karger & Stoesz, 2002). Clearly, the growth of these organizations is impressive and has had a strong impact on provision, availability, and quality of services. The following section will present the theoretical perspectives that explain the growth of these organizations and their role and function in the modern world.

THEORETICAL APPROACHES ON THE ROLE OF NONPROFIT ORGANIZATIONS

Several theories have attempted to explain the emergence of nonprofit human service providers as well as the trends described at the beginning of this chapter. In general, the relatively new theories can be categorized as "demand" theories, which focus on clients (the party that demands services) versus "supply" theories, which focus on providers (the party that "supplies" services). The demand theories explain why clients want services from nonprofit organizations and are willing to pay for those services. The supply theories describe the motivation and incentives that encourage groups of individuals (directors, entrepreneurs, and coalitions) to offer services in this organizational context. The demand theories, which are better known, include "government failure theory" (Weisbrod, 1977), "contract failure theory" (Hansmann, 1987), and "third-party government theory" (Douglas, 1987). With regard to supply theories, the main one is entrepreneurship theory (James, 1983, 1987; Young, 1983).

"Government failure theory" (Weisbrod, 1977) argues that in democratic regimes services are determined according to laws that derive from decisions adopted by a majority of voters. The services are appropriate for the "median voter," but they do not respond to a diverse population of clients who have special needs that are not met by the government. The vacuum is filled by nonprofit organizations that seek to provide services to the special needs of clients, and believe that in so doing they are realizing an ideology of philanthropy and altruism, besides enabling their clients to participate in political decisions about setting priorities and allocating resources.

The other theory, which was put forth by Hansmann (1980), a scholar of law from Yale University, maintains that the entry of nonprofit organizations into the field of service provision is part of the conditions created by "contract failure." Following Arrow (1963), he assumes that there is asymmetry in information between clients and providers, and that consumers feel unable to evaluate accurately the quantity or quality of the service a firm produces for them. Under such circumstances, a for-profit firm has both the incentive and the opportunity to take advantage of customers by providing less services to them than were promised and paid for. A nonprofit firm, in contrast, offers consumers the advantage that, owing to the nondistribution constraint, those who control the organization are constrained in their ability to benefit personally from providing low-quality services and thus have less incentive to take advantage of their customers than do managers of a for-profit firm (Hansmann, 1987, p. 29). Under these conditions, nonprofit organizations take advantage of the trust they are given by clients and enter new and existing service domains that increase their access to resources and capital.

Another demand theory that attempts to understand the role and function of voluntary nonprofit organizations was put forth by Salamon (1995). According to this theory, there is a division of labor between the government and nonprofit organizations. The government regulates the economy and society by assuming responsibility for setting general policies, for legislation that enables provision of services, and for (full or partial) financing of services. In addition, the government monitors, controls, and supervises the provision and quality of services while nonprofit organizations are responsible for providing services and for direct contact with clients, in that order. Governments intervene in crisis situations or, alternatively, when the nonprofit organizations face difficulties that prevent them from providing the amount and quality of services they are expected to offer. These difficulties, among others, include inability to mobilize resources, or to provide services to the populations that need them. Young (1999, 2000) provides support for this approach in his description of alternative models for relations between the government and nonprofit organizations. According to this model, the services provided by the organizations are viewed as supplementary, complementary, and adversarial. Along the same lines, Najam (1997) describes the relationships between the government and nonprofit organizations as confrontation, complementarity, and collaboration.

The main supply theory, "entrepreneurship theory" (James, 1987; Young, 1983), maintains that certain motives such as ambition, religious faith and altruism, or personal and social challenge can be best realized by initiating projects and by establishing nonprofit organizations that serve various populations whose needs have not been met by governmental agencies or local authorities. In fact, studies have shown that many nonprofit organizations were established by social entrepreneurs who witnessed the government's failure to provide services and sought to offer more flexible, efficient solutions to social problems. By establishing and heading their own organizations, they were also able to satisfy their personal motives and fulfill their ambitions (Schmid, Bargal, Korazim, Straus, & Hochstadt, 2001; Schmid, Bargal, & Hochstadt, 2003).

Based on these theories and on the changing context of social services, an attempt is made here to examine the goals and functions of nonprofit human service organizations and their contribution toward enhancing the well-being of disadvantaged and at-risk populations.

IDEOLOGY AND ESPOUSED GOALS OF NONPROFIT HUMAN SERVICE ORGANIZATIONS

Nonprofit human service organizations are considered to be ideologues, and their espoused goals are derived from the their raison d'être, which is to enhance the well-being of their clients. The following section presents these goals and then discusses the extent to which they are achieved.

First, Billis (1993) expressed the view that nonprofit organizations operate mainly in areas characterized by social ambiguity, where they have a comparative advantage over public, governmental, and for-profit organizations. In this connection, his main claim is that the distinctive and ambiguous hybrid structures of these organizations enable them to overcome problems of principal-agent gap, median voter reluctance, weak messages from politicians to staff, and lack of market interest. However, there are other interpretations of social ambiguity which shed light on the mission and goals of those organizations. According to these perspectives, ambiguity ensues for various reasons, including vague and inconsistent government policies for social, educational, health, and other services. Under these conditions, for-profit organizations avoid entering areas and domains where they cannot be ensured of the profits they expect to receive. By contrast, nonprofit organizations maintain an altruistic ideology of charity and concern for others, and perceive their mission and role as a "safety net" for people who are unable to find solutions to their problems and exigencies.

Second, nonprofit organizations function as pioneers that stake out the land and enter uncultivated, unknown domains. At the same time, they try to find innovative solutions for populations whose needs have not been met by governmental agencies. NPOs are thus perceived as innovative organizations that are not trapped by government bureaucracies and can therefore offer innovative experiments that the government would have difficulty implementing.

Third, nonprofit organizations support ideologies that aim to enhance the personal well-being of their clients. In so doing, they fulfill a social mission aimed at promoting justice, equality, and well-being for individuals, groups and communities (Kramer, 1987). In this context, they fulfill advocacy roles as agents of social control and social change (DiMaggio & Anheier, 1990; Teasdale, 1999), and as policy entrepreneurs (Najam, 1997). They represent groups of citizens-clients with special needs, and intervene on behalf of those who are unable to make their voices heard, while acting in areas of human and civil rights. They represent the government agencies where decisions are made and policies are determined, in order to channel resources to needy populations.

Fourth, nonprofit organizations enable their member-clients to express their views and raise their voices in protest. Moreover, they facilitate attainment of social goals by providing clients with an opportunity to participate in social struggles and conflicts. They are considered a democratic means of promoting values such as equal opportunity, equitable allocation of resources, support of disadvantaged populations, and responses to the needs of specific populations (Eisenberg, 2000). Government agencies are interested in establishing and preserving these organizations, since they act as a buffer and ensure social stability in the face of growing inequality and widening gaps between haves and have-nots.

Fifth, nonprofits–some of which originated in religious communities–emphasize the need for mutual support in addition to advocating the ideology of citizen participation. Their ideology reflects an orientation toward the community and commitment to solving social problems. As part of their social mission, they encourage development of community services, which offer an alternative to institutional services. They seek to change the existing balance of power and responsibility between the community on the one hand and the central and local authorities that control resources on the other. Nonprofit community service organizations aim to change this situation by encouraging processes of devolution and decentralization, in which the role of decision-making is transferred from the central government to community and neighborhood self-management organizations.

Finally, the ideology and ethic underlying their operation is to accept from their clients-consumers the price they are able to pay and provide to each consumer the services they need (Lewis, 1989, p. 10).

Undoubtedly, these are worthy and important goals, which go beyond the traditional roles of the government and its agencies. The nonprofit organizations value these goals, which represent the ideology that constitutes the ethical and moral basis for their service programs and activities. The question is whether they have succeeded in achieving those goals and in promoting the well-being of their clients, as they claim, or whether the goals have become myths that are not actualized. In the following section, an attempt will be made to analyze and evaluate the myths and to examine the extent to which they have been fulfilled in reality.

ARE THE IDEOLOGY AND ESPOUSED GOALS OF NONPROFIT HUMAN SERVICE ORGANIZATIONS ACTUALIZED?

First, regarding the contribution of nonprofit human service organizations toward diminishing social gaps and reducing the growth in inequality between haves and have-nots in Western countries. In my opinion, they have not achieved this goal, and inequality between different social strata has grown. There is ample evidence that the activities and programs run by these organizations are differential, encourage sectoralism, and in certain cases even perpetuate inequality between different target populations. There is reason to assume that by defining the needs of the respective target populations NPOs indeed overtly manifest selective and non-universal behavior. At times, these organizations delineate clear boundaries, which define the populations that are eligible for their services while rejecting all of those who do not meet the definitions, criteria, and requirements. The services they deliver are selective, and are not anchored in law or in legal rights enjoyed by the eligible groups–unlike the universal services provided by government authorities. Thus they may develop welfare cartels or supply oligopolies of social services. It is believed that nonprofit agencies focus on clients that conform with their respective service missions (Lipsky & Smith, 1989/90). In this vein, Knapp, Robertson, and Thomason (1990) argue that purchase and contracting of services by nonprofits has the potential for " . . . fragmentation, discontinuity, complexity, low-quality outputs, poorly targeted services, productive inefficiencies, horizontal and vertical inequities, wasteful duplication and inappropriate replication, secotiralism and paternalism" (pp. 213-214). Evers (1995) also argues that voluntary nonprofit organizations and purely voluntary organizations do not operate on principles of equity and equality. Rather, "services of voluntary organizations are often unreliable and unequally spread. They tend to exclude certain groups and are very different in quality" (p. 175).

Second, are nonprofits really innovative and creative in delivering social services compared to the bureaucratic, formal, rigid, and cumbersome governmental agencies? It is commonly believed that voluntary nonprofits reflect innovative thought, technology and services, and that they respond rapidly and efficiently to changes in their task environments. However, research findings indicate that this is not the situation. On the contrary, studies indicate that when nonprofit agencies are highly dependent on government resources, they tend to provide services mandated by law and in keeping with government policy (Schmid, 2001b). Moreover, nonprofit agencies as providers of government services have found that as long as they conform to government policy and regulations, they will be able to obtain the resources they need for their survival. Hence, they do not give priority to development of new programs and innovative service technologies (Davis-Smith & Hedley, 1993; Hoyes & Means, 1991), and the penalties they incur for failing to meet standards may inhibit innovation (Deakin, 1996, p. 119).

Third, it is also believed that the introduction of nonprofit agencies to the area of providing social services has the potential to increase the choice option for clients. The basic assumption behind government policy to contract out services with nongovernmental agencies states that clients will be offered a wider and more varied choice of service providers that will enable them to choose rationally according to their needs and financial capabilities. Allowing clients to select service providers may also empower them and increase provider dependence on them, while the resulting competition is expected to yield improved services and possibly reduce costs as well. Contrary to these expectations, however, research findings show that the choice option is only partially exercised by social service clients (Schmid, 1998, 2001b). Frail elderly clients, couples applying for adoption, students at residential boarding schools and others often become highly dependent on their caregivers or home care workers. Thus, they tend to resist change and usually do not complain even if they are dissatisfied with the services they receive. Moreover, the choice option is only available to clients who control the appropriate resources, i.e., to educated and sufficiently affluent people with access to information that is relevant to their needs. Those who lack sufficient and accessible information are limited in their ability to make choices, to compare the performance of provider organizations, and to evaluate them. This argument is supported by Knapp, Kendall, and Forder (1999), who report that beneficiaries of local authority and independent sector domiciliary care services did not exercise their option to choose between sectors or providers. Few had been consulted about service composition or timing, and most were happy to rely on care managers' judgments. These findings are also supported by other studies, which have demonstrated that contracting out increases neither choice nor user control (Hoyes & Means, 1991).

Fourth, compared with their for-profit competitors, nonprofit organizations enjoy a large extent of trustworthiness from their clients. Based on the clients' behavior under the "contract failure" theory described earlier (Hansmann, 1980, 1987), and under the conditions of the nondistribution constraint, it is believed that managers of nonprofits–unlike managers of for-profit agencies–are not motivated to make profits since they are prohibited from doing so. Any such profits must be invested in development of services for the benefit of their clients, who consequently place considerable trust in the organization's executives and workers. However, the evidence points to a different view of the behavior of nonprofit agencies and their executives. Recent events, including several scandals in nonprofit church-based organizations, provide incontrovertible evidence that the trust accorded to the nonprofit sector should be reconsidered from several perspectives (Gibelman & Gelman, 2001).

There is increasing evidence that directors of nonprofit organizations compensate themselves with high wages and fringe benefits because they are subject to the nondistribution constraint. In numerous organizations such as the United Way, the directors earn disproportionately higher wages than their workers, contrary to the ideology, goals, and spirit of the organization. In addition, it has been found that since the late 1980s, directors of hospitals used the surplus of income over expenditures and the support payments received from various sources to pay higher salaries to their professional staff instead of investing in service development (Lewis, 1989).

Moreover, most of the studies on differences between NPOs and FPOs have found that church-based organizations are the most trustworthy of all types of organizations (Weisbrod, 1998). However, an entirely different picture emerges from the events that have taken place over the past few years and from the findings of studies that have traced the activities of those organizations and compared their performance. The major scandals uncovered recently in numerous church-based organizations, which have revealed abuse and sexual harassment of young men by church leaders, demonstrate the unmitigated misuse of clients' trust in the services provided by those organizations. In brief, NPOs may exploit the implicit trust that their clients place in them and the lack of effective supervision and control by public boards in order to improve their directors' status, position, and salaries, as well as other benefits.

THE UNIQUE ORGANIZATIONAL IDENTITY OF NONPROFIT HUMAN SERVICE ORGANIZATIONS

The above discussion somewhat contradicts the basic assumptions and the rationale for the existence of nonprofit human service organizations that serve special needs and at-risk populations. Have these organizations actually succeeded in forming their own unique identity, or are they subcontractors of the government for provision of services, whose dependence on resources controlled by the government dictates their behavior (Young, 2001)? There is a growing body of evidence to support the latter argument that high dependence on government resources potentially affects their activity as gatekeepers, protestors, or advocates of at-risk and special needs populations (Schmid, 2001b). The more dependent they are on government funding, the less they engage in protest activities and advocacy–all at the expense of their mission and their organizational identity. In addition, as mentioned, dependence on government funding on the one hand and the coercive power of the government on the other cause nonprofit organizations to adopt behavior that conforms to the norms and standards set by the government, which detract from their ability to offer innovative programs and services (Bielefeld & Corbin, 1996). Moreover, even though there are those who would disagree with this argument (DiMaggio & Powell, 1983; Gronbjerg, 2001), the coercive power of the government encourages bureaucratic, formal behavior among nonprofit human service organizations. Thus, they become not only a "shadow government" (Wolch, 1990), but also a "government B" under a somewhat different guise. Moreover, competition with for-profit organizations influences their organizational behavior and poses a potential risk to their unique identity. Over the past two decades, dozens of articles have analyzed the differences between the nonprofit and for-profit sectors in numerous areas such as services for children, adolescents, people with disabilities, and health services (for a comprehensive review, see Schmid, 2000). Research findings clearly indicate that the distinctions between the sectors are becoming blurred as a result of several interesting processes. First, the organizations operate in similar environments, are subject to the same regulations, use the same service technologies, employ the same types of workers, serve client populations with similar needs, and are becoming more bureaucratic and political. Second, nonprofit organizations have begun to emulate their for-profit counterparts, and have assimilated service technologies and administrative techniques like those of for-profit providers (Austin, 2000; Salamon, 1993). The process of commercialization has also given rise to "disguised nonprofits," which are legally defined as nonprofits, but essentially operate as profit-making firms (Weisbrod, 1998).

Under these circumstances, can nonprofit human service organizations potentially lose their identity while devaluing their mission and the quality of their services? It is argued here that even in changing environments characterized by the intensive penetration of for-profit organizations, nonprofit organizations still play a major role in delivery of social and welfare services to populations at risk that have been adversely affected by the government's policy to diminish its role in the provision of services. In our view, nonprofit human service organizations have an exclusive domain for the provision of social services, and they should emphasize their distinctive virtues and added value compared to governmental agencies and for-profit firms (Salamon, 1995). They have to position themselves in areas characterized by structural ambiguity, which both governments and for-profit organizations are reluctant to enter. Specifically, for-profit organizations may be forced to lower the quality of their services in those areas in order to ensure themselves of a profit. Thus, nonprofit organizations need to operate in areas where they have a relative advantage, which enables them to realize their identity and achieve their mission while attaining the trust of their clients without exploiting their weakness and naivete. In so doing, they need to adhere strictly to codes of professional ethics and abide by the values and ideology that they represent. They have to be cautious about developing "poor," low-quality services for disadvantaged populations, and maintain high standards of service quality that will be a model for governments and for-profit organizations. They need to make better use of their relative advantage, which is defined as the asset of human resources, by developing their professional and volunteer staff me   ˈ ˑ
are known to be committed to the organization's goals and clien
the motivation to provide high-quality services. It has been fo·
profit workers enjoy a relatively high level of functional autono
ables them to develop their competencies and give the organiz

advantage over its competitors (Schmid et al., 2003). In the midst of intensive change, and in a market economy where the fittest have the best chances of survival, nonprofit organizations play a major role as they represent and reflect values of collective responsibility and social justice. These organizations therefore act as a counterweight against governmental organizations and for-profit agencies, which place the benefit of their owners before the benefit of their clients.

This special volume is one of the few attempts to present the work of leading scholars and scientists, who analyze and evaluate various organizational and structural dilemmas related to the functioning of nonprofit human service organizations. I have no doubt that this collection of articles will enhance the knowledge and arouse the interest of social policy-makers, theoreticians, researchers, students, practitioners, and others in the field.

The first article by Brilliant and Young presents the changing identity of federated community service organizations. In the article, they examine the experience of these organizations in the United States from the end of the 19th century to the present day. The differential experiences of several community service organizations illustrate various possible identities for federated organizations.

The second article, by Cnaan, Sinha, and McGrew, describes and analyzes the role of congregations as social service providers. The authors explain why faith-based care is so paramount in the United States and discuss the political developments in faith-based efforts. They also deal with key administrative challenges, including issues of capacity, cultural characteristics, and organizational behavior.

Netting, Nelson, Borders, and Huber present an interesting perspective on volunteer and paid staff relationships, which examines what administrators in social work can glean from theory and research on the topic. They draw their observations from the conceptual literature on volunteerism, as well as from their experience with one nationally mandated program that utilizes ninety percent volunteers and ten percent paid employees.

The two articles that follow deal with the implications of welfare-to-work services. The first one, by Hasenfeld and Powell, is based on a study which showed that contracts have placed these agencies in a difficult task environment that has severely restricted their autonomy. In order to cope with their environment, these agencies have developed very similar welfare-to-work programs that are consonant with the dominant institutional rules in the employment services sector. Their findings also analyze how these agencies are trying to maintain their distinctiveness, and suggest that government contracts with nonprofit agencies may prevent them from achieving the objectives they are contracted to fulfill. The second paper by Murloy and Tamburo discusses the environmental turbulence and organizational change in nonprofit organizations delivering welfare-to-work services. Using the political economy theory as a conceptual framework, the literature review suggests that nonprofits are experiencing organizational change and frequent turbulence on four key dimensions–interorganizational relationships, mission and philosophy, resource dependencies, and target populations. The article analyzes each dimension, then deals with the implications of the changes for social work managers, practitioners, educators, and researchers.

Gibelman uses media reports that trace the cycles of public sentiment as expressed through the media. The author analyzes the capabilities of public, nonprofit, and for-profit providers, in addition to discussing the failures of those sectors and identifying their common themes. The data indicate that all of the sectors have been found wanting.

Tropman and Shaefer's article deals with executive calamity in the nonprofit sector. The authors discuss the issue of nonprofit executive problematics, which can be defined as behavior of executives that causes harm to themselves and to their organizations, e.g., inappropriate personal use of agency resources, embezzlement, and sexual acting out. Their research expands the study of "derailment" by exploring cases in which the misbehavior of executives causes extensive damage to themselves, their families, and their agencies.

In the next article, Schmid and Nirel explore what makes the difference between nonprofit and for-profit organizations. Based on their longitudinal study of the home care industry, they suggest that structural properties such as age indeed affect the differences between organizations in the two sectors. However, they also indicate that type of ownership generates the differences as well as the dynamics between age and ownership.

The concluding article by Weiss and Gal discusses the preferences of social work graduates for employment in various sectors of the welfare economy. Their findings indicate that the private nonprofit sector was given the highest preference by graduates in most countries, while for-profit employment was not given the highest preference in any country.

I am confident that the articles in this special volume provide the reader with a comprehensive body of knowledge, research findings, and information on organizational and structural dilemmas faced by nonprofit human service organizations, based on a broad range of perspectives and sources. In the midst of rapid changes, and in light of the transitions witnessed by these organizations, it is essential to continue to explore and study the dilemmas that concern them. The knowledge we develop will enable the organizations to improve their performance and enhance the well-being of their clients.

REFERENCES

Arrow, K. (1963). Uncertainty and the welfare economics of medical care. *American Economic Review, 53*, 941-973.

Austin, M. (2003). The changing relationship between nonprofit organizations and public social service agencies in the era of welfare reform. *Nonprofit and Voluntary Sector Quarterly, 32(1)*, 97-114.

Austin, J. (2000). Strategic collaboration between nonprofits and businesses. *Nonprofit and Voluntary Sector Quarterly, 29(1)*, 69-97.

Ben-Ner, A. (1986). Nonprofit organizations: Why do they exist in a market economy? In S. Rose-Ackerman (Ed.), *The economics of nonprofit institutions* (pp. 94-113). New York: Oxford University Press.

Berger, P.L., Neuhaus, R.J., & Novak, M. (1996). *To empower people: From state to civil society*. Washington, D.C.: American Enterprise Institute.

Bielefeld, W., & Corbin, J.J. (1996). The institutionalization of nonprofit human service delivery: The role of political culture. *Administration and Society, 28*, 362-389.

Billis, D. (1993). Sector blurring and the nonprofit centers: The case of the United Kingdom. *Nonprofit and Voluntary Sector Quarterly, 20(3)*, 241-257.

Cnaan, R.A. (2002). *The invisible caring hand: American congregations and the provision of welfare*. New York: New York University Press.

Cordes, J., Henig, J.R., & Twombly, E.C. (2001). Nonprofit human service providers in an era of privatization: Toward a theory of economic and political response. *Policy Studies Review, 18(4)*, 91-110.

Davis-Smith, J., & Hedley, R. (1993). *Volunteering and the contract culture*. Berkamsted, UK: Volunteer Centre.

Deakin, N. (1996). What does contracting do to users? In D. Billis, & M. Harris (Eds.), *Voluntary agencies, challenges of organization and management* (pp. 113-129). London: Macmillan.

DiMaggio, P.J., & Anheier, H.K. (1990). The sociology of nonprofit organizations and sectors. *Annual Review of Sociology, 16*, 137-159.

DiMaggio, P.J., & Powell, W.W. (1983). The iron cage revisited: Institutional isomorphism and collective rationality in organizational fields. *American Sociological Review, 48*, 147-160.

DiMaggio, P.J., Weiss, J.A., & Clotfelter, C.T. (2002). Data to support scholarship on nonprofit organizations: An introduction. *American Behavioral Scientist, 4(10)*, 1474-1492.

Douglas, J. (1987). Political theories of nonprofit organizations. In W.W. Powell (Ed.), *The nonprofit sector: A research handbook* (pp. 43-54). New Haven, CT: Yale University Press.

Eisenberg, P. (2000). The nonprofit sector in a changing world. *Nonprofit and Voluntary Sector Quarterly, 27(2)*, 325-330.

Evers, A. (1995). Part of the welfare mix: The third sector as an intermediate area. *Voluntas, 6(2)*, 159-182.

Frumkin, P. (2002). Service contracting with nonprofit and for-profit providers. In J.D. Donahue, & J.S. Nye Jr. (Eds.), *Market-based governance* (pp. 66-87). Washington, D.C.: Brookings Institution Press.

Gibelman, M., & Gelman, S.R. (2001). Very public scandals: Nongovernmental organizations in trouble. *Voluntas, 12(1)*, 49-66.

Gronbjerg, K.A. (2001). The U.S. nonprofit human service sector: A creeping revolution. *Nonprofit and Voluntary Sector Quarterly, 30(2)*, 276-297.

Gronbjerg, K.A., & Salamon, L.M. (2002). Devolution, marketization, and the changing shape of government-nonprofit relations. In L.M. Salamon (Ed.), *The state of nonprofit in America* (pp. 447-470). Washington, D.C.: Brookings Institution Press.

Hammack, D.C. (2001). Introduction: Growth, transformation, and quiet revolution in the nonprofit sector over two centuries. *Nonprofit and Voluntary Sector Quarterly, 30(2)*, 157-173.

Hansmann, H. (1980). The role of nonprofit enterprise. *Yale Law Journal, 89*, 835-901.

Hansmann, H. (1987). Economic theories of nonprofit organization. In W.W. Powell (Ed.), *The nonprofit sector: A research handbook* (pp. 27-42). New Haven, CT: Yale University Press.

Hopkins, B. (1992). *The law of tax exempt organizations*. New York: Wiley.

Hoyes, L., & Means, R. (1991). *Implementing the White Paper on community care*. Bristol, UK: School for Advanced Urban Studies.

James, E. (1983). How nonprofits grow: A model. *Journal of Policy Analysis and Management, Spring*, 350-365.

James, E. (1987). The nonprofit sector in comparative perspective. In W.W. Powell (Ed.), *The nonprofit sector: A research handbook* (pp. 397-415). New Haven, CT: Yale University Press.

Karger, H., & Stoesz, D. (2002). *American social welfare policy*. Boston: Allyn & Bacon.

Knapp, M.R., Kendall, J., & Forder, J. (1999). Is the independent sector important in social care? *PSSRU Bulletin, 11*, 14-17.

Knapp, M., Robertson, E., & Thomason, C. (1990). Public money, voluntary action: Whose welfare? In H. Anheier, & W. Siebel (Eds.), *The third sector* (pp. 138-218). Berlin: DeGruyter.

Kramer, R.M. (1987). Voluntary associations and the personal social services. In W.W. Powell (Ed.), *The nonprofit sector: A research handbook* (pp. 240-257). New Haven, CT: Yale University Press.

Kramer, R.M. (2000). The third sector in the third millennium. *Voluntas, 11(1)*, 1-23.

Lewis, H. (1989). Ethics and the private nonprofit service organization. *Administration in Social Work, 13(2)*, 1-14.

Lipsky, M., & Smith, S.R. (1989-90). Nonprofit organizations, government, and the welfare state. *Political Science Quarterly, 104(4)*, 625-648.

Mishra, R. (1990). *The welfare state in capitalist society*. Toronto: University of Toronto Press.

Najam, A. (1997). *The 3 C's of NGO-government relations: Confrontation, complementarity, collaboration*. Unpublished manuscript. Boston University.

Putnam, R.D. (2000). *Bowling alone: The collapse and revival of American community*. New York: Simon & Schuster.

Salamon, L.M. (1993). The marketization of welfare: Changing nonprofit and for-profit roles in the American welfare state. *Social Service Review, 67(1)*, 16-39.

Salamon, L.M. (1995). *Partners in public service*. Baltimore: Johns Hopkins University Press.

Salamon, L.M. (Ed.). (2003). *The state of nonprofit America.* Washington, D.C.: Brookings Institution Press.

Salamon, L.M., & Anheier, H.K. (Eds.). (1992). In search of the nonprofit sector I: The question of definitions. *Voluntas, 3(2),* 125-151.

Salamon, L.M., & Anheier, H.K. (Eds.). (1997). *Defining the nonprofit sector: A cross-national analysis.* Manchester, UK: Manchester University Press.

Salamon, L.M., Anheier, H.K., List, R., Toepler, S.S., & Sokolowski, W. (1999). *Global civil society: Dimensions of the nonprofit sector.* Baltimore: The Johns Hopkins Comparative Center for Civil Society Studies.

Schmid, H. (1998). *Evaluation of the functioning of home care organizations delivering services to the frail elderly.* Jerusalem, The Hebrew University of Jerusalem (Hebrew).

Schmid, H. (2000). For-profit and nonprofit human services: A comparative analysis. *Social Security, 6,* 161-179 (Special English Edition).

Schmid, H. (2001a). *Neighborhood self-management: Experiments in civil society.* New York: Kluwer Academic/Plenum Publishers.

Schmid, H. (2001b). Evaluating the impact of legal change on nonprofit and for-profit organizations: The case of the Israeli long-term care insurance law. *Public Management Review, 3(2),* 167-189.

Schmid, H. (2003). Rethinking the policy of contracting out social services to nongovernmental organizations: Lessons and dilemmas. *Public Management Review, 5(3),* (forthcoming).

Schmid, H., Bargal, D., Korazim, Y., Straus, E., & Hochstedt, M. (2001). *Voluntary nonprofit human service organizations delivering services to children and adolescents: Areas of activity and structure.* Jerusalem: The Hebrew University of Jerusalem (Hebrew).

Schmid, H., Bargal, D., & Hochstedt, M. (2003). *Voluntary nonprofit human service organizations delivering services to the elderly.* Jerusalem: The Hebrew University of Jerusalem (Hebrew).

Smith, S.R., & Lipsky, M. (1993). *Nonprofits for hire.* Cambridge, MA: Harvard University Press.

Taylor, M. (2002). Government, the third sector and the contract culture: The UK experience so far. In U. Ascoli, & C. Ranci (Eds.), *Dilemmas of the welfare mix* (pp. 77-108). New York: Kluwer Academic/Plenum Publishers.

Teasdale, K. (1999). *Advocacy in health care.* London: Blackwell Science.

Tuckman, H.P. (1998). Competition, commercialization, and the evolution of nonprofit organizational structures. *Journal of Policy Analysis & Management, 17(2),* 175-194.

US Census Bureau. (1997). *Economic Census: Health Care and Social Assistance.*

Weisbrod, B.A. (1977). *The voluntary nonprofit sector.* Lexington: D.C. Heath and Company.

Weisbrod, B.A. (Ed.). (1998). *To profit or not to profit: The commercial transformation of the nonprofit sector.* New York: Cambridge University Press.

Wolch, J. (1990). *The shadow state: Government and voluntary in transition.* New York: Foundation Center.

Young, D.R. (1983). *If not for profit, for what?* Lexington, MA: D.C. Heath and Company.

Young, D.R. (1999). Complementary, supplementary or adversarial: A theoretical and historical examination of government-nonprofit relations in the U.S. In E.T. Boris, & C.E. Steurele (Eds.), *Government and nonprofit organizations: The challenges of civil society*. Washington, D.C.: The Urban Institute.

Young, D.R. (2000). Alternative models of government-nonprofit sector relations: Theoretical and international perspectives. *Nonprofit and Voluntary Sector Quarterly, 29(1)*, 149-172.

Young, D.R. (2001). Organizational identity in nonprofit organizations: Strategic and structural implications. *Nonprofit Management and Leadership, 12(2)*, 139-157.

The Changing Identity of Federated Community Service Organizations

Eleanor Brilliant, PhD
Dennis R. Young, PhD

SUMMARY. Organizational identity is that which is central, distinctive, and enduring about an organization. Clarity and consensus about organizational identity is an essential element in setting successful long term strategy in nonprofit organizations. At the same time, changing environmental conditions require that identities, and concomitant strategies, be revisited over time, in order to ensure survival and growth. This paper examines the experiences of an important subset of nonprofit organizations–community-based federations in the United States as they have evolved from the end of the 19th century to the present day. These organizations originally emerged as vehicles for the more efficient collection and distribution of charitable contributions and provision of related services, but over time their identities have evolved in important ways. The differential experiences of United Ways, alternative funds, Catholic Charities, and United Jewish Communities illustrate various possible identities for such federated organizations. The future success of

---

Eleanor Brilliant is affiliated with the School of Social Work, Rutgers University. Dennis R. Young is affiliated with Case Western Reserve University and the National Center on Nonprofit Enterprise.

[Haworth co-indexing entry note]: "The Changing Identity of Federated Community Service Organizations." Brilliant, Eleanor, and Dennis R. Young. Co-published simultaneously in *Administration in Social Work* (The Haworth Social Work Practice Press, an imprint of The Haworth Press, Inc.) Vol. 28, No. 3/4, 2004, pp. 23-46; and: *Organizational and Structural Dilemmas in Nonprofit Human Service Organizatons* (ed: Hillel Schmid) The Haworth Social Work Practice Press, an imprint of The Haworth Press, Inc., 2004, pp. 23-46. Single or multiple copies of this article are available for a fee from The Haworth Document Delivery Service [1-800-HAWORTH, 9:00 a.m. - 5:00 p.m. (EST). E-mail address: docdelivery@haworthpress.com].

http://www.haworthpress.com/web/ASW
Digital Object Identifier: 10.1300/J147v28n03_02

these organizations depends on successful adaptation of their identities to contemporary conditions, and the implementation of new strategies consistent with, and supportive of, those identities. *[Article copies available for a fee from The Haworth Document Delivery Service: 1-800-HAWORTH. E-mail address: <docdelivery@haworthpress.com> Website: <http://www.Haworth Press.com> © 2004 by The Haworth Press, Inc. All rights reserved.]*

KEYWORDS. Organizational identity, community federations, social services, United Way, alternative funds, religious federations, organizational evolution, organizational change

INTRODUCTION

Federated community service organizations date back to the late nineteenth century in the United States. The first coordinated fund raising campaign in what became the United Way movement was organized in Denver in 1887. The first coordinated fund raising effort in Jewish philanthropy arose in Boston in 1895. Catholic Charities and other religious fund raising federations have equally long histories. In contrast, the myriad of "alternative funds" which address human rights, environmental and minority interests, the arts, and other issues not embraced by the mainstream health and human service federations, are generally of more recent vintage.

The concept of coordinated fund raising is straightforward. By avoiding duplication and competition, charities can exploit economies of scale, and use resources more effectively. This idea lies at the root of all federated community service organizations. However, as various factors have come into play–demands of groups not represented by the mainstream federations, demands by donors for a say in how their contributions are expended, and public demands for more effective deployment of philanthropic funds to address social problems–federations have revisited their core identities over time and sometimes assumed very different postures than the ones with which they began.

This paper examines the evolution of alternative organizational identities by four principal groups of federated community service organizations–United Ways, United Jewish Communities, Catholic Charities, and so-called "alternative funds." First, we review the concept of organizational identity, and then we describe several different prototype identities that federated community service organizations have embraced over their histories. With these stereotypes in mind, we examine the histories of the four federation groups, the issues precipitating evolution in their identities, and the strategic issues these organizations face as they resolve their identities for the future.

METHODOLOGY

This paper is based on a broad scan and close reading of historical and organizational literature, current web sites, specific organizational reports, limited participant observation, and selected personal interviews. Our intent is to provide a qualitative overview of the historical evolution of the selected groups of federations, and to introduce the concept of organizational identity to the analysis of these organizations so as to demonstrate the utility of this concept for understanding the strategic issues with which these organizations struggle and the dilemmas they now face. In this sense, the current study is exploratory in nature. We anticipate that the conceptual framework offered here can be the basis for future research which would entail more systematic collection of quantitative and case study data and lead to analysis and comparison of many different kinds of community and regional service federations.

ORGANIZATIONAL IDENTITY

Organizational identity has been defined as that which is "central, distinctive and enduring" about an organization (Albert and Whetten, 1985). Identity becomes important when organizations face very hard decisions or challenging situations, such as birth, loss of a key element or a founding leader, accomplishment of a long standing mission or circumstance that renders the mission irrelevant, a period of rapid expansion or retrenchment, or a change in corporate status, e.g., a merger or takeover. It is under such circumstances that organizations search their collective souls to determine who they are and what business they are in (Albert and Whetten, 1985). Such circumstances feature struggles between groups defending old identities and others promoting new ones, and they lead to the evolution of identities to address new environments and challenges (Whetten and Godfrey, 1998). Thus the concept of enduring identity has to be reconciled with the demands of organizational change.

The organization literature distinguishes "identity" from "image," the latter reflecting how the organization is perceived by outsiders (Dutton and Dukerich, 1991). In contrast, identity is an internal construct, reflecting the view of insiders (Gioia and Thomas, 1996). Moreover, it is a dynamic concept whose adaptation helps an organization accomplish change (Gioia, Schultz, and Corley, 2000). Scholars have commonly expressed organizational identities in terms

of metaphors, following the lead of Albert and Whetten (1985), who characterized universities as struggling with alternative identities of "church" and
"business." This approach has been applied to nonprofit associations (Young,
2001a), other nonprofit organizations (Young, 2001b), community organizations (Golden-Biddle and Rao, 1997), mental health organizations (Stone,
1996) and religious welfare organizations (Stone and DeWaard, 1998).

Organizations often struggle with multiple identities (Albert and Whetten,
1985), because additional roles may be imposed on them from the outside or
because they have difficulty shedding old identities while cultivating new
ones. Scholars differ on whether the maintenance of multiple identities is necessarily dysfunctional. Some argue that multiple identities can be useful in dealing with conflicting environmental pressures (Stone, 1996) while others ob-
serve that they can be successfully managed (Pratt and Foreman, 2000). In any
case, scholars have identified several strategies that organizations use to manage multiple identities, including compartmentalization, finding a higher level
(meta)identity that successfully integrates existing identities, and allowing
one or more identities to slowly decay (Whetten and Godfrey, 1998; Pratt and
Foreman, 2000). Overall, the concept of organizational identity illuminates
how nonprofit organizations sometimes struggle to restructure or "reinvent"
themselves in order to survive and prosper in a changing environment. The
resolution of multiple identities is often a key facet of these struggles. This is
certainly the case for community service federations.

ALTERNATIVE IDENTITIES OF FEDERATED
COMMUNITY SERVICE ORGANIZATIONS

Federated community service organizations operate largely at local or regional levels, although many belong to national umbrella associations. While
concentrated in the human services, they operate in diverse fields including environmental conservation and the arts. Some focus on particular population segments, such as Black United Funds; others are concerned with social change for
various marginalized groups in the community, e.g., Greater Cleveland Community Shares or Community Shares of Louisiana.

The nominal *raison d'etre* for federated community organizations is that
they are more efficient vehicles for generating net charitable contributions
than the alternative of recipient charities competing for those funds. Elimi-
nating duplicate fund-raising expenditures and exploiting economies of scale
reduces the cost of raising donations. While this economy lies at the root of
community service federations, other rationales have contributed to their development over time. For example, some federations are powerfully positioned

to influence the allocation of resources among local charities, obligating them to help ensure that those resources are distributed effectively in their communities and efficiently utilized by recipient organizations. Pressures from the donor community to have a say in the designation of their gifts also supports federations in facilitating such choices.

Even in the current, dynamic environment of competition for charitable resources, federations may enjoy considerable discretion in the identities they adopt and how they position themselves in their communities. The present challenges follow from adapting historical identities to present circumstances, and in some cases shaping new identities for the future. The following identities have characterized the historical development of various federations, and all appear to be in play at the present time:

Fiscal Intermediary. Federated community service organizations can conceive of themselves essentially in mechanical terms—as efficient solicitors of funds, and distributors of those funds among affiliated service organizations according to some agreed upon formula or procedure. This is the classical manner in which United Ways have operated in the past. Once accepted as members, local agencies file financial statements signaling their fiscal needs, these reports are reviewed by federation staff and board members, and applicants receive an allocation to address that need. Strategic goals are limited to target levels for community fund raising, and criteria for inclusiveness and fairness in distributing funds to affiliated service organizations.

Economic Regulator. Having been placed in the position of collecting financial statements from participating service agencies, it is a relatively small step for federations to assume an overseer role. Financial statements can be audited, programmatic data analyzed, and judgments made about a recipient organization's performance. From there it seems natural to reward those organizations that perform well and discipline those that perform poorly. Hence, federated community service organizations can take on the role of economic regulator and quality assurer, pressuring poor performers to improve, close up shop, or merge with other organizations. In recent years, much of the pressure for local nonprofit social service agencies to combine with one another has come from federations seeking greater returns for their donors on dollars they allocate to recipient organizations.

The economic regulator identity puts greater demands on both governance and administration. Board members must be able to absorb criticism, make difficult judgments with political implications, and stand by their policies. These demands require greater inclusiveness in governing bodies to ensure the perception of fairness, than if the organization were simply a Fiscal Intermediary. Staff too must have more capacity to analyze the cost-effectiveness of services of recipient organizations.

Community Problem Solver. As federations cohere into more systematic arrangements, they may expand their focus to addressing community problems as a whole, rather than simply supporting or overseeing organizations that deliver services in the community. The Community Problem Solver identity puts further pressure on governance and staffing. It requires setting community service priorities, making judgments on how to effectively address those priorities, and determining which organizations would make best use of available funds. Ultimately, Community Problem Solvers depart from the traditional mode of making annual allocations to all member organizations, instead making grants selectively according to programmatic priorities. They come to resemble community foundations, requiring staff knowledgeable in community needs, governing bodies capable of assessing and defending the fairness and efficiency of alternative community investments, and sometimes looking for partner organizations (e.g., corporations and foundations) with which to engage in collaborative community projects.

A variant of the Community Problem Solver identity is the Social Change Agent. In particular, some alternative funds are more laser-like in their focus on certain social causes or social justice issues as they apply to particular communities. In this variation, more emphasis is placed on funding advocacy groups and activities directed at social change, rather than solely traditional services, and board membership is chosen with great regard to ideological commitment or the need for diversity.

Charitable Mutual Fund. The recent trend towards donor choice suggests a fourth possible identity for federated community service organizations–that of manager of individual donor funds. In this conception, the function of the federation is to offer an attractive portfolio of charitable "investments" to potential donors so that they are inclined to give as much as possible and have the information they need to make intelligent decisions. Under this identity, staff must be efficient compilers and marketers of charitable offerings. The governing board must be responsive to preferences of various donor segments in the community so that they can influence the kinds of charities brought into the portfolio. The financial allocation process becomes more routine, directing funds to charities designated by donors, supplemented by rules to allocate non-earmarked contributions.

In summary, it is clear that the alternative identities of federated community service organizations have distinctly different implications for their strategic choices. Moreover, all of the major groups of federations are in flux, with all of the forgoing identities currently in play and many individual federations moving from one identity to another, or trying to balance more than one identity at a time.

THE UNITED WAY

The United Way system celebrates its origins in Denver in 1887 when, in a period of societal change and proliferating services, religious and philanthropic leaders came together to reduce duplication and create one combined fund-raising appeal. The new association embraced the identity of Fiscal Intermediary, with the intention of raising funds more efficiently and dividing them among member agencies. In 1913, a group of city officials, businessmen, and professionals in Cleveland also adopted the idea of a joint federated fund-raising campaign. Unlike Denver, the Cleveland Federation of Charities and Philanthropies employed professional staff and sought widespread community involvement. Cleveland has been called the first modern community chest (Lubove, 1969; United Way of America, 1977) although in this period financial federations were developing in other cities as well. In what would become paradigmatic, associations based on broader concepts of community welfare coordination and study had also emerged, such as the Central Council of the Associated Charities in Pittsburgh (1908). By 1917, the Federation of Charities and Philanthropies absorbed the Welfare Federation of Cleveland (Foundation Center of Cleveland, 2002). The combined organization embodied multiple identities, including early concepts of Economic Regulator and Community Problem Solver, in addition to Fiscal Intermediary. During this period financial federations spread across the country with added momentum from the "War Chests" created in World War I.

In the next decades, welfare councils (Councils of Social Agencies) and federated fund-raising campaigns continued to grow nationwide. However, the relationship between financial federations and councils varied among communities. By 1950, there were 1270 community chests and slightly over 400 community councils (Social Work Year Book, 1951, cited in Harper and Dunham, 1959, p. 355). It is not clear how many councils were sub-units of a community chest. In fact, a policy statement approved by the national Board of the Community Chests and Councils (1950) stated that "(V)arious structural arrangements are possible for the relationship of community planning and financing groups . . . " (United Funds and Councils of America, 1959). Whatever the arrangement, the three identities of Fiscal Intermediary, Economic Regulator and Community Problem Solver were often manifested separately, either in different organizations, sub-units of the same organization, or with different personnel.

From the beginning, financial federations embraced the Fiscal Intermediary identity and were intended to serve as buffers between recipient agencies and donors, particularly with regard to business solicitations (Watson, 1922).

Nevertheless, the function of Economic Regulator was so closely allied with chest activity that chest staff could scarcely avoid this identity. Still, expansion of the Community Problem Solver identity was problematic because financial federations focused on fund-raising, and their resources were allocated to a limited group of member agencies. The issue was stated explicitly in a study carried out by a citizen's group of a local combined federation:

> There is an incongruity in combining responsibility for over-all planning with that of financing a small minority of total health and welfare services. (Citizens Study Committee, n.d., cited in Pfeiffer, 1959)

Community chests' identities became even more complicated when national health agencies proliferated after World War II. Companies were besieged by appeals from new health causes and community chest hegemony in local campaigns was threatened. By 1949, corporate concerns and community chest self-interest coalesced in a new donor driven image for federated fund raising: the United Fund. This concept spread across the country, as community chests took the new name–United Fund–and sought to enroll national health agencies, generally with little success. In practical fact, United Fund meant inclusion of the American Red Cross and a new emphasis on giving by employees. United Funds generally had monopoly access in corporate workplaces, and the use of the check-off for worker donations also accelerated. However, the issue of inclusiveness in employee campaigns became increasingly troublesome through the next decades (Brilliant, 1990; Glaser, 1993).

United Funds were a shift from former reliance largely on corporate donations as part of general community campaigns, to a new emphasis on employee donations through unified company-workplace campaigns. Thus, during the 1950s, both the image and identity of financial federations as Community Problem Solvers, or leaders of consensus community planning efforts, tended to have less salience. In addition, this identity was soon undermined by other challenges. In the 1960s and early 1970s the numbers of nonprofit organizations in the United States expanded greatly (Weisbrod, 1988), assisted by available federal funding. Thereafter, the planning roles of community federations were diminished even more by increasing government sponsorship of local coordinating initiatives such as those of the War on Poverty (1965) or mandated social service planning in Title XX (1974). Consequently in the 1970s the (renamed) United Way system struggled to maintain local planning efforts. Many local United Ways developed new methods of planning and allocation of resources, with enhanced citizen review processes that incorporated regulatory and planning activities. These latter activities involved some United Ways working with government agencies to leverage both corporate leadership and available dollars. Although local United Way actions did not keep up with United Way of America rhetoric on the subject of planning, in a difficult financial period many United Ways absorbed their separate local planning councils, and some United Ways used priority studies as a means to parcel out limited resources (Brilliant, 1990).

In the next decade United Ways' image as Fiscal Intermediary was threatened by emerging causes and competing federations, like Black United Funds, arts funds, and women's funds. Growing out of the civil rights movement, a new diversity in workplace philanthropy also was encouraged by the National Committee for Responsive Philanthropy (NCRP); demands by workers for choice in giving paralleled the development of more activist funds. After a series of court decisions and congressional legislation, United Way monopoly of workplace campaigns was being eroded (National Committee for Responsive Philanthropy, 1987). Initially this change occurred primarily in public sector campaigns, starting with the Combined Federal Campaign (CFC) which already included three other groups (National Health Agencies, International Voluntary Agencies, and some independent Red Cross Chapters). Subsequently, the concept of donor choice spread to state and local government as well as to some corporate workplaces (National Committee on Responsive Philanthropy, Fall 1989; Winter, 1989; Fall 1990).

Despite these changes, United Ways seemed to retain their identities as Economic Regulator of their "member agencies." However, this became more tenuous when proliferating new agencies received donor choice funds without United Way budget review. Former competitors, the American Cancer Society and American Heart Association, were also becoming United Way affiliates without having to face the citizen review process. Finally, since United Way campaigns were growing slowly, and resources were being distributed more widely, member agencies developed other sources of support, including government funds. United Way support decreased continuously as a percentages of agency budgets (Brilliant, 1990), further undermining the identity and image of Economic Regulator for local United Ways.

In the last decade of the 20th century, faced with increased use of donor choice, and more funds going outside the United Way agency group, local United Ways developed several ways both to protect their image and adapt their identity. First, they revived the old community planning concept under new names, including Community Problem Solver or community building, as "value added" by the United Way. A national Task Force even adopted social change terminology, urging that United Way become a "preeminent community change agent" (United Way of America, October 1, 2001). Second, many United Ways attempted to head off donor designations outside the United Way system, by creating new methods for designating funds for priority community needs and emphasizing a United Way "community impact" (United Way of America, 1998). In connecting the idea of community needs and community problem-solving, United Ways proposed coalitions with other groups and developed special programs, often in partnership with corporations, like the early childhood initiative, Success by Six (United Way of America, May 3, 2001; October 1, 2001). Third, United Ways attempted to counteract defections in the workplace with a new emphasis on leadership gifts by individuals (Billitteri, March 9, 2000; United Way of America, 10/26/01). Fourth, in an effort to placate corporate leaders and deal with issues of accountability and efficiency, United Way of America undertook initiatives to promote nationwide standards, to handle corporate contributions centrally, and in what became an expensive failure, experimented with processing payroll deductions through one common system. These efforts threatened the autonomy of local United Ways, and their sense of being true community organizations (United Way of America, October 1, 2001; Varchaver, 2000; confidential interview, September 23, 2001).

New strategies require structural and tactical changes, which some flexible local United Ways have adopted readily (for example, Atlanta, Columbus, Los Angeles). To other United Ways however, losses of their primary identities of Fiscal Intermediary and Economic Regulator present more difficulties. The issue once again may turn on United Ways' self-concept as Community Problem Solver, considered to be the social work "heart" of United Way. This identity could be manifested through allocations made via the citizen review process, but also through separate planning efforts focused on community needs. After several weak fund-raising campaigns (Kaplan, 1995), there were undoubtedly fewer resources for planning. But at the same time there was increased recognition that partnerships and coalitions could be used to leverage available resources more effectively.

By the late 1990s, United Ways had revived the identity of Community Problem Solver as part of a paradigm shift. This new development appeared to be a way of compensating for the loss of the other two United Way identities, but it was also a way to market United Way services to donors. Newly defined, problem solving came to include designations to specified areas of need, like child welfare or criminal justice, as determined by United Way committees and other government and citizen groups. In effect this could bring donor choice dollars under control of local United Ways for reallocation. Therefore, in marketing the community problem solving role to corporations and individual donors, local United Ways would also bolster their identities of Fiscal Intermediary and Economic Regulator.

The end of the 1990s brought other challenges as well, perhaps the most significant of which was the emergence of e-giving. By allowing individual donors to give directly to charitable causes, e-giving could potentially undermine all three traditional United Way identities, but less so if United Ways were to control e-giving in employee campaigns through use of United Way software packages. Yet this development could lead to yet another United Way identity, that of Charitable Mutual Fund with "packaged" choices. In this new scenario United Ways, facing increasing competition from other federated funding groups, including a newly emerging Union Community Fund (Center on Philanthropy, 2001), might offer various packages of services and agencies, or cafeteria choices, along with a campaign-management role (United Way of America, 2000). Agency packages could include specialized social action funds, like women's funds, or the more viewpoint neutral America's Charities (more than 100 different kinds of agencies nationwide), along with more traditional groups, like their own affiliated agencies or health funds. Some United Ways, e.g., the United Way of the National Capital Area (Washington) and the United Way of Southeastern Pennsylvania (Philadelphia based) already seem to be doing this; they allow designations to America's Charities as part of the United Way campaign (Cordes, Henig, Twombly, and Sanders, 1999; Gondella interview, January 21, 2003). Adoption of a new Charitable Mutual Fund identity would be a radical change, not without risks. Among other questions are, would United Ways suffer further loss of identity if not focused solely on health and human services, what would happen to controversial causes in "packages" offered by United Ways, and would their inclusion cause problems with regard to the United Way identity as Fiscal Intermediary for corporate donors?

UNITED JEWISH COMMUNITIES

Historically, federated fund-raising in the U.S. Jewish community is founded on the identity of Fiscal Intermediary, and this identity maintains much of its relevance to the present day. According to United Jewish Communities (UJC), the national umbrella organization for Jewish federations (United Jewish Communities, 2002):

> In 1895, the Jews of Boston created a centralized, communal organization–later to become the Combined Jewish Philanthropies–which brought together under one umbrella all the different local fundraising groups. It offered the first one-stop philanthropy ever formed on this continent. Each welfare agency maintained its full independence and gained proportionate representation on the CJP board of trustees. . . . Jews in other cities quickly recognized the genius of the Boston federation, for it al-

lowed the community to raise more funds at less expense and distribute them more wisely to meet greater needs. Today there are nearly 200 federations across North America. . . .

While Jewish federations were conceived for their efficiency in community fund-raising, they were also motivated by overall philanthropic goals and, as cited, the possibility of distributing funds "more wisely to meet greater needs." In this sense, the Jewish federations manifest the Community Problem Solver identity. Locally organized, with a strong national superstructure, the federations embrace a concept of community that includes Jews, locally and elsewhere, as well as non-Jewish neighbors in their local communities. Community Problem Solver appears to have become the primary identity of Jewish federations, as they address the social and human service needs of Jews and others in their local communities, international needs such as the plight of Soviet and Ethiopian Jews in recent years, and assistance to Israel. The problem solving approach is manifested through strategic planning at the community level as well as systematic allocation of raised funds according to community-wide priorities set by the federations' volunteer committees and boards of trustees (United Jewish Communities, 2002). This arrangement emerged over time as joint fund-raising efforts came together with collaborative efforts among Jewish human service organizations. For example, in St. Paul, Minnesota, the United Jewish Fund and Council (UJFC) was formed in 1943 as a merger of The United Jewish Fund of St. Paul (the fund raising organization) with the Council of Jewish Social Organizations (the association of Jewish service agencies) which had "provided a common meeting ground for all Jewish communal organizations in St. Paul, to avoid duplication of services and to set priorities regarding growing needs in the community" (United Jewish Fund and Council of St. Paul, 2002).

While the Community Problem Solver identity appears to be the central driving concept for federations belonging to United Jewish Communities, with Fiscal Intermediary as a strong secondary identity, the Jewish federations have also pioneered the cultivation of individual donors, to the point where the identity of Charitable Mutual Fund has become relevant and significant. The Jewish Community Federation of Cleveland may have been the first to employ the concept of donor-advised funds, and donor advised funds have become a prominent part of the fund-raising arsenal of federations nationwide. That arsenal quite clearly includes a variety of arrangements designed to permit individual donors to decide upon, or strongly influence, the allocation of their own charitable contributions, with the federation serving as intermediary. In particular, these arrangements help federations deal with the division between donors who want to concentrate resources on international and Israel-related needs and those more concerned with the needs of the American Jewish community. Federations encourage individualized contributions by marketing "alternatives to private foundations"–allowing donors to avoid the tax-related penalties of private foundation status by operating within the federation framework. These alternatives include (United Jewish Communities, 2002):

- Donor-Advised Philanthropic Funds which offer "active family involvement in the process of allocating resources to meet needs in the Jewish and general communities . . . "
- Designated Endowment Funds which "create a permanent legacy, perpetuating your ideals and your name . . . "
- Supporting Foundations which "are independent, charitable corporations providing a unique vehicle for involvement in philanthropy . . . "

While technically, the federations control these funds and could allocate their resources according to overall federation priorities, in fact, the process is much more subtle. In essence, federations maintain the faith of donors while addressing overall federation priorities, by offering a strong advisory structure within which resource distribution decisions are made. This is very much in the spirit of the Charitable Mutual Fund identity, yet still fairly consistent with the dominant identity of Community Problem Solver.

Recently, a change in the name of Jewish Federations to United Jewish Communities seems to suggest a joining of the identity of local Community Problem Solver with concern for international communities of Jews. However, the maintenance of this identity still depends on balancing pressures from both the provider community of autonomous Jewish human service organizations, and a donor community with significant numbers of major donors who can take advantage of options that offer considerable discretion in allocating their charitable resources. By themselves, providers might want to limit the federations' role to efficient fund raising and allocation (its Fiscal Intermediary identity) while donors might want to limit federations' role to that of assistance with administration of their charitable funds (the Charitable Mutual Fund identity). The success of the Jewish federations in maintaining the dominant Community Problem Solver identity appears to hinge on the essential commonality of goals among providers and donors regarding the welfare of the Jewish community, as well as the democratic mechanisms that federations employ for donors, volunteers, and social service executives to participate in the formulation of community priorities and in the decision making process for allocating charitable resources. In addition, integration of the Charitable Mutual Fund identity helps to ameliorate differences in priorities within the donor community.

CATHOLIC CHARITIES

Catholic Charities are local and regional groupings of human services organizations organized under the dioceses of the Roman Catholic Church in the United States. These federations have historically manifested the identity of Community Problem Solver, collections of agencies organized under auspices of the dioceses to address human needs in their respective communities. Most started with the establishment of specific agencies and programs addressed to particular community needs, often initiated by groups in local parishes or by particular religious orders within the church, and evolving into coordinated systems of fund-raising and service delivery. Thus, Fiscal Intermediary and Economic Regulator emerged as secondary identities as the service delivery organizations grew in number, complexity, and autonomy, and were able to benefit from coordinated fund-raising through an annual campaign (Catholic Charities Annual Appeal) and other mechanisms of charitable solicitation. Still, the emphasis on "systematic" and "community-focused" remains a key characteristic of Catholic Charities organizations, even as they have become more complex and multifaceted. The experience of Cleveland Catholic Charities appears to be typical in this respect (Catholic Charities of Cleveland, 2002):

> For nearly 80 years Catholic Charities has provided health and human services to the most vulnerable in the Diocese of Cleveland. Over the years, the Catholic Charities system which is part of the Diocesan structure of the Secretariat for Catholic Charities Health and Human Services, has evolved and adapted to the changing environment in which we raise funds, deliver services and carry out our work . . . We are continually examining our services and our mission . . . to better serve the needs of the people in our diocese. Over the past several years we have laid the ground work for establishing an integrated system of services to more efficiently manage facilities and fashioning better means to interface with parishes.

Similar evolutions characterize other Catholic Charities organizations, including Portland, Oregon, Houston, Minneapolis-St. Paul, Los Angeles, St. Louis, Boston, New York, Toledo, and Washington, D.C. (see referenced web sites; also, Dolan, 1998). All cite histories which begin with individuals or groups in the diocese organizing a program or agency to address a particular social need or problem (depending on the historical and local issues of the founding period), and feature subsequent periods of proliferation in the numbers of programs and agencies, and periods of consolidation. These histories reflect an evolution of the Catholic Charities organization towards becoming more systematic in the assessment of community needs and the development and coordination of programmatic initiatives over time. These scenarios result in Catholic Charities federations integrating Fiscal Intermediary and Economic Regulator identities, as the system grows and decentralizes, but the overall systematic Community Problem Solver identity seems not to have been lost in this evolution. In large part this identity is grounded in the systemic character of the Catholic Church with which it is affiliated. In essence, Catholic Charities organizations are part of the local church hierarchy and as such its resource decisions are controlled by the diocese administered by the local bishop. Donors are asked to contribute to the system-wide Catholic Charities appeal, not to designate the uses of their gifts, though they may choose to give separately, on their own, to institutions within the system.

One development, however, that potentially may transform the identities of Catholic Charities organizations is the development of diocesan foundations. The Cleveland diocese in particular has taken the lead in organizing its new Catholic Diocese of Cleveland Foundation which " . . . coordinates fund raising for all schools, agencies, and organizations owned and operated by the Diocese . . ." (Catholic Diocese of Cleveland Foundation, 2002). What is most interesting about this development is that it begins to transfer authority for resource allocation to donors through donor advised funds. These funds operate as follows:

> The named advisors may submit written grant recommendations on up to 6 percent of the fund's fair market value. Advisors are encouraged to consult with CDFC staff about organizations or projects to support and the staff will work with donors to identify potential grantee organizations or projects of interest to the donors. Recommendations are advisory only and the CDFC staff and board will review the recommendations . . . Grantmaking is expected to primarily support Diocesan and other Catholic organizations within [local] counties. However, selected grants may be recommended for any organization whose mission is consistent with the moral and social teaching of the Church . . .

The introduction of the CDFC and its donor advised funds begins to move Catholic Charities towards the Charitable Mutual Fund identity where resource allocation priorities are decided by donors, in a decentralized but advised manner, from the older model of allocation according to centrally-determined system priorities. Some apparently believe that this is the wave of the future for Catholic Charities because it inches towards lay control of resources and is potentially much more attractive to modern Catholic donors who prefer to make their own charitable decisions. As resource development becomes more difficult in the current Catholic Church environment, this new model may become all the more compelling. The logical extension of this identity is that Catholic Charities would move from a systems planning/Community Problem Solver role to a financial management role for its affiliated organizations and would allow the delivery system to evolve in response to donor-perceived preferences. However, this future remains speculative.

ALTERNATIVE FUNDS

There is no published comprehensive history of the alternative fund movement, and its history is not well known. Indeed, unlike United Way and religious federations, alternative funds did not start as an identified group of federated organizations, and they have developed into a multi-faceted complex group of federations. The so-called "movement" is of rather recent origins, essentially starting after the tumultuous 1960s. The amounts raised by alternative funds are growing, but still relatively small. According to the National Committee for Responsive Philanthropy (2003), in their fall 2001 campaign alternative funds raised more than $222 million while essentially for the same campaign year (2001-2002) United Ways reported $3.95 billion raised (United Way of America, 2003), although these are not entirely unduplicated amounts.

Among the earliest alternative funding federations were two "partners" in the combined federal employee campaign (CFC) that started in 1964 (Brilliant, 1990): International Voluntary Agencies (now International Service Agencies) and the National Health Agencies. However, by the end of the 1960s, other more activist funds began emerging out of the civil rights awakening of that decade. Some of these were targeted for the needs of particular groups such as the first Black United Fund (the Brotherhood Crusade in Los Angeles, 1968), the MS Foundation (1973), and the Astraea Lesbian Foundation in New York (1977), as well as The People's Fund in 1971 (now Bread and Roses) (National Alliance for Choice in Giving, 2003). While not really formalized federations of agencies, these funds certainly perceived themselves as Fiscal Intermediaries since they passed funds from donors to recipient organizations. In their grant-making activities they tended to conceive of themselves as Economic Regulators as well, but undoubtedly their primary identity was that of Social Change Agents for particular community needs or special populations, e.g., the black community, the poor, or women. Arguably by extension this could include a broader Community Problem Solver identity, since the conditions affecting these populations were problems which the community needed to confront.

In this period other federations also developed in the workplace, separate from the United Way. Two notable examples were the Associated-in-Group Donors-United Givers (AID) group in the high tech industries in California, and the Cooperating Fund Drive in Minneapolis, St. Paul. They each served as a Fiscal Intermediary between donors and recipients, but since they offered a packaged choice to the United Way, they also contributed to the latter's potential Charitable Mutual Fund identity. In the late 1970s, the United Way was partially successful in sidetracking the AID group (Brilliant, 1990), which has since morphed into Independent Charities of America (Ronnie interview, January 17, 2003). Meanwhile, in a more hospitable setting, in 1980 the Cooperative Fund Drive gained access to company workplaces, offering side-by-side cafeteria choice campaigns with the United Way.

The number of "nontraditional funds" seeking workplace access increased in the early 1980s. Community-based social justice workplace federations spread nationwide, with a particular growth spurt in 1987 after Congress passed permissive legislation regarding CFC admission for advocacy groups (National Committee for Responsive Philanthropy, Fall 1989). Soon thereafter the burgeoning group of workplace funds and federations created their own national association, the National Alliance for Choice in Giving (NACG). The National Alliance was formed to seek workplace access for its members and break United Way domination for funding of "traditional health and welfare agencies" (National Alliance for Choice in Giving, 2003).

By 2002, NACG membership included 52 federations and funds in 34 states (National Alliance for Choice in Giving, 2003). Its membership included an Asian Pacific Community Fund, the United Latino Fund, two women's federations, and a few other targeted social justice funds. However, the bulk of its membership were progressive grassroots federations affiliated loosely with the name (or concept) of "Community Shares," and state environmental funds, many with the name Earth Shares.

NACG members include local, regional, and statewide funds and financial federations that have social change agendas and participate widely in public employee campaigns. Although all of NACG's members are progressive in orientation, they have different structures, and there is really not one single identity for groups as diverse as statewide environmental funds, the local Action for Boston Community Development, or the Caring Connection. Still members share common identities largely around the double thrust of Fiscal Intermediary and Social Change Agent. Moreover, as community-based federations, many of the members of NACG also serve as Charitable Mutual Funds, offering donors choices among agencies concerned with substantive issues like women's needs or the environment. Many of these federations are less likely to take on the identity of Economic Regulator; as grass roots organizations they have small staffs and, of necessity, must emphasize raising funds.

Not all the groups generally referred to as social justice or alternative funds are members of the National Alliance. There are many other diverse groups in the Combined Federal Campaign and also increasingly in corporate workplaces. These groups include: (1) traditional federations formed primarily for the CFC public sector campaigns, such as the International Service Agencies; (2) national health agencies and combined local health appeals; (3) America's Charities, the National Service Group added to the CFC in the 1980s, which has since grown exponentially (America's Charities, 2002); and (4) other loosely affiliated federations, like the Independent Charities of America, that participate in various workplace campaigns. In addition to serving as Fiscal Intermediaries, these federated groups promote giving through donor choice in a way akin to Charitable Mutual Funds. Many also have some sense of identity as Economic Regulators, since they require structural and fiscal accountability documentation from their members.

In addition, there are 29 arts funds, about 18 local Black United Funds (and their national organization), and the funds in the Women's Funding Network, which also includes some workplace federations (National Committee for Responsive Philanthropy, 2003). The women's funds, more than 90 in all, evidence multiple identities; they function as Fiscal Intermediaries, and explicitly talk about re-granting foundation contributions to their members. However, like the Black United Funds, for the most part they tend to emphasize their Social Change Agent identity (Brilliant, 2000; Perlmutter and Kramer, 2001). With the encouragement and assistance of their national organization, the Women's Funding Network, most of these funds also conceive of themselves as Economic Regulators, and, like other social justice funds, they may embrace the identity of Community Problem Solver.

SYNTHESIS AND CONCLUSION

The four groups of federated community service organizations differ substantially in the way their identities have evolved over time. Table 1 briefly summarizes these alternative histories, in a necessarily simplified manner that conceals much of the subtlety of these evolutions.

The four federation groups also differ substantially in how their identities influence their thinking and approaches to strategic issues. Alternative funds embrace new social perspectives and are still evolving. Many of them consider

TABLE 1. Evolution of Organizational Identities of Community Service Federations

	United Way	Catholic Charities	Jewish Federations	Alternative Funds
Late 19th Century through WWII	FI is dominant; ER and CP emergent	CP dominates with FI as strong secondary identity	FI is dominant; CP and ER emerge	***********
Late 1940s through early 1960s	FI and ER dominate; CP declines	CP is dominant; FI maintained and ER emerges	CP grows; FI remains dominant; ER is secondary	FI emerges in federal campaign and community health appeals; some CP in community health appeals
Mid 1960s through 1970s	FI and ER maintained; CP threatened	CP remains dominant; FI and ER maintained	CP becomes dominant; FI and ER maintained	FI emerges and dominates; CP/SA emerges
1980s-present	ER and FI declining; CP resurrected; CM emerges	CP remains dominant; FI and ER maintained; CM begins to emerge	CP is dominant; FI and ER maintained; CM emerges and gains strength	CP/SA and FI co-exist as dominant identities for various federations; aspects of CM emerge and develop

Key: FI: Fiscal Intermediary
         ER: Economic Regulator
         CP: Community Problem Solver
         CM: Charitable Mutual Fund
         SA: Social Change Agent

themselves Community Problem Solvers in addition to Social Change Agents, although they also can function simply as Fiscal Intermediaries. Catholic Charities federations have succeeded as systematic Community Problem Solvers, centered on social needs in their parishes; however, they are facing new conceptions of donor control that may push them to integrate a version of the Charitable Mutual Fund identity in order to maintain community support. Similarly, United Jewish Communities federations have coalesced around a Community Problem Solver identity, while successfully integrating the traditional Fiscal Intermediary identity. More recently they have emphasized Charitable Mutual Fund identities to accommodate efficiency considerations and individual donor preferences within a coherent planning framework. United Ways seem to have struggled more than other federations in resolving multiple identities all strongly embedded throughout their history. Less secure in their roles of Fiscal Intermediary and Economic Regulator, these organizations are now struggling to regain prominence as Community Problem Solvers while facing pressures to reinvent themselves as broad-based Charitable Mutual Funds.

The experiences of the four groups of federations are similar in a number of ways which illustrate the centrality of organizational identity in managing for long-term survival and success. First, it is clear that as complex organizations, members of all four groups have struggled in reconciling multiple identities and new and changing circumstances over time. Implicitly and explicitly organizational identities serve as fundamental frames of reference for these federations, allowing them to weather storms in their economic and social environments while keeping their essential character and purpose in mind. Certainly clarity and relative stability of identity helped the Catholic and Jewish federations to prosper over many decades. For much of their history, United Ways enjoyed special status and stability from a combination of continued support from major corporate stakeholders and a strong community presence that included attachments to provider agencies. Still, United Ways have been forced to adapt new strategies and to reshape their identities in response to an increasingly diverse and changing charitable landscape. Indeed, flexible adaptation and revisiting of identities is a part of the story of all federated community service organizations and has accounted for much of their resilience, although too much adaptation causes tensions in maintaining a core organizational identity.

Second, the complexity of these organizations appears to require that they do indeed manifest multiple identities, yet manage these identities in ways that avoid organizational schizophrenia. This seems to favor one identity predominating as the overall "meta-identity" at any given time, and preferably over long periods of time. For Catholic Charities and for United Jewish Communities, this is clearly the Community Problem Solver identity, and for the Alternative Funds, it is probably the Social Change Agent identity. For United Ways, settling on the dominant meta-identity has been a continuing concern. This is part of the reason why a consistent name and prominent logo are significant both for reaffirming internal identity and projecting a strong external image.

Finally, experience in the four groups of federations makes clear that identities do not evolve in a vacuum nor can they remain functional without successful accommodation to the environments in which federations operate. While nonprofit organizations may not be subject to quite the same competitive pressures that force businesses into common molds in order to sell their products on the basis of market demands, neither do nonprofits have complete discretion to determine their identities without external reckoning. This is certainly the case for federations which depend on organizational members and broad bases of contributors. As such, identity formation entails juxtaposition and resolution of the viewpoints of key stakeholders, including social service providers, donors, and business, religious and community groups. When the interests of key stakeholders are aligned with a common notion of the essential purposes of the federations, a coherent identity can drive strategic decisions. Without such alignment, drift, conflict, and a clouded identity are more likely. To one degree or another, all of the studied federated community service organizations require continuing self-examination in order to adapt their foci and promote their ideals in a changing world. Indeed, the ability to balance flexibility with a coherent and acceptable organizational identity may ultimately mean the difference between future impact and success, and probable irrelevance and failure.

REFERENCES

Albert, Stuart, and David A. Whetten, "Organizational Identity," in L.L. Cummings and Barry M. Staw (eds.), *Research in Organizational Behavior*, volume 7, Greenwich, Connecticut: JAI Press, 1985, pp. 263-295.

Beene, Betty S., "Perceptions of Organizational Structure and a Nonprofit System's Operations in a Changed Environment: A Descriptive Case Study." Dissertation submitted for the degree of Doctor of Education. The George Washington University, 2001.

Billitteri, Thomas J. "United Ways Seek a New Identity," *The Chronicle of Philanthropy*, March 9, 2000, pp. 1, 21-26.

Brilliant, Eleanor L. *The United Way*, New York: Columbia University Press, 1990.

Brilliant, Eleanor L. "Women's Gain: Fund-Raising and Fund Allocation as an Evolving Social Movement Strategy." *Nonprofit and Voluntary Sector Quarterly*, 29 (4), December 2000, 554-570.

Center on Philanthropy, Indiana University. *Giving USA 2001: The Annual Report in Philanthropy for the Year 2000*. Indianapolis, IN: AAFRC Trust for Philanthropy, 2001.

Cordes, Joseph J., Jeffrey R. Henig, and Eric C. Twombly (with Jennifer L. Saunders), "The Effects of Expanded Donor Choice in United Way Campaigns on Nonprofit Human Service Providers in the Washington, D.C. Metropolitan Area, " *Nonprofit and Voluntary Sector Quarterly*, 28:2, June 1999, pp. 127-151.

Dolan, Jay P. "Social Catholicism, " chapter 26 in David C. Hammack (ed.) *Making the Nonprofit Sector in the United States*, Bloomington: Indiana University Press, 1998, pp. 188-202.

Dutton, Jane E., and Janet M. Dukerich, "Keeping an Eye on the Mirror: Image and Identity in Organizational Adaptation, " *Academy of Management Journal*, Vol. 34, No. 3, pp. 517-554, 1991.

Gioia, Dennis A., and James B. Thomas, "Identity, Image and Issue Interpretation, " *Administrative Science Quarterly*, Vol. 41, 1996, pp. 370-403.

Gioia, Dennis A., Majken Schultz, and Kevin G. Corley, "Organizational Identity, Image and Adaptive Instability, " *Academy of Management Review*, Vol. 25, No. 1, January 2000, pp. 63-81.

Glaser, John S. *The United Way Scandal: An Insider's Account of What Went Wrong and Why*. New York: John Wiley and Sons, 1993.

Golden-Biddle, Karen, and H. Rao, "Breaches in the Board Room: Organizational Identity and Conflict of Commitment in a Non-Profit Organization," *Organization Science*, Vol. 8, pp. 593-611, 1997.

Gondela, Rick (Director of Marketing and Communications, America's Charities). Interview, January 21, 2003.

Harper, Ernest B., and Arthur Dunham, *Community Organization In Action: Basic Literature and Critical Comments*. New York: Association Press, 1959.

Howe, Matt (Executive Director of National Alliance for Choice in Giving). Interview, January 15, 2003.

Kaplan, Ann. *Giving USA 1995: The Annual Report on Philanthropy for the Year 1994*. New York: AAFRC Trust for Philanthropy, 1995.

Local United Way Executive, Confidential Interview (telephone), September 23, 2001.

Lubove, Roy L. *The Professional Altruist: The Emergence of Social Work as a Career 1889-1930*. New York: Atheneum Press, 1969.

National Alliance for Choice in Giving. Appendix A, "NACG: A Brief History" and attached documents, including "Chronology of Workplace Giving Federation and Fund Development, 1971-2001," and "Democratizing philanthropy in the American workplace, " provided by the National Alliance for Choice in Giving.

National Committee for Responsive Philanthropy. *The Workplace Giving Revolution*. Washington, DC: Author, Fall 1987.

National Committee for Responsive Philanthropy. *The Workplace Giving Revolution: The New Era*. Washington, D.C.: Author, Fall 1989.

_____. President Signs CFC Legislation; Ends 11-Year Charity Drive Battle? In *Responsive Philanthropy*, The Newsletter of the National Committee for Responsive Philanthropy, Winter 1989.

_____. Special Report on Workplace Giving Alternatives: 10% and Growing. Washington DC: Author, Fall 1990.

_____. Charts with data on amounts raised by non-United Way, alternative funds and federations, provided by National Committee for Responsive Philanthropy, January 2003.

Perlmutter, Felice, and Vicki Kramer, . *Progressive Social Change Funds: Strategy for Survival*. Working Paper of the Aspen Institute Nonprofit Sector Research Fund. Washington, DC: Aspen Institute, 2001.

Pfeiffer, C. Whit. "Chest and Council Relations– The Case for Separate Councils." In Ernest B. Harper, and Arthur Dunham, *Community Organization in Action: Basic Literature and Critical Comments*, New York: Association Press, 1959, pp. 402-407.

Pratt, Michael G., and Peter O. Foreman, "Classifying Managerial Responses to Multiple Organizational Identities, " *Academy of Management Review*, Volume 25, No. 1, January 2000, pp. 18-42.

Ronnie, Kevin (Director of Field Operations, National Committee for Responsive Philanthropy). Interview. January 17, 2003.

Steketee, Nan (Former Executive Director, Center for Responsible Funding). Interview. January 18, 2003.

Stone, Melissa M. "Competing Contexts: The Evolution of a Nonprofit Organization's Governance System in Multiple Environments, " *Administration & Society*, Vol. 28, No. 1, May 1996, pp. 61-89.

Stone, Melissa M., and Jacelee DeWaard, "The Lutheran Welfare Society, 1905-1962: A Study of Contradictory Institutional Logics and Multiple Identities, " draft presented to Academy of Management, August 1998.

Strom, Stephanie."Questions Arise on Accounting at United Way," *New York Times,* November 19, 2002.

United Funds and Councils of America. Community Planning for Social Welfare–A Policy Statement (based on statement adopted by the Board of the Community Chests and Councils of America, 1950. In Ernest B. Harper, and Arthur Dunham, eds., *Community Organization in Action: Basic Literature and Critical Comments,* New York: Association Press, 1959, pp. 361-368.

United Way of America. *Community Impact: A New Paradigm Emerging.* (A White Paper on Change in the United Way Movement). Alexandria, VA: Author, 1998.

United Way of America. *Community Impact: Overview of Funding Systems* (A Handbook of Strategies and Practices 2000), Author: Alexandria, VA: 2000.

_____. *People and Events: A History of the United Way,* (Based on the manuscript of Elwood Street), Alexandria, VA: author, 1977

_____. Task Force on Strengthening the United Way System. *The Case for Action.* Draft Report, May 3, 2001.

_____. Task Force on Strengthening the United Way System. *Rising to the Challenge: How United Way will become America's preeminent community change agent.* Draft Report, October 1, 2001.

Varchaver, Nicholas. "Can Anyone Fix the United Way." *Fortune,* December 27, 2000, p. 171.

Watson, Frank Dekker. *The Charity Organization Movement in the United States,* New York: The MacMillan Company, 1922.

Weisbrod, Burton A. *The Nonprofit Economy,* Cambridge, MA: Harvard University Press. 1988.

Whetten, David A., and Paul C. Godfrey (eds.), *Identity in Organizations,* Thousand Oaks, California: Sage Publications, 1998.

Young, Dennis R. "Organizational Identity and the Structure of Nonprofit Umbrella Associations," *Nonprofit Management and Leadership,* Spring 2001, 11(3), pp. 289-304.

Young, Dennis R. "Organizational Identity in Nonprofit Organizations: Strategic and Structural Implications," *Nonprofit Management and Leadership,* 12(2), Winter 2001, pp. 139-157.

WEB SITES

America's Charities. Welcome to America's Charities. *www.charities.org/acbody1b.html,* retrieved January 8, 2002.

Catholic Charities: Archdiocese of Boston, *www.ccab.org,* December 19, 2002.

Catholic Charities of the Archdiocese of New York, *www.catholiccharitiesny.org,* December 19, 2002.

Catholic Charities: Archdiocese of St. Louis, *www.ccstl.org,* December 19, 2002.

Catholic Charities: Archdiocese of Toledo, *www.catholiccharitiesnwo.org*, December 19, 2002.

Catholic Charities of the Archdiocese of Washington, *www.catholiccharitiesdc.org*, December 19, 2002.

Catholic Charities of Cleveland, *www.clevelandcatholiccharities.org*, December 9, 2002.

Catholic Charities of St. Paul and Minneapolis, *www.ccspm.org*, December 19, 2002.

Catholic Charities of Houston, *www.catholiccharities.org*, December 19, 2002.

Catholic Charities of Los Angeles, *www.catholiccharitiesla.org*, December 19, 2002.

Catholic Charities of Oregon, *www.catholiccharitiesoregon.org*, December 19, 2002.

Catholic Charities USA, *www.catholiccharitiesusa.org*, December 9, 2002.

Catholic Diocese of Cleveland Foundation, *www.cdfc.org*, December 9, 2002.

Council of Jewish Philanthropies/Boston, *www.cjp.org*, December 20, 2002.

Foundation Center of Cleveland. *http://fdncenter.org*, January 4, 2003.

Jewish Community Federation of Cleveland, *www.jewishcleveland.org*, December 9, 2002.

Jewish Community Foundation, Minneapolis Jewish Federation, *http://twincities.ujcfedweb.org*, December 20, 2002.

Minneapolis Jewish Federation, *www.jewishminnesota.org*, December 20, 2002.

National Committee for Responsive Philanthropy, *www.ncrp.org*, January 18, 2003.

UJA-Federation of New York, *www.ujafedny.org*, December 20, 2002.

United Jewish Communities, About UJC, *www.ujc.org*, December 9, 2002.

United Jewish Fund and Council of St. Paul, *http://twincities.ujcfedweb.org*, December 20, 2002.

United Way of America, *www.national.unitedway.org*, January 19, 2003.

_____. 2000-2001 CAMPAIGN RESULTS (Highlights), *http://national. unitedway. org*, October 26, 2001.

Congregations as Social Service Providers: Services, Capacity, Culture, and Organizational Behavior

Ram A. Cnaan, PhD
Jill W. Sinha, PhD, MDiv
Charlene C. McGrew, MSW, ThM

SUMMARY. Social welfare is traditionally discussed as a mixture of public, private, communal, and familial enterprise. Indeed, most textbooks and programs focus on the changing balance between these four circles of care. In the United States, a fifth and recently prominent circle of care exists and plays a major role, namely congregation-based social service provision. In this article, we first explain why faith-based care is so paramount in the United States, including a short discussion about the political developments in faith-based efforts. We then show the scope of congregational involvement in social service provision based on a large

Ram A. Cnaan is Professor and Director, Program for the Study of Organized Religion and Social Work. Jill W. Sinha serves as a post doctoral fellow at Princeton University, Department of Sociology. Charlene C. McGrew is a Doctoral Student, School of Social Work, University of Pennsylvania.

Address correspondence to: Ram A. Cnaan, PhD, Professor and Director, Program for the Study of Organized Religion and Social Work, University of Pennsylvania, 3701 Locust Walk, D-19, Philadelphia, PA 19104-6214 (E-mail: cnaan@ssw.upenn.edu). The authors wish to thank the Pew Charitable Trusts and the Buford Foundation for technical and financial support that were necessary for the completion of this study.

[Haworth co-indexing entry note]: "Congregations as Social Service Providers: Services, Capacity, Culture, and Organizational Behavior." Cnaan, Ram A., Jill W. Sinha, and Charlene C. McGrew. Co-published simultaneously in *Administration in Social Work* (The Haworth Social Work Practice Press, an imprint of The Haworth Press, Inc.) Vol. 28, No. 3/4, 2004, pp. 47-68; and: *Organizational and Structural Dilemmas in Nonprofit Human Service Organizations* (ed: Hillel Schmid) The Haworth Social Work Practice Press, an imprint of The Haworth Press, Inc., 2004, pp. 47-68. Single or multiple copies of this article are available for a fee from The Haworth Document Delivery Service [1-800-HAWORTH, 9:00 a.m. - 5:00 p.m. (EST). E-mail address: docdelivery@ haworthpress.com].

47

study of congregations. The rest of the article is dedicated to key administrative challenges regarding this mode of social service provision with a focus on their capacity, cultural characteristics, and organizational behavior. The latter topic is divided between start-up of new projects by congregations and issues related to running social programs in congregational settings. We conclude with a summary and discussion about the place of congregations as social service providers in the American welfare arena. *[Article copies available for a fee from The Haworth Document Delivery Service: 1-800-HAWORTH. E-mail address: <docdelivery@haworthpress.com> Website: <http://www.HaworthPress.com>* © *2004 by The Haworth Press, Inc. All rights reserved.]*

KEYWORDS. Congregations, faith-based social services, administrative challenges, alternative social services delivery, welfare-mix

INTRODUCTION

At the dawn of the 21st century, many welfare states are discussing the need to shift the balance in their welfare programs. Moving from a massive reliance on the public sector, these states are increasingly investigating the role of three other players: the private sector (both employers and private providers), the local community, and the family (Ascoli & Ranci, 2002). In the past quarter century, almost all Western democracies are shifting their welfare costs from the government to other sectors, a process known as devolution (Lipsky & Smith, 1989-90). The United States clearly led the way toward devolution. Starting with smallest percentage of GDP publicly allocated for welfare services, under the guise of the "new federalism," the American government shifted welfare provision responsibility to the states and from them to cities and counties (Conlan, 1998). Yet, today what is most unique about the American welfare state is the push to use faith-based social providers and especially local religious congregations (Cnaan et al., 2002; Hodgkinson, Weitzman, Kirsch, Noga, & Gorski, 1993).

To understand the role of religious groups in social service provision, a few facts should be clarified. First, the United States may justly lay claim to be the most religious of all modern democracies. According to the World Value Survey, conducted from 1990 to 1993, more people in the United States (82%) defined themselves as religious than did those in any other country (*The Economist*, 1995). In a 1993 CNN/USA Today/Gallup poll, 71 percent of Americans reported membership in a church or synagogue, and 41 percent reported attendance at a church or synagogue in the seven days prior to the poll (McAneny & Saad, 1993). A more recent study by the Pew Research Center for the People and the Press (2001) found that Americans show high rates of religious observance. Six out of ten Americans attend religious services (not including weddings and funerals) at least once a month, while 43 percent attend at least weekly. Overall, slightly less than half the public (46%) said they attended church in the previous seven days. Cnaan, Gelles, and Sinha (2002) found that even teens in the United States report high religiosity, with 86 percent claiming that religion is important in their lives, 67 percent report attending worship services at least monthly, and 41 percent report membership in a faith-based youth group.

Second, in addition to congregations, America has the widest range of active religions and denominations. It is estimated that there are 2,000 religions and denominations active in the United States. However, this religious presence is often overlooked when discussing the contributions of community organizations.

Community organizations most often refer to neighborhood associations, human service organizations, branches of city-wide groups, civic associations, small businesses, tenants' associations, ecological preservation groups, police precincts, city units (those stationed in the neighborhood and those only serving the neighborhood), libraries, community centers, public schools, private schools, and gangs, each representing certain interests. It is surprising that we neglect to include the most prevalent and longstanding community institution, namely local religious congregations. Other religious groups in the community, including religious schools (Catholic and many others), faith-based social groups, para-church groups, Bible reading/study groups, and house churches contribute to the presence of faith-based groups in the community. In communities that have witnessed a decline or disappearance of employers and community organizations over the late twentieth century, faith groups that have remained in the community are crucial (Fabricant & Fisher, 2002).

In his in-depth study of the institutional ecology of four Los Angeles neighborhoods, John Orr (1998) discovered that there were "an average of 35 religious congregations and 12.5 religiously-affiliated nonprofit corporations per square mile, far more than the number of gasoline stations, liquor stores, and supermarkets combined" (p. 3). Similarly, in our study of West Philadelphia, we found 433 places of worship in an area of 13 square miles, approximately the same ratio of congregations to square mile found by Orr in Los Angeles (Cnaan & Boddie, 2002). Botchwey (2003) studied a small segment of Philadelphia's most blighted neighborhood. In an area of seven contiguous census tracts (1.3 square miles and 400 households), she found 62 active organizations. Of these 62 organizations, only 23 percent (14) were non-faith-based.

The remaining organizations were either congregations (41, or 66%) or faith-based organizations (7, or 11%). In other words, not only are Americans very religious, but religious organizations in the United States are the most prevalent community institution.

Given the preponderance of congregational involvement and sheer volume of congregations in America (estimates range from 250,000 to 400,000), their geographical distribution, and the devolutionary trends in this society, it is clear that faith-based groups, especially congregations, will be harnessed to provide social services (Cnaan & Boddie, 2002; Smith & Sosin, 2001). Signs of this movement are visible. After Charitable Choice legislation passed in 1996, making it more possible for faith-based groups to apply for public funding to provide certain services, the legislation was extended twice; once to include Community Services Block Grants (1988) and once to include drug abuse treatment programs (2000). In 2001, President Bush established the White House Office of Faith-Based and Community Initiatives, and in late 2002, he signed an executive order barring all federal agencies from discriminating against religious organizations when awarding social service money.

Congregations and other faith-based organizations are encouraged to move into the field of social welfare provision when resources are cut and needs are rising. Consequently, religiously affiliated agencies are experiencing new obligations as they are pressured to compensate for declines in public spending. For example, clients and other constituencies are urging some faith-based agencies to increase their material assistance effort as income maintenance support declines (Smith & Sosin, 2001).

Whether and to what extent congregations can increase their service provision remains at large in the debate. The unique administrative and managerial characteristics of congregations may well be part of their strength, while at the same time limit their capacity. Harris (1995) contended that congregations are a unique subset of voluntary associations with a few special characteristics. We take this argument one step further, asserting that congregations are so distinct that they should be singularly defined and studied.

The purpose of this study is to provide an overview of congregations as social service providers in America and review their organizational characteristics. We deal with congregations as unique social service providers as opposed to other types of nonprofits or public service providers. We focus here on the formal social service provided by congregations ranging from after school programs to health clinics and from summer camps to homeless shelters. These services significantly complement and reduce the need for public social services. In this era of devolution and increased reliance on faith-based organizations, it is essential for the social service administration community to know how to collaborate with, and even within, faith-based social services providers.

This study will enable social service administrators to work better with faith-based social service providers of all types.

In this paper, after describing the methods for our study, we provide the reader with information of services provided by congregations, followed by an analysis of their capacity as social service providers. We continue by discussing the organizational culture of congregations as social service providers, followed by two sections about organizational behavior–starting up programs and maintaining social programs. We conclude with a discussion of the congregations as a social service agency. We should note at the outset that congregations are extremely heterogeneous and diverse. While we treat them as a single entity here, we recognize the risk of overgeneralization and overlooking variation and regional and theological differences.

METHODS

Background and Sampling

Data collection took place from 1998 to 2001. It was difficult to identify all congregations in Philadelphia, as there is no complete accurate list with all or even most of the city's religious congregations; neither is there an agreement on how to define a congregation (Cnaan et al., 2002). After almost three years of study, we estimate the number of congregations in Philadelphia to be approximately 2,119. To develop a working list of congregations, we merged two data files: the City of Philadelphia Property Tax list and the Yellow Pages list of congregations. In order to identify unlisted congregations, we applied three methods. First, we requested lists from every denomination and interfaith organization in the region. We received fifteen different lists. We merged these with our master file manually since congregations often use various names and may give more than one address or list a clergy residence. Second, in every interview, we asked clergy members or key-informants to identify and provide contact information for any congregations with which they collaborate. Given that the interviewers were paid per completed interview, they had an incentive to identify new congregations and add them to the master list. We also enlisted our advisory board, composed of religious leaders throughout the city, to review the list and supply information about missing congregations. Finally, our research interviewers canvassed neighborhoods block-by-block to identify possibly unlisted storefront churches and other congregations not on our master file. In the process we discovered many congregations, especially those of ethnic minority, that were unlisted. These combined approaches brought us closer to a complete master list. Our list now consists of

2,119 distinct congregations. Of this list, we interviewed 1,392 congregations (66%).

Procedures

Trained research assistants or the authors contacted congregations to solicit their participation. All interviewers received both a lengthy orientation and weekly group in-service training about the history and overview of the study, its benefit to the congregations and broader community, ways to use and disseminate data, and an introduction to the survey instruments. Each interviewer was given a training manual with the above information and specifications and clarification for the survey instruments. Weekly in-service meetings were held to discuss problems and insure inter-rater reliability. Mock interviews were held monthly and a trained data entry person detected mistakes and inconsistencies in the data.

When a congregation agreed to an interview, the interviewer went and engaged the senior clergy or his/her representative in a face-to-face interview. On average, interviews lasted three or more hours. At times the interview included a group of people in the congregation such as the clergy, lay leaders, and an administrator. Given that many questions were written for experienced interviewers, interviews were conducted face-to-face in the congregational setting. No telephone or written responses were accepted.

Instrumentation

In carrying out this study, we used a comprehensive range of research instruments. The first instrument is the *Core Questionnaire*. The Core Questionnaire is a ten-page instrument designed to elicit information regarding the history and background of the congregation. The key areas covered in this instrument are: the congregation's religious affiliation, theological and political orientation, history, membership, financial affairs and budget, governance, future plans, physical layout, and relationships with the local community and other institutions that are active in the area.

The second part of the interview is the *Inventory of Programs*. It was compiled after reviewing numerous reports and interviewing experts in congregational social services. The instrument ascertained information about the congregation's areas of social service involvement (that is, non-religious services to society). The interviewer covered 215 areas of possible social and community involvement. For each possible area of social service, it was assessed if the service is provided at all, formally or informally, by the congregation or by someone else, on the congregational properties or elsewhere, and if it is the congregation's program or supports another organizations' program. The interview focused on the past year (past 12 months) to include annual and seasonal programs such as summer camp, and to assure similar coverage for all congregations regardless of the time of year in which the interview took place. This inventory of social programs served as a means to help interviewees cover all their social programs and involvement.

The third part of the interview is the *Specific Program Form*. This instrument was used to gather information about the most important and resource-laden social service programs provided by the congregation, up to a maximum of five programs. The interviewee was asked detailed questions about a program's history, ownership, staffing, beneficiaries, frequency, and cost. To determine a program's overall cost, seven items were used to compile a replacement value (value of space used for the program; clergy, staff and volunteer hours; cash support; in kind support; and utilities costs). Due to the length of interviewing time, congregations with more than five social programs were asked to choose only the five "most representative of their work," and to tell us briefly about other services or programs provided.

RESULTS

What Services Do Congregations Provide?

Congregations are highly involved in social service provision (Cnaan & Boddie, 2001). Almost nine of every ten congregations, regardless of size and ethnic composition, are engaged in at least one social service provision. Often the service is quite modest—meeting the need of some twenty community residents in programs such as after school recreational programs and food pantries. A host of other local studies show similar findings (cf. Ammerman, 2001; Billingsley, 1999; DiPietro & Behr, 2002; Grettenberger & Hovmand, 1997; Hill, 1998; Hodgkinson et al., 1993; Jackson, Schweitzer, Blake, & Cato, 1997; Printz, 1998; Silverman, 2000) with one often-quoted exception (Chaves, 1999).

Our social service inventory of 215 possible congregation services included only those programs that went beyond solely religious services such as prayer meetings or worship. It included programs that were administered formally by the congregation, occurred on its property, or with help from outside the congregation. Of the 215 services, each and every program was offered by at least a few congregations. While we are sure that the tapestry of congregation-based services is a rich and diverse one, it also deserves further study.

The most commonly served groups were children and youth, the elderly, people who are homeless, and people who are poor. Almost half the congregations reportedly offer food pantries, and more than a third of the congregations offer summer day camps, recreational programs for teens, and clothing closets. About a quarter of the congregations offer music performances, soup kitchens, and educational tutoring. Other commonly offered programs included: international relief and sick/homebound visitation (22% each), prison ministry, programs for gang members, and choral groups (21% each), and after school care and support for neighborhood associations (20% each).

On average, we found that each congregation provides at least 2.5 distinct programs. These programs served some combination of members and non-members. On average, each congregation sponsored programs that served 39 members of the congregation and 63 community residents who are not members of the congregation. In other words, congregations tend to serve others more than their own members at a ratio of two to three. This ratio shows congregations serving others rather than existing as "exclusive clubs."

On average, 16 members of each congregation (this figure includes paid staff and volunteers) are involved in social service delivery, and they are joined by nine volunteers who are not members of the congregation. This ability to recruit a large volume of volunteers, even from among non-members, sets congregations apart from many social service organizations and highlights one of their strongest advantages over traditional social services providers.

Almost all congregations (1192, or 85.6%) informed us that they hold worship or prayer services in collaboration with other religious groups. A large percentage of congregations collaborated with other faith-based organizations to develop and deliver community service programs (870, or 62.5%). Somewhat surprisingly, more than half of the congregations (781, or 56.2%) reported collaborating with secular organizations for the purpose of delivering a service or running a program. The collaborating organizations may be government agencies, local universities, neighborhood associations or community organizations. The purposes of the collaborations often include sharing space, sharing financial resources, or sharing staff and supplies. Interestingly, congregations often elect to worship with others, but also willingly cooperate to help people in need.

What is the value of social labor contributed by congregation volunteers, clergy, and staff? The answer can be provided by estimating the replacement value of the social services provided by the congregations on their properties, using their own financial resources and volunteers. By replacement value we do not mean the amount it costs for a congregation to run their programs in terms of dollars. What we mean is the amount it would cost others to provide the same services or programs at the level stipulated if they did not have congregational property and member volunteers at their disposal. To illustrate, if a congregation pays a mortgage for a building in which a social program is held, the value of the space is a congregational contribution, which in real terms, has a cost and a financial value. Similarly, if a clergy member invests time in a social program, his or her salary should be recognized as paid by the congregation which enables him or her to spend time providing community-oriented services.

The monthly replacement value of an average Philadelphia congregation is estimated at $9,821.06. We converted the monthly values into annual values (multiplying the sum of $9,821.06 by 12 months), and thereby obtained an annual replacement value of $117,852.72. Given that our work so far shows that there are 2,119 congregations in Philadelphia, and assuming (as we do) that our sample of 1,392 congregations is highly representative of the city's congregations, we assess the annual replacement value of the entire body of congregations in Philadelphia at $249,729,914. In other words, congregations' annual contribution to Philadelphia's quality of life is estimated at a quarter billion dollars. It can be shown that this estimate is quite conservative and the real value is possibly higher (Cnaan & Boddie, 2001).

In order to understand the congregational replacement value in context, we must assess the City of Philadelphia's annual commitment to social care. In 2002, the City of Philadelphia spent $473,525,933 for services to children and youth through the Department of Human Services, $14,902,777 for services to the homeless through the Department of Adult Services, and $34,258,043 for services to the community through the Department of Recreation. In other words, the total social services budget of the city of Philadelphia is $522,686,573 which includes space, salaries, and administration costs as well as direct services. Thus, the congregational replacement value reported above equals 47.8 percent of the annual City budget. When the two grand sums are combined, about one third of the cost to maintain quality of life in Philadelphia is voluntarily provided by local religious congregations.

Finally, we asked, "What percentage of the annual operating budget is earmarked for social services?" as opposed to operation costs or member development. Of the congregations that answered this question, the mean was 21.6 percent. That is, about two-fifths of the congregations' annual budget (excluding capital campaigns and schools) is designated to contribute to the quality of life of people in the community and in the city beyond the cost of maintaining the congregation property and staff.

The previous sections of this article demonstrated that relying on faith-based groups to provide social services is an inevitable and rational component to the American quest to reduce welfare costs and enhance efficiency. Given that so many Americans believe in God and attend religious congregations indicates that numerous congregations are spread throughout the country, and every person has access to any number of them. We also demonstrated, based on our census of congregations in Philadelphia, that many congregations are heavily involved in social service provision. In fact, many human service organizations deny new clients eligibility for services if they have not first sought assistance from their own or a near by congregation. De-facto, American congregations turned out to be the national and local safety net, and public opinions show that most Americans expect congregations to provide welfare services to needy people (Pirog & Reingold, 2002). Now that the political and public discourse focuses on faith-based groups as the "new kid on the block" to provide services to the poor and disadvantaged, a question has emerged about their organizational behavior: What do we know about their capabilities and organizational strengths and weaknesses?

THE CONGREGATION AS A SOCIAL SERVICE ORGANIZATION: CAPACITY, CULTURE, AND ORGANIZATIONAL BEHAVIOR

This section of the article will be divided into three key sub-themes. First, we will discuss congregational capacity in terms of membership size, funds, and other key resources. Second, we will discuss the unique cultural background that governs most congregations. Third, we will discuss issues pertaining to organizational behavior with two key subheadings: start-up of new projects by congregations and issues related to running social programs in congregational settings.

Capacity: Size, Community Base, Ethnicity, Budget, and Location and Space

Size. Among the congregations in this study, membership size ranges from a low of six members to a high of 13,000 members. On average, 247 people attend at least one worship service per week per congregation. The average size of active members (people attending at least monthly) of the congregations is 346 individuals including children. In order to achieve reliability, we ask all congregations to include children even if they are not officially viewed as members. It should be noted that when children are excluded, half the congregations in our study report a membership of less than 100 members. Our mean membership size is increased by a group of mega-churches (congregations attracting more than 1000 members each). This number, which is corroborated by other studies (Dudley & Roozen, 2001), suggests that many average-sized congregations have relatively few adult members who can implement social programs. While size can be deceiving, we found a correlation between size and involvement in social service provision. Additionally, the existence of a full time clergy was also associated with social service involvement. Congregations without at least one full-time clergy where less likely to be involved in providing services than congregations with one or more full-time clergy. In other words, not all of the 2119 congregations in Philadelphia are equally poised to deliver social services.

Community Base. On average, almost half (44.5%) of all congregation members live within ten blocks of the congregation's site, 37.5 percent live within the city limits but beyond a ten-block radius, and 18 percent live outside of the city limits. Many people in the community told us that faith communities are considered hubs of trust and islands of peace and support within their communities. Among African American communities, the role of the congregation is particularly prominent. In an analysis of the National Survey of Black Americans, Taylor, Thornton, and Chatters (1987) report that 82.2 percent of African American adults who were surveyed said that the Black church has helped the condition of Blacks in America. The definition of "help" included but was not limited to: promoting of positive feelings; sustaining and strengthening; personal assistance; providing moral guidelines for behavior; personal or social help; and providing a sense of unity and gathering place in the community.

These findings imply that among nonprofit and community organizations, congregations are the most community-based social service organization, and their members have intimate understanding of the changing needs of people in the community. The only other community-attached organization is the public school. However, in urban America, schools are often distrusted or extremely distressed, with the community viewing them either as filled with outsiders who are not committed to the neighborhood, or who are unable to help (Sanders, 2000).

Ethnicity. An overwhelming majority of congregations (89.9%) reported that at least 75 percent of their members belong to one racial or ethnic group. The majority of the congregations in this sample were Black congregations (54.9%) and white congregations (26.2%). The sample also included Hispanic congregations (5.3%) and Asian-American congregations (3.5%). The high proportion of congregations that represent primarily one ethnicity suggests that congregations remain divided by ethnic lines, and to some extent, by class. As such, one may wonder if people of different ethnic groups and class-bases feel welcome to utilize services from homogenous social service providers, such as congregations. However, our observations did not reflect this to be a problem. Furthermore, social services offered by various human service organizations are often provided by staff that is of a class and/or race that is different from that of the clients (Fong & Gibbs, 1995).

Budget. Three out of ten congregations (31 percent) reportedly have annual budgets of less than $50,000 and an additional quarter (26 percent) have a budget of between $50,000 and $100,000. A similar percent (23%) of congregations reported having a budget between $100,000 and $200,000, another 14 percent reported having a budget of between $200,001 and $500,000, and a slightly smaller number (6%) reported having a budget between $500,000 and $1,000,000. Only a small number of congregations (2 percent) reported having a budget of more than a million dollars a year. The reported budgets do not include building funds or school budgets.

Budget size is an important variable in explaining the scope of social services involvement, and our findings above suggest that over half of congregations have annual budgets of less than $100,000. Given that for congregations, social service provision comes second to worship and maintenance, one wonders how feasible it is for such congregations to provide an additional formal program either at their own expense or by applying for a public grant. While almost all of them provide social services, the services are often small scale programs that rely on volunteers and use congregational space.

Location and Space. One of the noted assets that congregations bring to the social service arena is space. Congregations are dotted throughout communities and the majority own one or more buildings. Four-fifths (81.8%) of the congregations in our study own their properties and are able to use them for any use they see fit. Only 11.5 percent of the congregations have no space of their own. These congregations rent space from other congregations (guest congregations), use hotel halls, schools, and other spaces donated by willing owners. A little over half of the congregations (51.4%) reported using more than one property and about one of these congregations (14.2%) own three or more buildings. Often, additional buildings house schools, day care centers, day missions, youth programs, or homeless shelters. In many cases, space within these buildings is available for social programs throughout the week for community groups, community meetings, or local service delivery.

Large numbers of properties owned by the congregations are old buildings and thus suffer from structural problems that may inhibit social service delivery. For example, 17.2 percent of our sample reported roof leaks and need of repairs, and 13.9 percent reported leakage through walls or floors. In addition, the following building distresses were reported by congregations: wall stress and cracks (6.5%), electrical problems (5.2%), heating and cooling problems (8.3%), and problems meeting city codes (4.0%). The large majority of the congregations (69.4%) reported no building problems. It is reasonable to con-take time from work to pray and thank God. Faith interweaves into the planning, delivery and alteration of social services. Congregational members are used to having people in their building who are theologically like-minded and with whom they can discuss faith and God, and as such, are comfortable with blending faith and social service. As shown by several studies, congregations have varied styles of delivery and overt religious talk, actions, or symbols may or may not be an observable part of the social service (Sider, Olson, & Unruh, 2002).

Congregations tend to carry out their ministries alone. As Cnaan and colleagues (2002) found, congregations do not view themselves as an arm of the state or any other group, but rather as an independent body that acts upon its own cues. The major reason to offer a social program was consistently "acting out people's faith." Most often, a program evolves when a member of the congregation, usually a clergy or lay leader, observes a need and shares his or her observations with the congregation. What follows is usually a discussion about the problem and the congregation's desire and ability to help. While many such initiatives/testimonials go nowhere, some materialize into programs designed to help those in need. Since this initiative for serving comes from within the congregation, it is unlikely that those engaged in delivering the service will attempt to find partners. While many congregations have members who volunteer or assist community and nonprofit organizations, congregations like to "own" their social programs. That is, helping others in need becomes a collective spiritual endeavor borne out through congregational ministry. The idea of sharing a ministry or program delivery with an outside or non-religious organization is far less common. Even when it is obvious to local faith communities that the needs are greater than their capabilities, there is a proclivity to go at it alone and resistance to calling upon other groups to partner in program delivery. To be fair, 36.3 percent of congregations in our sample are partners in interfaith or non-religious collaborations; however, among the listed social programs 66.1 percent are carried by the congregation alone. Furthermore, as noted above 62.5% of the congregations reported to collaborate with faith partners and 45.7% with secular partners to provide social services.

Another notable characteristic of many congregations is that they work informally and without protocol. People react to whatever is needed and the idea of a bureaucracy seems impersonal and even threatening to members. For example, many congregations do not have personnel policies and view them with some wariness. In general, we found that people are hired with a handshake and are told about salary and benefits, but the expectation is that the person will be immersed into the congregation, often along with their families. In most congregations there are no formal procedures for employee evaluation.

sider that these sacred properties may be available for social service d
when not used for worship, religious classes, and other sacramental pur[
Overall, congregations in urban America are characterized by being
They are located in every community and are accessible to local resi
Most congregations are relatively small in size, which often translates in[
vices that are very personal in nature. Meanwhile, few congregations are
in size and resources. For the most part, congregations remain ethnically
regated–a fact that engenders trust and enhances the fabric of mutual ;
tance which is foundational for serving others. A majority of congregaı
are not financially strong, yet, on average, they allocate more than one-fif[
their budgets to social programs and services.

Cultural Background

As noted, the neglect of faith-based groups in the social work literatı
leaves us with limited knowledge on how to work with these groups, and h[
to collaborate with them on joint projects. For example, harnessing the uniq[
contributions of communities of faith requires sensitivity to their characte
appreciation of their faith, and willingness to work with organizations th[
simultaneously adhere to an "organizational" authority and to a "higher" authorit[
(Chaves, 1998). The "higher" authority is often dominant in determining wha[
services will be offered and under what conditions. In some cases, religiou$
beliefs or doctrines may result in refusing to serve people who live certain lif[
styles. A related situation may be that if the mission of the religious congregation or religious group changes so does their social service offering. It is imperative to understand that congregations' primary raison d'etre is worship
and religious life, followed by organizational survival. Though congregational theologians rightly suggest that providing social services is an inherent
and crucial part of being a congregation, the practical reality for most congregations is that providing social services is tertiary and depends on successful
maintenance of the first two functions of the congregation.

A clergy that we interviewed used the following analogy about understanding religion in the context of a congregation: "For us religion is everywhere.
When you make a pancake you see an egg next to the flour, margarine, and
sugar. Focus on this egg. When the pancake is done, the egg is in it, but you do
not see it. So, for us is religion. It is everywhere, and yet you can't see it but
you know it is there, respect it, and know that without it there is no pancake."
What this clergy is referring to is the pervasiveness of religion in everything
they do. In the name of religion, a congregation may start a social service and
the focus of a program will change when the spirit moves it. Furthermore, in
congregations it is common for people (staff, lay people, and clients alike) to

Salary raises and dismissals are done informally without scheduled periodic reviews.

In addition, congregation staff, while possibly having professional experience, often have limited or no experience in external (aside from members) fund-raising, grant proposal writing, or formal program development and evaluation. Further, as congregations are exempted from filing an IRS report, many operate without strict accounting of their finances (Jeavons & Basinger, 2000).

In contrast to congregations' informality, professionals in human service organizations are often hired to perform a specific set of skills. They use their training and education to execute clearly defined tasks and responsibilities. Congregations, however, tend to have people who not only are volunteers, but may become involved in any number of overlapping activities. The same set of people who plan Sunday music may also organize food distribution. It is common for anyone in the building to be called upon to help with certain tasks that require more hands. One will see the senior clergy fixing the boiler and carrying boxes of food. Therefore, volunteers are utilized not only for their professional training or education but for whatever is needed for the congregation to provide a service.

Unlike formal service organizations, in congregation programs, time spent visiting, chatting, and relating is valued and accepted as strengthening the membership or the quality of the service. Using paid time for work-related or task-specific functions is expected, and time spent "relating to others" is minimized. While it is common for the congregation members to do whatever is needed whenever it is needed, human service organization employees may see such expectations on them as an intrusion, violation of their contract, or an interference in their ability to complete the task for which they were hired.

Organizational Behavior

The last section of this article discusses issues of organizational behavior. We divided this section into two sub-sections. We first discuss issues pertaining to start up of new programs by congregations followed by discussing the day-to-day management of social programs by congregations.

Starting-Up Social Programs

The process through which congregations versus secular organizations arrive at social service delivery is diametrically opposed. Secular human service organizations often respond to donor preference or the availability of public grants to fund their activity. Every nuance of the funding stream influences service options and scope of care. Congregations, on the other hand, often depend on internal resources and use members' desires, volunteers, and available space as the cornerstone of their services. In our study, we asked interviewees about how some 3,922 different programs were initiated. In almost two-thirds of the cases the initiation came from the pastor (64.7%), followed by congregational members (28.2%), congregational committee (12.3%), and congregational staff (7.5%). Note that in some cases these percentages are overlapping as a program can be initiated by a variety of actors. A decision of whether and in what area to develop services is based on being compelled by a need, confirming it with others, forming a group to plan a service, and then carrying out a program. There is almost never a commitment to an external agency, and hence the service may be modified or cut as needed. In sharp contrast, very few congregational programs were initiated by a call from the outside or a funding opportunity. Outside initiators may include diocese or judicatories (3.9%), human service organizations (1.9%), neighborhood associations or coalitions (1.6%), other congregations (1.1%), government agencies (0.9%), and others (4.3%). When we viewed all programs and compared in-house initiation versus externally-encouraged initiation, the difference is extremely large. The overwhelming majority of congregational programs are initiated in-house (91.8%) as compared to externally initiated (11.5%).

Local religious congregations, with few notable exceptions, have limited resources and operate at maximum capacity. That is, the budget and other resources are maximized. Often the hope is that nothing will break, and that there will not be any need for extra expenses. By far, the majority of congregations that we interviewed indicated that their financial situation was "sound or struggling" (90.2%), as indicated by a tremulous balance between expenditures and income, and only 9.8 percent reported to be financially strong. This stretching of financial and other resources puts the congregation in a vulnerable situation. Collaborating with others exposes vulnerabilities and limits the congregation's flexibility to deal with crises as they come. For example, if a congregation makes a commitment to pay for food at a certain joint event, and then its heating system fails, the priority will be given to fixing the heating system and not to supporting the joint event. Being uncertain of how many times crises like this may occur, and having very tight budgets influences many congregations to shy away of collaborating with others, and with others who have abundant resources.

Members of faith communities, particularly clergy, are circumspect about the intentions of external groups, especially the government. Most outside partners, foundations, academic institutions, city units, and human service organizations are viewed as short-term partners who find the community and congregation trendy, but who will disappear as soon as something even trendier will be declared. Often, external commitment is limited for the duration of a project or the duration of a grant. Community residents and congregation members and their relatives who live in the community are attached to it for decades, and they have seen many external partners come and go. Hence, their immediate understanding and expectation is for the external people to use the community for something that they need, and then leave it with no real progress. This perception makes congregations less hospitable to partnership with external organizations and further enhances the intended isolation of congregations.

Running Social Programs in Congregations

Congregations rarely have to record or report the way they provide services, or who is eligible and partakes of a social service. Given that the majority of programs are planned, financed, and implemented "in-house," little reporting takes place and no formal reporting is required. In many cases, annual reports or committee meetings devote little more than a paragraph or a few sentences to update other members on the outcomes of a program. This informality and lack of attention to detailed recording makes the service provision more personal and enables congregations to serve people without strict adherence to eligibility criteria. Secular human service organizations, which draw their resources from public funds or foundations, are required to monitor service delivery and document client contacts and services. As such, the service may take on a formal and regulated flavor compared to congregations' delivery.

In an evaluation of a TANF program in New York City that was faith-based, Rock (2002) noted that clients described frontline workers as more friendly and respectful. These workers, although paid employees, were also congregation members who felt ownership for the service as part of their faith. Similarly, Goggin and Orth (2002), in a study comparing faith-based and secular service provision for interim housing, observed that faith-based organizations were perceived as being more holistic in their service through trying to address all a client's needs rather than just focusing on housing. In this study, clients perceived front-line staff at most faith-based organizations as more caring than staff at the government agency. Clients described faith-based staff with words such as dedicated, nurturing and loving.

Congregations, as noted above, are prevalent in communities and range from very small to very large. A human service organization that wishes to collaborate with them may find it difficult to approach all of them. Thus, when planning a collaboration, human service organizations select a few congregations and ignore the rest. This potentially leaves hundreds of congregations feeling snubbed and resentful. Collaboration with one congregation may indicate to the many others that the human service organization did not want to work with them. Often local rivalry and turf building prevent larger collaborations from existing in the same community.

Similar to all human interactions, collaborations are frequently drawn along lines that advance the status of certain clergy. The decision to join or partner with another group is often filtered through "what good it will do to me and my congregation." However, such collaborations potentially open up the door for wider community participation and representation from many sub-groups that otherwise would be excluded. Additionally, a congregation's involvement in local coalitions may be limited to the congregation's support of the coalition with funds and formal endorsement but not with their members' spirit, enthusiastic volunteering, and commitment (Pipes & Ebaugh, 2002).

Congregations often lack experience in strategic planning. A congregation's plans and ideas may be inappropriate or unrealistic according to human service organizations standards. As noted, most programs in congregations evolve naturally and with little formal planning. Similarly, a decision to close down a program is not based on formal planning but on member preferences or changing needs. When asked about a decision to close down a program, many clergy responded that "the fit between the program and the congregational 'call' is no longer there." In the event that the demand for service increases beyond the congregational capacity, a key decision must be made: "Shall we relinquish control of our 'ministry' to an external source or keep providing services below the level of demand?" In other words, enlarging the scope of care implies inviting nonreligious service providers or other congregations to join in. This is not a simple choice, as enlargement also signifies that the program is no longer owned by the congregation but is shared with others (Smith, 2002).

Many of our interviewers preferred smaller-scale, intimate service provision and maintained services as congregation-owned programs. This may stem from the ideal as social service provision as a means of "actualizing faith" in which benefiting a larger number of needy people is beyond the traditional scope of ministry. This does not imply an uncaring approach, but highlights the preference of maintaining a spirited and personalized mode of care rather than a formal bureaucratic attitude towards recipients of help.

DISCUSSION AND CONCLUSIONS

As shown above, congregations in America are the most prevalent and trusted community organizations. These hubs of social concern and pro-social human nuclei are woven like a thick tapestry all over America. Given the high level of religious involvement of Americans, and the country's very limited welfare program, it is natural for faith communities to extend their involvement in local social service provision as a manifestation of members' faith. The political elite in America is as religious as other residents and is all too fond of the potential embedded in faith-based care. As such, since 1996 the visibility and role of congregations and other faith-based organizations in providing publicly-funded social services is on the rise. Yet social work and other human service disciplines know very little about the work of these organizations and their organizational characteristics.

As we demonstrated, based on a one-city census of congregations, congregations' contribution to people's quality of life is immense. Funding this level of care by other means in Philadelphia would cost at about a quarter of a billion dollars and would mean uprooting a rich web of social care and connectedness and the comprehensive network of referrals and informal care that go with it. In fact, in America, it does not overstate the reality to assert that the only real community organization capable of reaching every person in need on an on-going basis is the local religious congregation.

As suggested, communities of faith bring with them a wealth of resources that many traditional human service providers lack. They are located in the heart of the community and almost on every block. They have physical space that is maintained for religious purposes on weekends and evenings but is often available for community-oriented programs at no or low cost. Congregations usually have a pro-social perspective and wish to improve the quality of life in the community. They demonstrate endurance in terms of being in the community for a long time and credibility for consistently attempting to help neighbors. Additionally, congregations have access to potential volunteers that can be asked to join collaborative social programs (Wineburg, 1988).

However, viewing them as social service providers ought to be done with great respect and understanding of their unique organizational characteristics. Their first raison d'etre is to provide a communal framework for their faith. Faith undercuts every aspect and activity of a congregation. People come together in search of spiritual fulfillment, and social service provision is only one aspect of that quest and a means for its actualization. As such, social services are very important, but not the primary concern of the collective.

Human service organizations can work with congregations, use their space, and harness their volunteers, but they have to be cognizant of faith communities' identity and role in the community. We have listed some key issues pertaining to working with congregations and understanding their unique nature. However, one should also keep in mind that all organizations are not the same. Congregations vary in size, membership, resources, and religious commitment. Some are very theologically liberal and some are very prescriptive. The level of religious commitment and delivery style influences social care and willingness to collaborate with public entities and groups of other faith traditions.

Finally, it should be noted that as impressive as congregations are in the social services arena, they cannot be a substitute for the public sector. It is not known whether most religious congregations are capable of, or desire to expand their current provision of various services. This unknown factor suggests that any expectation that religious congregations can be a panacea for reduced public welfare spending is premature and unwise. For those congregations who are able to and wish to expand their current social programs, it appears that time, technical assistance, and supportive funding are required for congregations to provide high-quality, stable, and lasting services (Sinha, Cnaan, Jones, & Dichter, 2003).

Congregations can well complement the government commitment for people in need. They can reduce public expenditure but only at the margins. An expectation that such diverse and often small organizations can substitute for government welfare is unrealistic and dangerous. While social service administrators will benefit from knowing and in some cases collaborating with these organizations, be aware of their strengths and weaknesses. It should be understood that congregations possess their own sets of resources and limitations and cannot be expected to carry the load of American welfare on their shoulders.

REFERENCES

Ammerman, N. T. (2001). *Doing Good in American communities: Congregations and service organizations working together.* Hartford, CT: Hartford Institute for Religion Research, Hartford Seminary.

Ascoli, U., & Ranci, C. (2002). *Dilemmas of the welfare mix: The new structure of welfare in an era of privatization.* Dordrecht, The Netherlands: Kluwer.

Billingsley, A. (1999). *Mighty like a river: The Black church and social reform.* New York: Oxford University Press.

Botchwey, N. (2003). *Exploratory research on local secular and faith-based organizations in one Lower North Philadelphia high poverty neighborhood.* Unpublished dissertation, University of Pennsylvania, PA.

Chaves, Mark. (1998). Denominations as dual structures: An organizational analysis. In N. J. Demerath, P. D. Hall, T. Schmitt, & R. H. Williams. (Eds.). Sacred companies: Organizational aspects of religion and religious aspects of organizations (pp. 175-194). New York: Oxford University Press.

Chaves, M. (1999). Religious congregations and welfare reform: Who will take advantage of charitable choice? *American Sociological Review, 64,* 836-846.

Cnaan, R. A., & Boddie, S. C. (2002). Charitable choice and faith-based welfare: A call for social work. *Social Work, 47,* 247-235.

Cnaan, R. A., with Boddie, S. C., Handy, F., Yancey, G., & Schneider, R. (2002). *The invisible caring hand: American congregations and the provision of welfare.* New York: New York University Press.

Cnaan, R. A., & Boddie, S. C. (2001). Philadelphia census of congregations and their involvement in social service delivery. *Social Service Review, 75,* 559-589.

Cnaan, R. A., Gelles, R. J., & Sinha, J. W. (2002). *Is religion relevant for teenagers? Impact of religion on risk behavior.* Paper presented at the Annual Meeting of the Society for the Study of Religion. Salt Lake City, Utah. November 1-3, 2002.

Conlan, T. (1998). *From new federalism to devolution: Twenty-five years of intergovernmental reform.* Washington, DC: Brookings Institution.

DiPietro, M., & Behr, G. (2002). *Social services in faith-based organizations: Pittsburgh congregations and the services they provide.* Pittsburgh: The William J. Copeland fund.

Dudley, C. S., & Roozen, D. A. (2002). *Faith communities today: A report on religion in the United States today.* Hartford, CT: Hartford Seminary.

The Economist, (1995, July 8). The counter-attack of God. *The Economist,* 19-21.

Fabricant, M., & Fisher, R. (2002). Agency based community building in low-income neighborhoods: A praxis framework. *Journal of Community Practice, 10*(2), 1-22.

Fong, L. G. W., & Gibbs, J. T. (1995) Facilitating services to multicultural communities in a dominant culture setting: An organizational perspective. *Administration in Social Work, 19*(2), 1-24.

Grettenberger, S., & Hovmand, P. (1997, December). *The role of churches in human services: United Methodist churches in Michigan.* Paper presented at the 26th annual meeting of the Association for Research on Nonprofit Organizations and Voluntary Action, Indianapolis, IN.

Goggin, M. L., & Orth, D. A. (2002, October). *How faith-based and secular organizations tackle housing for the homeless.* Paper presented at The Roundtable on Religion and Social Welfare Policy, Washington, D.C.

Harris, M. (1995). Quiet care: Welfare work and religious congregations. *Journal of Social Policy, 24,* 53-71.

Hill, R. B. (1998). *Report on study of church-based human services.* Baltimore: Associated Black Charities.

Hodgkinson, V. A., & Weitzman, M. S., with Kirsch, A. D., Noga, S. M., & Gorski, H. A. (1993). *From belief to commitment: The community service activities and finances of religious congregations in the United States, 1993 Edition.* Washington, DC: Independent Sector.

Jackson, M. C. Jr., Schweitzer, J. H., Blake, R. N., Jr., & Cato, M. T. (1997). *Faith-Based Institutions: Community and Economic Development Programs Serving Black Communities in Michigan.* Kalamazoo, MI: Michigan State University.

Jeavons, T. H., & Basinger, R. B. (2000). *Growing givers' hearts: Treating fundraising as ministry.* San Francisco: Jossey-Bass.

Lipsky, M., & Smith, S. R. (1989-90). Nonprofit organizations, government, and the welfare state. *Political Science Quarterly, 104,* 625-648.

McAneny, L., & Saad, L. (1993). Strong ties between religion commitment and abortion views. *The Gallup Poll Monthly, No. 331*, 35-43.

Orr, J. B. (1998). *Los Angeles religion: A civic profile.* Los Angeles: University of Southern California, Center for Religion and Civic Culture.

Pew Research Center for the People and the Press. (2001). *Faith-based funding backed, but church-state doubts abound.* Retrieved on January 10, 2003, from Http:/www.people-press.org/re101rpt.htm.

Pipes, P., & Ebaugh, H. R. (2002, October/November). *Coalition ministries and the provision of social services: Data from a national survey.* Paper presented at the Annual meeting of the Society for the Study of Religion, Salt Lake City.

Pirog, M. A., & Reingold, D. A. (2002). *Has the social safety net been altered? New roles for faith-based organizations.* Bloomington, IN: Perspective No. 8, An Occasional Series Published by The Office of the Dean School of Public and Environmental Affairs, Indiana University.

Printz, T. J. (1998). *Faith-based service providers in the nation's capital: Can they do more?* Policy Brief No. 2 in Charting Civil Society, Center on Nonprofits and Philanthropy, Washington, DC: The Urban Institute.

Rock, J. (2002, October). *Stepping out on faith: New York City's Charitable Choice demonstration program.* Paper presented at The Roundtable on Religion and Social Welfare Policy, Washington, D.C.

Sanders, M.G. (Ed.). (2000). Schooling students placed at risk: Research, policy, and practice in the education of poor and minority adolescents. Mahwah, NJ: Lawrence Erlbaum Associates, Inc.

Silverman, C. (2000). *Faith-based communities and welfare reform: California religious community capacity study.* San Francisco: Institute for Nonprofit Organization Management, University of San Francisco.

Sider, R. J., Olson, P. N., & Unruh, H. R. (2002). *Churches that make a difference: Reaching your community with good news and good works.* Grand Rapids, MI: Baker Book House.

Sinha, J. W., Cnaan, R. A., Jones, D. L., & Dichter, S. (2003). Analysis of a collaborative faith-based demonstration project: The unique capacity of congregation- and community-based collaboration. In the Independent Sector (Ed.). *The Role of Faith-based Organizations in the Social Welfare System Spring Research Forum Working Papers* (pp. 159-168). Washington, D.C.: Independent Sector Roundtable on Religion and Social Welfare Policy.

Smith, K. K. (2002). *Manna in the wilderness of Aids: Ten lessons in abandonment.* Cleveland: The Pilgrim Press.

Smith, S. R., & Sosin, M. R. (2001). The varieties of faith-related agencies. *Public Administration Review, 61*, 651-670.

Taylor, R. J., Thornton, M. C., & Chatters, L. M. (1987). Black Americans' perceptions of the sociohistorical role of the church. *Journal of Black Studies, 18*, 123-138.

Wineburg, R. J. (1988). Welfare reform: What the religious community brings to the partnership. *The Journal of Volunteer Administration, XVI, 2*, 19-26.

Volunteer and Paid Staff Relationships: Implications for Social Work Administration

F. Ellen Netting, PhD
H. Wayne Nelson, Jr., PhD
Kevin Borders, PhD
Ruth Huber, PhD

SUMMARY. In this article, we examine theoretical perspectives and studies on volunteer and paid staff relationships to determine what administrators in social work can glean from theory and research. We also draw from the conceptual literature in the area of volunteerism, as well as our experience with one nationally mandated program that utilizes 90% volunteers and 10% paid employees. Implications for social work administration include recognizing the culture of one's program or organization and the norms associated with volunteerism, as well as understanding the nature of psychological contracting for both paid employees and volunteers. Guidelines for assessing volunteer/paid staff culture are provided. *[Article copies available for a fee from The Haworth Document Delivery Service: 1-800-HAWORTH. E-mail address: <docdelivery@haworthpress.com> Website: <http://www.HaworthPress.com> © 2004 by The Haworth Press, Inc. All rights reserved.]*

F. Ellen Netting is Professor, Virginia Commonwealth University, School of Social Work. H. Wayne Nelson, Jr. is Assistant Professor, Towson University, Department of Health Science. Kevin Borders is Instructor, and Ruth Huber is Professor, Kent School of Social Work, University of Louisville.

[Haworth co-indexing entry note]: "Volunteer and Paid Staff Relationships: Implications for Social Work Administration." Netting, F. Ellen et al. Co-published simultaneously in *Administration in Social Work* (The Haworth Social Work Practice Press, an imprint of The Haworth Press, Inc.) Vol. 28, No. 3/4, 2004, pp. 69-89; and: *Organizational and Structural Dilemmas in Nonprofit Human Service Organizations* (ed: Hillel Schmid) The Haworth Social Work Practice Press, an imprint of The Haworth Press, Inc., 2004, pp. 69-89. Single or multiple copies of this article are available for a fee from The Haworth Document Delivery Service [1-800-HAWORTH, 9:00 a.m. - 5:00 p.m. (EST). E-mail address: docdelivery@haworthpress.com].

http://www.haworthpress.com/web/ASW
© 2004 by The Haworth Press, Inc. All rights reserved.
Digital Object Identifier: 10.1300/J147v28n03_04

KEYWORDS. Volunteerism, human resources, roles, personnel management, paraprofessionals

Volunteer management trainers tell us that one of the most frequent requests they receive is to assist organizations and groups in dealing with volunteer and paid staff relationships. This is not surprising, given the numbers of health and human service organizations that use volunteers and given the multiplicity of roles they perform.

Popular media carry reports about how voluntary organizations here and abroad are having to consider how to deliver services more flexibly, with implications for the mix of volunteers and paid staff (Bowgett & Salvage, 2001; George, 1997; Rickford, 1994). For example, organizations such as Traveler's Aid (McComb, 1995) and the American Red Cross (HLC.internet, 1996) are focusing on better communication links between paid staff and volunteers. Common Cause suspended its magazine, closed its offices in several smaller states, and anticipated that volunteers would take the place of paid staff (Victor, 1997). Studies on the American Cancer Society revealed "a delicate balance . . . between volunteers and paid staff members" (Wandersman & Alderman, 1993, p. 67).

An ongoing theme in the volunteerism literature is that paid staff often resist the introduction of volunteers (Brudney, 1990). McCurley and Lynch (1996) suggested that such resistance may be particularly threatening when older volunteers with experience and credentials bring their expertise to an organization and assume similar roles as paid staff. "Conventional wisdom has held that volunteer programs spare agency budgets and raise the level of services that organizations are able to provide, but jeopardize paid positions and relationships with staff" (Brudney & Gazley, 2002, p. 525-526). However, Brudney and Gazley went on to demonstrate that conventional wisdom is not always supported in empirical studies. Thus, paid staff and volunteer relationships, like most relationships, are likely to be more complex than one might assume at first glance.

To address this complexity, we begin with a brief historical background. Next we provide a theoretical framework followed by earlier studies on volunteer and paid staff relationships to determine what administrators in social work can glean from previous research. We also draw from the conceptual literature in the area of volunteerism, as well as our experience with one nationally mandated program that utilizes 90% volunteers and 10% paid employees. Our intent is to draw implications for today's social work administration, within the context of a rich history of volunteerism.

HISTORICAL CONTEXT

In the U.S., the profession of social work emerged as a volunteer activity in both Charity Organization Societies and social settlements, with volunteers performing both direct and macro practice roles. As social work professionalized, the use of volunteers in direct practice roles "was sharply curtailed . . . Consequently, between the 1920s and 1960s, professional social workers became the primary providers of services" (Perlmutter & Cnaan, 1993, p. 78). Volunteers certainly continued as members of boards of directors and federated funding agencies, but when they participated in direct service provision they were more likely to be involved in non-professional activities such as facilitating self help groups (Perlmutter & Cnaan, 1993).

As the social work profession matured, particularly during the 1960s and 1970s, social work professionals hung onto their newly acquired status. Volunteers redirected their efforts and although they were used, a number of forces worked to alter their previous roles. Proponents of the women's movement argued that women were exploited as volunteers, and that these traditional roles should be replaced with paid positions. Additionally, the Civil Rights Movement opened new roles for persons of color to participate in social movements, advocacy efforts, and social change (Ellis & Noyes, 1990; Perlmutter & Cnaan, 1993).

In the 1980s, Hauser and Schwartz (1980) wrote about ways to counteract resistance to the use of volunteers by paid staff. They contended that if workers understood "the differences between professional and volunteer roles, the nature of a volunteer development system, the self-actualization aspect of volunteering, the volunteer as mediator and advocate, and the growing value of professional-volunteer relationships" (p. 595) that their resistance could be overcome. Seeing resistance as rooted in historical misunderstandings associated with the value-laden Lady Bountiful tradition and professional territoriality, Hauser and Schwartz sought to confront the "the covert and overt, conscious and unconscious resistance of professional paid staff" to the use of volunteers. They cited a 1972 study on the differential use of volunteers in public welfare that indicated that paid staff were more receptive to volunteers if they had been volunteers themselves (Stewart, Pollance, & Blenkner, 1972, as cited in Hauser & Schwartz, 1980). The problems associated with professional resistance were elucidated as Hauser and Schwartz revealed the lack of preparation that professionals had for (a) working with volunteers, (b) the concerns of the National Information Center on Volunteerism about the persistent problem of paid staff and agency non-support of volunteers, and (c) the National Organization of Women's 1974 resolution to discourage women from volunteering.

Concern over resistance was particularly relevant during the 1970s and 80s (Strickler, 1987) when there were attempts by political leaders to use volunteers to replace striking workers (Ellis & Noyes, 1990). "Today the practice of substituting volunteers for paid employees has been outlawed for the most part in both private practice and public law" (Brudney & Gazley, 2002, p. 528).

During the 1990s there arose a renewed interest in using volunteers in human service arenas, particularly in light of inadequate fiscal resources. Perlmutter and Cnaan (1993) viewed this trend with "an underlying and critically important assumption . . . that volunteers cannot replace professionals" (p. 80). They surveyed 470 volunteers from 105 human service organizations and found that volunteers were involved in a broad array of roles. Their findings revealed a hierarchy of roles: "direct practice only; direct practice coupled with administrative support; direct practice and administrative support combined with advocacy; and, finally, the inclusion of all four roles" (p. 89). This hierarchy was associated with the educational levels of volunteers and with volunteers who participated in more than one human service organization. The hierarchy was also associated with methods of recruiting, orienting, and retaining volunteers.

As the decade progressed, the push to use volunteers culminated in the "1997 first-ever Presidents' Summit for America's Future, a historic meeting that brought unprecedented attention to volunteerism in service to the nation's young people" (Brudney, 1999, p. 385). Brudney reflects on his attendance at this event, revealing his disappointment in "the lack of attention to, or even interest in, the lifeblood of much of the sector: volunteer management" (p. 391). Brudney reminded us that the enthusiasm and motivation associated with volunteering must be joined with solid implementation skills in how to translate that energy into the day-to-day operation of volunteer programs. This translation requires the commitment of paid staff to oversee and support volunteers in their efforts.

Today "volunteering has never been more critical" (Govekar & Govekar, 2002). The Independent Survey on Giving and Volunteering (2001) indicated that 44% of adults volunteer (89.9 million Americans) at an annual estimated value of $239 billion. The rich and growing literature on volunteers crosses disciplinary boundaries. There are complex and diverse models pertaining to why volunteers do what they do (Govekar & Govekar, 2002; Smith, 1994). We point the reader to these sources as excellent overviews of volunteer labor and behavior. However, we shall focus specifically on a theoretical framework followed by those studies that compare volunteers and paid staff or attempt to examine volunteer/paid staff relationships.

THEORETICAL FRAMEWORK

Relationships between volunteers and paid staff can be viewed as a highly interpretive venture in that the intent is to understand how dynamics, interactions, motivations, and attitudes come together within some type of setting. According to Burrell and Morgan (1979), interpretivists see the world as a result of human consciousness. Reality, then, is a "network of assumptions and intersubjectively shared meanings that are always in flux due to the shaping of multiple individual perspectives" (Netting & O'Connor, 2003, p. 187). Therefore, an interpretive view of volunteerism recognizes the complexity and changing nature of relationships.

Theories that are based on interpretive assumptions are often referred to in both the studies and conceptual literature on volunteers and paid staff. These theoretical perspectives tend to be of two types, those focused on understanding psychological perceptions of volunteer roles and those concerned with organizational behavior. Both are critically important because they assist in understanding how individuals perceive their volunteer and paid roles, as well as how these sets of perceptions fit within the organizational context.

Theories focused on understanding human behavior address the psychological dimensions of volunteerism, including why people engage in the process of volunteering and how this engagement impacts others. Status characteristics theory, for example, suggests that paid employees inevitably enjoy greater prestige in mixed volunteer/paid staff organizations (Karr, 2000), with paid staff tending to identify and treat volunteers as pseudo-employees (Ashcraft & Kodrowicz, 2002). Status characteristics theory is built on the concept of status, which comes from those characteristics that people bring to their work and other situations and that impact how they engage with others (Berger & Zelditch, 1993). Status characteristics can include ascribed statuses such as race, gender, and age, but they can also include achieved statuses such as being designated as a volunteer or as a paid staff member. Once named "volunteer" or "staff" member, these statuses or categorizations take on meanings that lead to new identities (Rosenblum & Travis, 2000).

Recognizing the importance of how persons perceive their volunteer status, Farmer and Fedor (1999) focused on the psychological contract which is "an individual's beliefs regarding the terms and conditions of a reciprocal exchange agreement between that person and another party" (Rousseau, 1989, as cited in Farmer & Fedor, 1999, p. 350). A psychological contract is one that exists in a person's perception, it is a series of beliefs and assumptions that are held about the relationship. "Individuals hold beliefs about what they are obliged to provide, what the other party is obliged to provide, and how well the other party fulfills its obligation" (Farmer & Fedor, 1999, p. 350). Given the perceptual nature of psychological contracting, contracts may vary greatly along a defined, economic set of agreements to heavily value-laden and emotional concerns of an interpersonal nature. Since contracts are developed between the individual and the work setting, they are somewhat individualistic. They are also based on trust which means that perceptions about what constitutes a violation will differ depending on the interpretation of the contractee. The concept of psychological contracting is relevant to status characteristics theory in that it focuses on how individuals interpret the meaning of their volunteer (or paid) roles. Workers in organizations use status characteristics in assessing their work and the work of others, in shaping their interactions, and in determining psychologically what the interactions mean.

As important as it is to understand the psychological and status dimensions of volunteerism, this understanding is incomplete without placing these dynamics within context. Within the interpretive paradigm (Burrell & Morgan, 1979) is organizational culture theory. References to organizational culture are so integrated into the empirical and conceptual literature on volunteers and paid staff that it is almost taken for granted because organizational culture theory provides a contextual understanding of the multiple settings in which volunteers and paid staff interact.

Schein (1992) defines organizational culture as "a pattern of shared basic assumptions that the group learned as it solved its problems of external adaptation and internal integration, that has worked well enough to be considered valid and therefore, to be taught to new members as the correct ways to perceive, think, and feel in relation to those problems" (p. 12). Schein's definition holds clues to the interface between organizational culture and status characteristics theory. For example, if differences between the status of volunteers and paid staff are accentuated, then the setting within which they relate will maintain clear distinctions. Perceptions of those distinctions will become part of the underlying assumptions of the culture. If paid staff see volunteers as difficult to manage, as drains on their time, and as having less status than they, then those cultural assumptions may become so ingrained that they become subconscious. Volunteers who enter such a culture will pick up on those assumptions, from the behaviors of staff and other volunteers as well as cues from other cultural artifacts. Paid staff may not even recognize that they are projecting those assumptions through their behaviors.

Organizational culture theory offers the potential for understanding the settings in which volunteers engage with paid staff. In settings that began as volunteer-run operations, the concept of volunteerism may be deeply ingrained in the cultural roots. Conversely, in highly professionalized settings in which volunteers were recruited after programs were up and running, norms surrounding the use of volunteers may be palpably different. It is our contention that organizational culture theory, combined with concepts such as psychological contracting and status characteristics, hold potential for administrators who want to understand the complexity of how volunteers fit within the context of their organizations. In the sections that follow, the importance of interpretive theoretical assumptions will be evident as researchers examine various aspects of volunteer and paid staff relationships.

STUDIES OF VOLUNTEERS AND PAID STAFF

Studies of volunteers and paid staff can be generally categorized as follows: (a) attempts to examine differences and similarities in job attitudes and motivation between employees and volunteers; (b) studies focusing on participation and withdrawal of volunteers; and (c) the optimal mix of volunteers and paid staff. As we briefly examine each of these, we caution the reader to recognize that there is inevitable overlap among these three areas. They are not mutually exclusive.

Job Attitudes and Motivation

In the late 1970s and early 1980s a number of writers examined job attitudes and motivations of paid staff and volunteers. Gidron (1983) revealed the importance of recognizing that employees and volunteers are committed in different ways to an organization, given the free will nature of volunteerism. He went on to point out that volunteers were essentially assuming roles that were indistinguishable from those performed by paid staff (Gidron, 1987). Moore and Anderson (1985) decried the lack of research on volunteer motivation, and studied the need satisfaction for Canadian health service volunteer workers compared to paid employees in the same settings. Using Maslow's hierarchy, volunteers appeared to have more higher order needs met in the performance of their roles than did their paid counterparts.

Pearce (1983) examined how volunteers and paid workers in similar settings varied in terms of motivation and job attitudes. She commented that "unfortunately, there is very little organizational behavior research on volunteers or on the comparison of volunteers and employees" (p. 647). She paired organizations staffed predominately by volunteers and those staffed by paid employees: two newspaper operations, two poverty relief agencies, two family planning clinics, and two city fire departments. She found that volunteers were "more likely to report that they work for the rewards of social interaction and service to others, that their work is more praiseworthy, and that they are more satisfied and less likely to leave their organizations" (p. 650). Pearce (1993) continued her work on differences between volunteers and paid employees into the 1990s, examining differences in organizational citizenship between contract workers and employees. Over the last decade we have learned more about volunteer motivations (see for example, Clary, Snyder, & Stukas, 1996).

Liao-Troth (2001) extended the research on paid employees and volunteers. He wondered if Pearce's research could be interpreted differently in that the differences were not necessarily between volunteers and paid employees, but among the organizational cultures of the workgroups studied. Surveying paid and volunteer workers in similar roles within one hospital setting, he built on Pearce's work as well as the work being done on psychological contracting. He conducted his study in one setting, unlike Pearce's work, surveying 108 employees and volunteers doing similar job tasks in a medical center. Although the findings of his work do not negate Pearce's earlier work, Liao-Troth found that volunteers and paid staff performing similar work roles in the same setting have similar job attitudes about psychological contracting, affective commitment, and organizational justice. He also acknowledged that a medical setting is more formalized than many other settings in which volunteers are used. Thus, highly trained volunteers may be treated almost like employees.

Participation and Withdrawal

Differentiating what is known about paid from unpaid work environments, Galindo and Guzley (2001) tested the Volunteer Satisfaction Index (VSI), designed to measure job satisfaction among volunteers. Testing the index with 327 volunteers, factor analyses revealed four dimensions of volunteer job satisfaction: organizational support, participation efficacy, empowerment, and group integration. Further analysis indicated that participation efficacy and group integration were significantly correlated with volunteer satisfaction and the intent to remain on the job.

Van Dyne and Ang (1998) studied workers in Singapore, finding that full-time employees differed from contingent workers. Employees were more likely to engage in organizational citizenship actions, had more psychological contract expectations, and were more affectively committed to their roles than contingent workers. Laczo and Hanisch (1999, as cited in Liao-Troth, 2001) found that paid workers and volunteers doing similar tasks in a museum setting varied. Paid employees were more likely to engage in job withdrawal, whereas volunteers were more likely to participate in organizational citizenship behaviors. This is intuitively logical since volunteers perform their duties by choice and the very nature of what they do is a citizenship (without compensation) behavior.

Hopkins (2002) defined the concept of organizational citizenship behavior as "'extra-role activities' that are not formally required by the job, such as assisting supervisors and coworkers with their duties, working extra hours when needed, and making innovative suggestions to improve quality" (p. 2). Hopkins randomly surveyed 120 child and family service employees, finding that more citizenship behaviors were positively related to organizational support, opportunities for development, quality performance on the job, and professional education. Although she did not look at paid staff as well as volunteer organizational citizenship behaviors, she raised an important point–that employees engaged in roles that went beyond their official job requirements and expectations. This raises questions about what assumptions employees bring to their positions in terms of psychological contracting.

Originally conceived as a tool for considering how employees or paid workers view relationships with their work environment, Farmer and Fedor (1999) used psychological contracting to examine volunteer behavior. They contended that work on psychological contracting is cross-cultural, given a number of studies conducted in numerous countries. Volunteer relationships with nonprofit agencies are reflected in "(1) (sic) expectations that volunteers hold, (2) the nature of the contract, and (3) how violations are perceived and responded to" (p. 353). They proceeded to develop a table of contract differences between employees and volunteers based on three categories: "those that are structured or role-related in nature; those that concern worker attitudes, values, and motivations; and those involving differences in prevalent human resource management practices" (p. 353). What becomes evident is that employment and volunteer contracts are vastly different because expectations and beliefs are different. Farmer and Fedor conducted their study in a national, nonprofit health advocacy organization. They conducted semi-structured interviews with executive committee volunteers in diverse geographical areas, then surveyed 451 volunteers. Findings indicated that volunteers tie participation to their views of how well the nonprofit organization meets its obligations. But findings also highlighted the vast differences in psychological contracts in volunteers versus other types of workers. "Because volunteers' reasons for affiliation with the voluntary organization are primarily symbolic, not material, the 'coin' in which they see themselves 'paid' is also symbolic" (Farmer & Fedor, 1999, p. 362).

Nelson, Netting, Borders, and Huber (2002) examined reasons why volunteers terminated (withdrew) from the Long Term Care Ombudsman Program in one state. A telephone survey of 147 former Oregon volunteer ombudsmen was conducted, using four current volunteer interviewers. Four open ended questions were asked concerning factors that were most discouraging, most meaningful, influenced one's leaving, and that might have encouraged one to stay. Findings revealed that quality of supervisory support was a concern to these former volunteers. Perceived deficits in this area were revealed when former volunteers were asked about the most discouraging aspects of the job, and program factors concerning supervisory support accounted for 22% of the responses. Dissatisfaction with supervision was also evident. When asked reasons for leaving the program, responses suggested discontent with supervision as cementing volunteers' decisions to discontinue their volunteer services. Desire for better staff support leads the list of factors that would have encouraged continued service.

Keith and Schafer (2002) surveyed 778 volunteers and examined 694 applications volunteers filled out prior to becoming ombudsmen. They were interested in comparing the difficulties the volunteers anticipated experiencing before service with the actual experiences ombudsmen had after serving. They found that "applicants substantially underestimated the amount and type of difficulties they would experience" (Keith & Schaffer, 2002, p. 421). The most pronounced differences between anticipated experiences and actual events were related to time constraints, difficulties from working with ill and frail elders, and the lack of perception of job difficulties. Time requirements are an important reason why volunteers resign (Caro & Bass, 1995, as cited in Keith & Schafer, 2002). Keith and Schafer (2002) noted that these other issues are critical ones to be addressed in volunteer training. These findings (Keith & Schaffer, 2002; Nelson et al., 2002) reflected a nationwide concern about inadequate supervisory assistance in Long Term Care Ombudsman Programs (Harris-Wehling, Feasley, & Estes, 1995; Nelson, 2002).

A mailed survey of factors affecting volunteer long-term care ombudsmen's organizational commitment and burnout in one state was conducted with 255 volunteers. Results revealed that non-contest roles were more psychologically satisfying than those in which conflict was a given. The authors stressed that role ambiguity (job confusion) can be reduced by sufficient training and supervisory support (Nelson, Pratt, Carpenter, & Walter, 1995). This study underscored the importance of the psychological contract, particularly in light of Farmer and Fedor's (1999) findings about volunteer participation as symbolic.

Optimal Mix of Volunteers and Paid Staff

Numbers of volunteer long term care ombudsmen increased from 3,306 in 1982 (American Association of Retired Persons [AARP], 1994) to over 13,000 in 1999 (MacInnes & Hedt, 1999). This growth is somewhat misleading because it derives more from the number of states using volunteers, which grew from 29 to 38 between 1984 and 1987 (Schiman & Lordeman, 1989), than from growth in the ratio of volunteers to the number of nursing home residents serviced. Ombudsmen fill an important service gap by stretching outreach efforts that would otherwise depend on a tiny number of paid staff: 1 for every 2,698 nursing home beds (Harris-Wehling et al., 1995).

Concerned about a dearth of literature on ombudsman staff mix and potential conflicts between paid staff and volunteers, Huber, Netting, and Paton (1993) collected and analyzed secondary, aggregated data from multiple sources with the goal of providing an overall, national picture of the relationship between the ombudsman program's 8,665 volunteers and known variables of complaint handling in long term care facilities. Recognizing tremendous difficulties in locating accurate data, they concluded that programs with more volunteers tended to identify and investigate more complaints, but actual complaint resolution appeared to be more likely when the responsibility rested with paid staff.

Following the initiation of a new national database not in existence at the time of the 1993 study, Netting, Huber, Borders, Kautz, and Nelson (2000) accessed data previously collected by six states to focus on the use of volunteers and paid staff complaint investigations. These data revealed differences in the types of complaints received, the sources of complaints, and the percentage of complex (difficult) complaints investigated by volunteers and paid staff. These differences were viewed as resulting in a natural triaging that occurred among volunteers and paid staff, so that complaints viewed as difficult to verify and resolve were automatically given to paid staff. Having a national database now provides an opportunity to explore more fully the roles of both volunteers and paid staff and to gain a clearer picture of what is happening in the ombudsman program.

Duncombe and Brudney (1995) designed their study to locate the ideal mix of volunteer and paid staff firefighters so that cost could be optimized. The methodology that emerged from their study allowed them to determine the least cost of staff and volunteer mix. Even though their guidelines are applied to fire protection, they contended that the results of their analysis would be instructive to public administrators in other service domains.

More recently, Brudney and Gazley (2002) provided a glimpse into the conventional wisdom about volunteer programs saving money and providing more services, but also threatening paid staff positions. Their focus was on the impact of volunteers based in the US Small Business Administration's (SBA) volunteer program, Service Corps of Retired Executives (SCORE). They focused on three commonly held assumptions about volunteerism: cost savings, service expansion, and negative impact on paid staff. This latter area relates directly to the subject of this paper. Brudney and Gazley (2002) unpacked the underlying assumption about negative impact on paid staff into two major concerns: that employees resist the introduction of volunteers and that volunteers will replace paid employees. Brudney and Gazley (2002) used both qualitative and quantitative methods to focus on SCORE from 1954-1995. They found no evidence that management staff viewed SCORE volunteers in a negative or resistive manner. However, managers often had difficulty accommodating their own workloads when they had a large influx of volunteers. "In sum, this analysis suggests that SCORE volunteers were readily accepted into the SBA. SBA officials supported the SCORE volunteers and lobbied consistently for expanded funding for he program" (p. 532). If problems did occur in the SCORE program, they were related to issues of volunteer management when implementation indicated that best practices were not being used.

Studies of paid staff and volunteers across the world and in arenas beyond human services are appearing in the literature. For example, Thorley (2000) examines the competing roles of volunteers and professionals in the breast-feeding field, whereas Seippel (2002) focuses on the roles of volunteers and professionals in Norwegian Sport Organizations. These studies reveal differences across types of organizations, reinforcing the importance of determining volunteer paid staff mix and of recognizing the fit of this mix within the context of organizational culture.

IMPLICATIONS FOR SOCIAL WORK ADMINISTRATION

Training in how to handle volunteer and paid staff relationships continues to be a frequent request made to volunteer management experts. Administrators, managers, and agency staff are obviously making these requests, leaving little doubt that these relationships require time and attention in any organization in which there is a mix of employees and volunteers. Yet, relationship building and dealing with complex human relationships is a theme in any human service context, regardless of whether the participants are paid or are donating their skills and talents. Perhaps many of the difficulties and perceived relationships between volunteer and paid staff exist when one fails to recognize that, like staff, volunteers are not "free" and the organizational culture does not fully appreciate the nature of volunteerism.

In terms of job attitudes and motivation, the research is somewhat mixed. Whereas Pearce (1983, 1993) found differences in volunteer and paid staff motivations and job attitudes, she did not look at volunteers and employees co-existing in the same organizations. Therefore, Liao-Troth (2001) determined that it could be possible that these differences were as much a function of differences in organizational culture, as of differences between volunteers and paid staff. Organizations run predominately by paid staff and those that are volunteer-run would reflect different sets of assumptions. These assumptions could then be reflected in the minds of employees and volunteers as well. Thus, Liao-Troth examined one setting (a hospital) in which volunteers and employees looked much more similar, and in which the volunteer program was very formalized.

In studies examining participation, withdrawal, and even termination, additional insights are revealed. A theme that emerges is that of psychological connectedness. Concepts such as organizational citizenship and psychological contracting are introduced in which the interpretive nature of work (whether volunteer or paid) becomes important to one's understanding. In a museum setting, volunteers were more likely to participate in citizenship behaviors, whereas employees tended to withdraw. Farmer and Fedor (1999) talked about the differences in volunteers' assumptions and beliefs than in what employees assumed and believed about their organizations. The symbolic nature of contracting became evident in their research. Studies about long-term care ombudsmen who terminate services (Nelson et al., 2002) and about role ambiguity (Nelson et al., 1995) appear to reinforce the importance of psychological contracting. Hopkins' work (2002), although focused solely on employees and organizational citizenship, complicates the mix in that the employees she surveyed were actually performing activities that went beyond paid expectations.

In studies that sought to identify the optimal mix of volunteers and paid staff, differences were seen in the roles performed by volunteers, particularly when performing tasks that generated a great deal of conflict (Netting et al., 2000). Yet the reasons these volunteers often terminate related not to resistance of their being there, as much as to their feeling the need for more staff support. Rather than encountering resistance, they may feel neglected. Brudney and Gazley (2002) found no evidence that management staff viewed SCORE volunteers in a negative, resistive manner. It is important to note that the volunteers and paid staff in both the ombudsman and SCORE programs were part of national mandates in which the use of volunteers has been an acceptable part of the program culture from the beginning.

In light of paid staff and volunteer relationships, the literature revealed a predisposition to assume that conflict will occur and that paid staff will be resistant. Empirical evidence, however, does not fully support this assumption. Yet the empirical evidence has occurred in settings having cultures more conducive to receiving and accepting volunteer roles–the ombudsman program, SCORE, and hospitals. Whereas the ombudsman program and SCORE are governmentally mandated public volunteer programs, hospitals have been notoriously formal in their volunteer programs. Volunteers in hospitals are often treated so similarly to employees that they almost perform as paid staff, thus differences in their expectations might not be apparent. For example, in a sunbelt city where older persons volunteered in hospital settings, a volunteer dared not miss a day of "work" given that a long waiting list of potential volunteers awaited the invitation to participate, bumping current volunteers out of the limited number of slots available.

So what do these studies, combined with the conceptual literature on volunteerism, tell us? The literature over time has emphasized the importance of managing volunteers. There are historical pieces in the social work literature that provide excellent commentary on volunteer management (see for example Haeuser & Schwartz, 1980) as well as contemporary articles (see for example Marx, 1999). Marx (1999) provided a very helpful listing of what administrators can do to recruit and supervise volunteers, so we will not repeat these here. There are also helpful tips about volunteering on various websites such as the ENERGIZE, Independent Sector (2001), or the Points of Light Foundation, as well as practical books on volunteer management (see for example Connors, 2001; McCurley & Lynch, 1998; Macduff, 1996; Scheirer, 1993) and journals designed for practitioners such as *The Journal of Volunteer Administration*. An excellent resource is the 161-page-long 2002 Volunteer Management Bibliography developed by Steve McCurley, offered free of charge and available on the ENERGIZE website (www.energizeinc.com/art/biblio.html).

If one theme permeates the volunteerism literature, it is that volunteers require the commitments of time and resources if administrators want to have quality programs. This is not a new theme in that is has been the mantra of almost any writer, trainer, or researcher in the field. What appears to be somewhat new is the importance of understanding the concept of psychological contracting and its relationship to organizational culture. Embedding the value of volunteerism and receptivity toward volunteers may be part of what administrators can do to promote and enhance volunteer and paid staff relationships. Yet administrators cannot control the varied assumptions and beliefs that volunteers bring to the psychological contract. These are very individualistic perceptions and must be respected as such.

An organizational culture predisposed to using volunteers is very different than one in which the incorporation of volunteers is an "add-on" to an already busy schedule. An organizational culture that treats volunteers like paid employees (hospitals, for example) may find that volunteers act very similarly to employees. Therefore, it is critically important for managers and administrators to recognize the norms associated with volunteerism within their settings.

A mainstay of the applied literature on volunteer management is the perennial concern about "volunteer staff relations" (Sloan, 1985, p. 94). Suspicious, uncertain, and often outright false perceptions between paid and nonpaid workers in the same organization, even, and perhaps, especially when they perform similar tasks, spark a great deal of harmful organizational conflict (Sloan, 1985). Some of this results from status differences between paid and nonpaid staff. Time worn assumptions about poor staff volunteer relationship norms have several explanations. From a staff perspective, these could be: (1) staff don't see how volunteers meet organizational needs, (2) staff don't see how volunteers help to sustain the organizational vision, (3) staff see volunteers as taking more time and trouble than they are worth, (4) staff see volunteers as generally less proficient, (5) staff may believe that volunteers are not well grounded in factual information, (6) paid staff are more valuable because they are getting paid for their work, (7) volunteers need to be spoon-fed, and (8) staff who may be threatened by volunteers. In this latter case, if nonpaid paraprofessionals can succeed in doing work that is similar to what paid staff do, then the professional's role is seen as being devalued in an economic sense, thus robbing it of its social currency (prestige), and perhaps even de-legitimizing it (Scheier, 1993). More specifically, Scheier asks how one can expect paid staff to be completely secure in managing or working with volunteers because, in doing so, one is asking them to forego the two major ways in which one oversees employees: pay and control.

Sloan (1985) argues that the tensions that arise from these perceived threats are sustained and enlarged by certain myths that volunteer and professional staff hold about one another. Just as staff have perceptions about volunteers, volunteers may have perceptions about staff. For example in some organizational cultures: (1) volunteers may believe that staff work for pay but volunteers work out of the goodness of their hearts; (2) volunteers may believe that staff don't really know what it's like in the real world, and volunteers do; and (3) staff will attempt to control activities whenever they can. Sloan (1985) concludes that these myths perpetuate inter-role conflict and lead some volunteer coordinators to look the other way when training and discipline are required.

Scheier (1993) argues that the antidote to these mutual volunteer/staff misconceptions, whether mythical or not, is to develop policies that promote the volunteers' support of the professional role, not diminish the role by having volunteers do exactly the same thing. Managers are advised to take time to explain the important contributions that volunteers can make in their programs and organizations. More recently Scheier (1999) explored the possibility of exterminating staff-volunteer conflict by developing autonomous volunteer roles devoid of paid staff or closely allied professional counterparts.

Our experience in working with volunteer ombudsman programs indicates that the roles played by volunteers must be carefully defined. Since this is an advocacy type program, volunteers have to be carefully screened because some volunteers will want to be friendly visitors in long term care facilities rather than advocates who have to feel comfortable with conflict. Volunteers do not come to their roles because they want to do paperwork, yet paid staff are responsible for reporting to higher authorities. Frustrations over volunteers who do not complete their paperwork on time or who do not appreciate the importance of reporting is a frequent source of staff complaints. On the other hand, volunteers feel frustrated by staff who impose structure on their activities. Role conflict is supported in the literature and in our experience as a problem between paid staff and volunteers. This is not a new concept but it appears to be a persistent one. Role clarity and conflict tie in with how the congruence of organizational culture and psychological expectations mesh within the setting.

When a survey of volunteers who had terminated with a state ombudsman program was conducted, we found that program factors that were most frequently cited as problematic were conflict with central office staff and lack of support (Nelson, Netting, Borders, & Huber, 2002). Yet in a highly structured, federally-mandated program, it seems obvious that volunteers can not create their own visions or deviate from regulations. It is this highly prescribed setting that may be the greatest source of volunteer and paid staff conflict since it is up to central office staff to oversee the program protocols and procedures. Anecdotally, we have observed that state ombudsmen typically feel that volunteers are a double-edged sword. They are the program's greatest asset, but also their greatest liability. They increase routine review, complaint volume, and the ability to reach out to more older residents in long term care facilities. Yet, they are hard to manage in a highly complex, narrowly prescribed, resource strapped, legally bound position.

Perhaps it is this paradox, this double-edged sword, that attributes to the tensions inherent in paid staff and volunteer interactions. We have seen denial of this paradox in situations in which the management of volunteers has been added on to the job descriptions of social workers in various agencies. The assumption in this situation is that there is not that much to managing volunteers. In actuality, depending on the culture of the agency and the ways in which volunteers and staff perceive one another, the social worker inherits a complex set of interactions. Even in settings in which the culture supports volunteerism, relationships can be tense if roles are not clarified.

Therefore, based on the literature and our experience, we propose a series of questions to guide an administrator or manager in assessing the organization's or program's paid staff/volunteer roles and relationships. This organizational assessment focuses on the concepts identified by writers in the field and pushes beyond the assumptions of conventional wisdom.

1. How did this organization/program begin? Were volunteers a part of its beginnings either in conjunction with paid staff or prior to the hiring of paid staff? Or were volunteers added later?
2. What are the historical roles of, and assumptions about, volunteers and paid staff in this organization's/program's culture? How have these roles and assumptions changed/diversified over time?
3. What are the current organizational/programmatic cultural assumptions and expectations about volunteers and paid staff roles and relationships?
4. Is volunteer recruitment congruent with organizational assumptions about the roles and relationships of paid staff and volunteers? For what roles are volunteers recruited?
5. Do paid staff and volunteers interact within this organization? Are there highly differentiated roles or is there a great deal of role overlap? Are volunteers used for tasks that staff can not do (i.e., serving on the board, legislative advocacy)?
6. Is the management of volunteers as formalized as the management of staff (job descriptions, roles defined, training provided, etc.)? Do managers of volunteers and managers of staff coordinate their efforts?
7. How do conflict and resistance between paid staff and volunteers play out in this organization? What is the source of any conflict and how is it addressed?
8. How does the organization assess the assumptions and beliefs (psychological contracting) that both volunteers and staff bring to their positions? How is this knowledge used in making sure that volunteers are supported?
9. What citizenship behaviors are performed by volunteers and staff? Are these behaviors evident in the actions of both volunteers and staff?
10. Do volunteers have the staff support and oversight that they need to do their jobs?
11. How is an optimal volunteer/paid staff mix determined for this organization? Does the current mix work well or is change needed?
12. How are volunteers and paid staff included in evaluating the quality of programs and services provided by this organization?

Not only may these questions be useful in assessing one's volunteer program, but they are questions for future research. Of particular importance to understanding relationships among paid staff and volunteers is recognizing the differentiation of their status characteristics, the psychological contracts that both bring to their roles, and the organizational culture in the setting under investigation. We contend that it is important to understand both the psychological and sociological dimensions of any setting in which paid staff and volunteers engage in order to effectively intervene.

CONCLUSION

Resistance of staff to volunteers is not a foregone conclusion. Studies indicate that in some organizations this resistance is not part of the organizational culture. It appears that level of resistance will vary, depending on cultural norms. Regardless, there is definitely an interest in understanding volunteer and paid staff relationships. Although this interest may be triggered by conflict and resistance, it is also about clarification, best practices, and quality volunteer management. If one point is repeatedly emphasized, it is that volunteers are not free–there is an investment to be made when one incorporates volunteers into an organization's culture.

Focusing on organizational or programmatic culture can provide insight into volunteer and paid staff relationships. Cultures will differ, as will psychological contracts (the assumptions and beliefs) that both employees and volunteers bring to their positions. Carefully assessing organizational/programmatic culture is a first step. Equally important is recognizing that psychological contracting is very individualistic and requires attention to detail. Not only are volunteers not free, but it is the talented volunteer manager/administrator who will recognize the diversity among psychological contracts and will listen for underlying assumptions and beliefs that define both volunteer and employee expectations.

REFERENCES

American Association for Retired Persons (AARP)/Legal Council for the Elderly. (1994). *Survey of state ombudsman programs.* Washington, DC: Author.

Ashcraft, K. L., & Kedrowics, A. (2002). Self-direction or social support? Nonprofit empowerment and the tacit employment contract of organizational communication studies (Abstract). *Communication Monographs, 69*(1), 88-110.

Berger, J., & Zelditch, M. (1993). *Theoretical research programs: Study in the growth of theory.* Stanford, CA: Stanford University Press.

Bowgett, K., & Salvage, J. (2001). Should we be recruiting volunteers to work in hospitals (pro and con viewpoints). *Nursing Times, 97*(7), 25.

Brudney, J. L. (1990). *Fostering volunteer programs in the public sector.* San Francisco: Jossey-Bass.

Brudney, J. L. (1999). The perils of practice: Reaching the summit. *Nonprofit Management and Leadership, 9*(4), 385-398.

Brudney, J. L., & Gazley, B. (2002). Testing the conventional wisdom regarding volunteer programs: A longitudinal analysis of the service corps of retired executives and the U.S. Small business administration. *Nonprofit and Voluntary Sector Quarterly, 31*(4), 525-548.

Burrell, G., & Morgan, G. (1979). *Sociological paradigms and organisational analysis*. London: Heinemann.

Clary, E.G., Synder, M., & Stukas, A. A. (1996). Volunteers' motivations: Findings from a national survey. *Nonprofit and Voluntary Sector Quarterly, 25*(4), 485-505.

Connors, T. D. (Ed.). (2001). *The volunteer management handbook*. New York: John Wiley & Sons.

HLC.internet. (1996, March 28). *HLC announces American Red Cross worldwide Internet/Intranet network*. Retrieved December 14, 2002, from http://wint.decsy.ru /alphaservers/digital/v0000355.htm.

Duncombe, W. D., & Brudney, J. L. (1995). The optimal mix of volunteer and paid staff in local governments: An application to municipal fire departments. *Public Finance Quarterly, 23*(3), 356-385.

Ellis, S. J., & Noyes, K. H. (1990). *By the people: A history of Americans as volunteers*. San Francisco, CA: Jossey-Bass.

Farmer, S. M., & Fecor, D. B. (1999). Volunteer participation and withdrawal: A psychological contract perspective on the role of expectations and organizational support. *Nonprofit Management and Leadership, 9*, 349-367.

Galindo, K. R., & Guzley, R.M. (2001). The volunteer satisfaction index: Construct definition, measurement, development, and validation. *Journal of Social Service Research, 28*(1), 45-68.

George, M. (1997). Precarious pounds: For cash-hungry voluntary organisations funding cuts can seem like the final straw. *Community Care, 1160*, p. 28.

Gidron, B. (1987). Integration of volunteer workers into formal human service agencies: An organizational theory perspective. *The Journal of Applied Social Sciences, 2*(2), 191-205.

Gidron, B. (1983). Sources of job satisfaction among service volunteers. *Journal of Voluntary Action Research, 12*(1), 21-33.

Govekar, P. L., & Govekar, M. A. (2002). Using economic theory and research to better understand volunteer behavior. *Nonprofit Management and Leadership, 13*(1), 33-45.

Haeuser, A. A., & Schwartz, F. S. (1980). Developing social work skills for work with volunteers. *Social Casework: The Journal of Contemporary Social Work*, 595-600.

Harris-Wehling, J., Feasley, J. C., & Estes, C. L. (1995). *Real people, real problems: An evaluation of the long term care ombudsman programs of the Older Americans Act*. Washington, DC: Division of Health Care Services, Institute of Medicine.

Hopkins, K. M. (2002). Organizational citizenship in social service agencies. *Administration in Social Work, 26*(2), 1-15.

Huber, R., Netting, F. E., & Paton, R. N. (1993). In search of the impact of staff mix on long-term care ombudsman programs. *Nonprofit and Voluntary Sector Quarterly, 22*(1), 69-91.

Independent Sector. (2001). *Giving and volunteering in the United States 200*. Retrieved December 5, 2002, from http://www.independentsector.org/programs/research/ gv01main.html

Independent Sector Nonprofit Information Center. (2002). Ten tips for wise volunteering. Washington, D.C.: Online. Available: http://www.independentsector.org.

Karr, L. B. (2000). Status and the volunteer: Employment standing as a status characteristic in organized associations (Abstract). Southern Sociological Society. Available: http://newfirstsearch.ocle.org. Retrieved 12/12/02.

Keith, P. M., & Schafer, R. B. (2002). Expected and actual difficulties of volunteer resident advocates in an ombudsman program. *The Journal of Applied Gerontology,* *21*(4), 421-436.

Liao-Troth, M. A. (2001). Attitude differences between paid workers and volunteers. *Nonprofit Management and Leadership, 11*(4), 423-442.

MacInnes, G., & Hedt, A. H. (1999). *Volunteers in the long term care ombudsman program: Training, certification and liability coverage.* Washington DC: National long Term Care Ombudsman Resource Center.

Macduff, N. (1996). *Volunteer recruiting and retention: A marketing approach, 2nd edition.* MBA Publishing.

Marx, J. D. (1999). Motivational characteristics associated with health and human service volunteers. *Administration in Social Work, 23*(1), 51-66.

McComb, M. (1995). Becoming a travelers aid volunteer: Communication in socialization and training (Special Issue on Ethnography). Communication Studies, 46(3-4), 297-317.

McCurley, S., & Lynch, R. (1996). *Volunteer management.* Downers Grove, IL: Heritage Art.

McCurley, S., & Lynch, R. (1998). *Essential volunteer management.* London, UK: Directory of Social Change.

Moore, L. F., & Anderson, J. C. (1985). Need satisfaction of paid and volunteer workers in health service occupations. In L. F. Moore (ed.), *Motivating Volunteers* (pp. 187-199). Vancouver B.C.: B.C. Ministry of Human Resources.

Nelson, H. W. (2002). *Ombudsman training and certification: Toward a standard of best practice.* Paper commissioned by the National Association of State Long Term Care Ombudsmen for the retreat: The Long Term Care Ombudsman Program: Rethinking and Retooling for the Future. (January 31-February 2, 2002). Supported by a grant from the Helen Bader Foundation. Peachtree City, GA.

Nelson, H. W., Netting, F. E., Borders, K., & Huber, R. (2002). Reasons for terminating service with the long term care ombudsman program: Implications for volunteer retention. Unpublished paper presented at the Association for Research on Nonprofit Organizations and Voluntary Action (ARNOVA), Montreal, Canada.

Nelson, H. W., Pratt, C.C., Carpenter, C.C., & Walter, K. L. (1995). Factors affecting volunteer long-term care ombudsman organizational commitment and burnout. *Nonprofit and Volunteer Sector Quarterly, 24*(3), 213-233.

Netting, F. E., Huber, R., Borders, K., Kautz, J. R., & Nelson, H. W. (2000). Volunteer and paid staff investigating complaints in six states: A natural triaging. *Nonprofit and Voluntary Sector Quarterly, 29*(3), 419-438.

Netting, F. E., & O'Connor, M. K. (2003). *Organization practice.* Boston: Allyn & Bacon.

Pearce, J. L. (1983). Job attitude and motivation differences between volunteers and employees from comparable organizations. *Journal of Applied Psychology, 68,* 646-652.

Pearce, J. L. (1993). *Volunteers: The organizational behavior of unpaid workers.* New York: Routledge.

Perlmutter, F. D., & Cnaan, R. A. (1993). Challenging human service organizations to redefine volunteer roles. *Administration in Social Work, 17*(4), 77-95.

Rickford, F. (May 11, 1994). Volunteers for social change. *The Guardian, 2,* 15(1).

Rosenblum, K. F., & Travis, T. M. C. (2000). *The meaning of difference.* 2nd ed. Boston: McGraw-Hill.

Rousseau, D. M. (1989). Psychological and implied contracts in organizations. *Employee Responsibilities and Rights Journal, 2*(2), 121-139.

Schein, E. H. (1992). *Organizational culture and leadership* (2nd ed.). San Francisco: Jossey-Bass.

Scheirer, I. H. (1993). *Building staff/volunteer relationships.* Available: http//www. energize.com. Retrieved 12/12/02.

Scheirer, I.H. (1999). Introductory notes on staff/volunteer relations. In Section XIV, The New Volunteerism Project, The Archival Collection of Ivan Henry Scheier. Available: http//academic.regis.edu/volunteer/Ivan/sect14.htm#Building. Retrieved 12/12/02.

Schiman, C., & Lordeman, A. (1989). *A study of the use of volunteers by long term care ombudsman programs: The effectiveness of recruitment, supervision, and retention.* Washington, DC: National Center for Long Term Care Ombudsman Resources: Administration on Aging, Cooperative agreement no 90-AT0401.

Seippel, O. (2002). Volunteers and professionals in Norwegian sport organizations. *Voluntas, 13*(3), 253-270.

Sloan, H. (1985). Managing a volunteer program for maximum effectiveness. In C. Ewig, & J. Griggs (Eds.). *Public Concerns Community Initiatives: The Successful Management of Nursing Home Consumer Information Programs.* (pp. 79-97). New York: United Hospital Fund of New York.

Smith, D. H. (1994). Determinants of voluntary association participation and volunteering: A literature review. *Nonprofit and Voluntary Sector Quarterly, 23*(3), 243-263.

Strickler, G. (1987). The social work profession's attitude towards volunteerism. *The Journal of Volunteer Administration, 5*(4), 24-32.

Thorley, V. (2000). Complementary and competing roles of volunteers and professionals in the breastfeeding field. *International Journal of Self Help and Self Care, 1*(2), 171-180.

Victor, K. (March 1, 1997). Lost cause? (Common cause). *National Journal, 29*(9), 410(4).

Van Dyne, L., & Ang, S. (1998). Organizational citizenship behavior of contingent workers in Singapore. *Academy of Management Journal, 41,* 692-703.

Wandersman, A., & Alderman, J. (1993). Incentives, costs, and barriers for volunteers: A staff perspective on volunteers in one state. *Review of Public Personnel Administration, 13*(1), 67-77.

The Role of Non-Profit Agencies
in the Provision
of Welfare-to-Work Services

Yeheskel Hasenfeld, PhD
Lisa Evans Powell, MSW, MPP

SUMMARY. The impact of government contracts on the structure and service technology of non-profit organizations is examined within the context of welfare reform. Forty-three non-profit organizations contracted to provide employment and related services to welfare recipients under the Welfare-to-Work Grants Program were studied. The results show that the contracts placed the agencies in a difficult task environment that severely restricted their autonomy. To cope with such an environment, the agencies developed very similar welfare-to-work programs consonant with the dominant institutional rules in the employment services sector. However, to maintain their distinctiveness in this sector, the agencies also focused their service technology on intensive case management centered on close relations between staff and clients. To isolate the rest of the organization from the contractual constraints and uncertainties, the welfare-to-work programs had minimal internal specialization and were only

Yeheskel Hasenfeld is Professor of Social Welfare, UCLA School of Public Policy and Social Research. Lisa Evans Powell is project manager at a social planning agency.

This study was made possible by a grant from the Aspen Institute Nonprofit Sector Research Fund.

[Haworth co-indexing entry note]: "The Role of Non-Profit Agencies in the Provision of Welfare-to-Work Services." Hasenfeld, Yeheskel, and Lisa Evens Powell. Co-published simultaneously in *Administration in Social Work* (The Haworth Social Work Practice Press, an imprint of The Haworth Press, Inc.) Vol. 28, No. 3/4, 2004, pp. 91-110; and: *Organizational and Structural Dilemmas in Nonprofit Human Service Organizations* (ed: Hillel Schmid) The Haworth Social Work Practice Press, an imprint of The Haworth Press, Inc., 2004, pp. 91-110. Single or multiple copies of this article are available for a fee from The Haworth Document Delivery Service [1-800-HAWORTH, 9:00 a.m. - 5:00 p.m. (EST). E-mail address: docdelivery@ haworthpress.com].

loosely coupled with other service units in the agencies. The findings suggest that government contracts with non-profit agencies may constrain them from achieving the very objectives they are contracted to fulfill. *[Article copies available for a fee from The Haworth Document Delivery Service: 1-800-HAWORTH. E-mail address: <docdelivery@haworthpress.com> Website: <http://www.HaworthPress.com> © 2004 by The Haworth Press, Inc. All rights reserved.]*

KEYWORDS. Nonprofit, welfare reform, contracting out

Non-profit agencies have had a long history of providing services to welfare recipients. Agencies with a strong commitment to serve poor people inevitably find many welfare recipients among their clients (on the early history of voluntary associations serving the poor see Skocpol, 1992). Others have had contractual relations with welfare departments to provide specific mandated services, such as childcare, remedial education, or vocational training (e.g., Kramer and Grossman 1987; Gronbjerg 1993; Smith and Lipsky 1993). The participation of non-profit agencies in welfare reform dates back to the early WIN programs, and has expanded considerably in scope with JOBS (Hagen and Lurie 1994). In particular, as welfare departments increasingly rely on employment and training services funded by the Work Investment Act (replacing The Job Training Partnership Act), non-profits in this sector have experienced a significant rise in the number of welfare recipients they are asked to serve. The passage of Temporary Assistance to Needy Families (TANF) with its strong emphasis on welfare-to-work has further intensified the demand for and the use of a broad array of services provided by non-profit agencies to assist welfare recipients overcome barriers to employment (e.g., DeVita 1999; Pavetti et al. 2000)

Nevertheless, non-profit agencies contracted to serve welfare recipients encounter a radically different environment than the one they had known prior to TANF. First, most of the recipients they serve are under a five-year lifetime limit (or less in some states) for receipt of aid, and a two-year limit (or less) to become employed. Second, the services they provide must concord with and reinforce the work-first ideology of TANF. Third, with the rapid decline of the welfare rolls, these agencies are asked to serve the more difficult cases, those with multiple employment barriers. Fourth, because of the many restrictions placed on welfare recipients, the agencies face a far more complex set of relations with the welfare departments than before. Finally, for many of these agencies, offering services under a work-first policy requires changes and adaptations in their own service ideologies and technologies. It also necessitates development of new inter-organizational relations needed in conjunction with these changes.

The changing environment triggered by TANF raises anew the general policy issue about the relationship between the voluntary sector and the state (Smith 1999). Specifically, does contracting in such an environment seriously compromise the unique role and mission of non-profit social service and employment agencies? Does government oversight lead to higher bureaucratization, reduced autonomy and threat to the quality of services as Smith and Lipsky argue (1993)? Or does contracting out, especially in the context of having to serve a highly heterogeneous welfare population with multiple employment barriers, enable the provision of services tailored to their particular needs as suggested by Salamon (1995)? Does contracting out encourage or discourage non-profit agencies to innovate and experiment with new service models?

In this study we attempt to address these policy issues by exploring the actual experiences of non-profit agencies that provide welfare-to-work services under the Welfare-to-Work Grants Program. We focus on welfare-to-work (WtW) programs because they are at the core of TANF, placing these agencies in an important role in its successful implementation. Authorized under the Balanced Budget Act of 1997, the aim of the grants program is to provide states and local governments with additional resources to serve the hardest-to-employ welfare recipients, especially in areas with high rates of poverty. A second aim of the act is to mobilize the resources of local Private Industry Councils (PICS) or Workforce Investment Boards on behalf of the work-first programs under TANF.

The original legislation required that 70% of the grants be spent on recipients who were: (1) long-term recipients or recipients within one year of reaching the TANF time limit, and who had at least two of three specific employment barriers– (1) (a) lack of a high school degree or GED *and* low reading and math skills, (b) substance abuse problem or (c) poor work history; or (2) non-custodial parents of children receiving welfare who also have at least two of the three barriers (for a review on the early implementation of WtW see Nightingale, Trutko et al. 1999; Perez-Johnson 1999). The 1999 WtW amendments relaxed the 70% requirement by removing the additional employment barriers from eligibility, in part, because agencies were unable to meet their enrollment targets. Currently, TANF recipients are eligible for WtW if they have received aid for at least 30 months, if they are within 12 months of reaching their TANF time limit, or if they have exhausted their receipt of TANF due to time limits. It also eased the rules about the eligibility of non-custodial parents (http:/wtw.doleta.gov/laws-regs/99amendsum.htm).

There are also restrictions on the range of services that can be provided under the grants. WtW funds can be used for job preparation, job creation, supportive services (such as childcare and transportation), and post-employment services such as job retention (including non-medical substance abuse treatment), post-employment education, training and career advancement activities. The original legislation prohibited the use of WtW funds for education and training as stand alone activities. They could be provided only to recipients who are employed. The 1999 amendments added vocational training and education as a separate allowable activity but limited to six months.

THEORETICAL PERSPECTIVE

To understand the organizational responses and adaptations of non-profit agencies to WtW, we use an institutional political economy perspective (e.g., Greenwood and Hinings 1996; Oliver 1997; Ruef and Scott 1998). It suggests that organizations survive and adapt by (a) developing organizational practices that conform to dominant institutional norms, rules and cognitive schema, and by (b) making strategic choices that enable them to sustain their unique niche and competitive advantage. Accordingly, we propose that the non-profit agencies will adopt organizational practices that conform to the dominant institutional norms, rules, and language of a "work-first" policy. They will do so in order to legitimize current and future flow of WtW resources. In particular, we suggest that non-profit agencies will constrain their service practices to reflect the "work first" policy even if their own internal ideologies may contradict it. Still, we also expect that agencies will attempt to preserve their distinct service practices by surrounding them with the symbols of "work first." From a strategic perspective, we expect the non-profit agencies to negotiate new inter-organizational relations to manage the resource dependencies they encounter in serving the targeted welfare population. These include ensuring the flow of funds, recruiting of participants, enlisting employers, and maintaining a service niche in a fairly competitive environment. Of particular importance would be their relations with the welfare department as the key organization in their task environment. The strategies used to manage these relations will be reflected in internal organizational practices, especially in the organization of their service technology. We expect that the agencies will attempt to develop hybrid service technologies that combine features from prevailing "work first" practices and their own distinct service practices (D'Aunno, Sutton et al. 1991). However, we also anticipate tensions and conflicts between the externally imposed practices and their internal client service culture. To address these, we expect the agencies to develop their WtW program either as a distinct organizational unit or as a self-contained set of practices that are loosely coupled with their other service practices. In doing so, the agencies can respond to the new environmental exigencies and yet buffer their other service components from them.

METHODOLOGY

We have selected all the non-profit agencies in Los Angeles and San Diego counties receiving WtW grants in 1999, whether from local, state, or federal sources either directly or through sub-contracts. The universe includes 41 agencies in Los Angeles and 19 agencies in San Diego for a total of 60 agencies. All the WtW programs are quite new–most of them (81%) have been in existence less than one year at the start of our study. Data on the implementation of the WtW programs were obtained through a semi-structured face-to-face interview with the directors of the program. The response rate to the interviews was 68 percent (n = 43). The interviews focused on such organizational issues as constraints of the grants on services and participants; inter-organizational relations with the welfare departments, employers and other service agencies; organizational experience in working with hard-to-employ welfare recipients; service delivery patterns; the internal structure of the WtW program; relation of the program to other units in the agency; and issues about measuring performance, among other topics. The analysis is based on both the qualitative and quantitative data obtained in these interviews.

A PROFILE OF THE AGENCIES

The agencies that have succeeded in obtaining WtW grants obviously have had strong ties to the employment services network, especially via the Job Training Partnership Act (JPTA). Only 11 agencies (26%) did not have a JTPA component prior to WtW. Moreover, almost all (98%) claim to have had some prior experience in serving welfare recipients, either as part of their JTPA caseload, or via their other services. The agencies generally frame their experience as working with poor people, although most acknowledge that the recipients referred to their WtW program present a more difficult challenge in comparison to their other clients.

As can be seen from Figure 1, the majority of the agencies (53%) specialize in the provision of employment services, remedial education and vocational training. These, especially the one-stop centers and the employment/education agencies, present the prevailing patterns of serving the unemployed. Historically, these agencies have not shown to be particularly responsive and effective in serving welfare recipients in general, and hard-to-employ recipients, in particular (e.g., Anderson, Burkhauser et al. 1993; Lafer 1994). Thirty-seven percent of the agencies can be classified as multi-service; in addition to employment services, they also offer a wide range of other services such as assistance with food and shelter, childcare, family counseling, and mental health services. These agencies may be particularly well positioned to provide, in integrated and innovative ways, the multi-faceted services the multi-problem recipients may need. The four single-service agencies in our sample specialize in a unique service, such as residential drug treatment, transitioning homeless families to permanent housing, or day care for Alzheimer patients.

The WtW grants to the agencies range from about $100,000 to $5,000,000 with an average grant of about $1 million (data were not available for nine agencies). The one-stop centers, on average, received the largest grant amount ($1.65 million), while the multi-service agencies, on average, received the lowest amount ($831,000). The size of the WtW program in all the agencies is fairly small. On average, the target caseload for the duration of the grant (usually 24 months) is 157 participants. It ranges from a low of 78 for the training

FIGURE 1. Type of Agencies Offering WtW Services

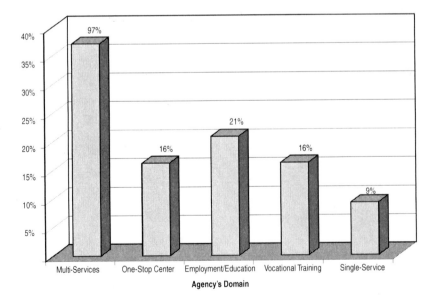

agencies to a high of 203 for the one-stop centers.[1] On average, the number of FTE staff allocated to the WtW program is 6.5.

Despite the heterogeneity of the agencies, almost all of them offer a fairly similar menu of WtW services (see also Pavetti et al. 2000). Almost all provide basic case management that consists of orientation, assessment, monitoring and referral to needed services. All the agencies that provide pre-employment services offer job club and job search, some form of work experience, and job placement. There are few variations; some may add motivational and self-esteem workshops. Those that provide post-employment services invariably offer On the Job Training (OJT), remedial education such as English as Second Language (ESL), or High School Equivalency Diploma classes (also known as GED), and access to vocational training. Here too, there are few variations; four agencies specialize in specific vocational training (e.g., security, childcare, truck driving), and several offer mentoring. Few agencies that have an on-site childcare program include it in their menu of WtW services.

MANAGING THE TASK ENVIRONMENT

The Grants Environment. In part, the commonality in the service menus of these agencies is a response to the grants' constraints. Agencies that provide pre-employment services must abide by a "work first" approach and cannot offer training or education to their participants as initial options. As one director put it, "We have to place in jobs first. We cannot do training first." Agencies that offer post-employment services can do so only if the participants are already working or engaged in allowable employment activities (i.e., community service programs, work experience programs, job creation through public or private sector employment wage subsidies, and on-the-job training).[2] It limits the ability of the participants to enroll in any comprehensive training or education program.

Most importantly, the similarity among the agencies is also a reflection of the measures of success imposed by the grants. The success of each WtW program is measured, first and foremost, by the proportion of recipients placed in jobs and secondly by the improvement in the wages of those given post-employment services. To be competitive, the agencies have to demonstrate a high degree of success. Most promise to place about 50 percent or more of the pre-employment recipients in unsubsidized jobs by the end of the grant year, and to achieve job retention of at least six months for well over 50% of those placed in a job. For recipients receiving post-employment services, most of the agencies promise to raise their wages, on average, by at least 10% within six months (i.e., $7.50-$8.64 per hour). When asked about expected program outcomes, a typical response was "50% placement in unsubsidized jobs, 75% retention at 6 months, and 50% go to better jobs."

As shown from recent studies of welfare-to-work programs, these goals are not readily achieved for many welfare recipients, let alone for recipients with multiple employment barriers (Freedman, Knab et al. 2000). To protect themselves from potential failure, the agencies have opted to emulate the service practices that are prominent and common in the employment services sector and especially its welfare-to-work sub-sector. In doing so, they try to insure that they could meet at least the prevailing rates of success in the sector. They can also justify and rationalize their programs as being consonant with the dominant and sanctioned service models of the sector.

Relations with the Welfare Department. The agencies must negotiate a set of relations with the county welfare department in order to (a) assure a steady flow of eligible ("certified") recipients, and (b) obtain approval of allowable service activities (i.e., services that can count as meeting the welfare-to-work requirement). In addition, the agencies depend on the county welfare department to pay for certain support services such as childcare and transportation. Most of the agencies in our study did not have prior established relations with the welfare department. Only three agencies have had substantial prior experience working with the welfare department.

Only 14% of the agencies claim to have good working relationship with the welfare department; 18.6% of the agencies experienced initial difficulties but have gradually worked them out. Still, 67.4% of the agencies continue to experience significant difficulties. In part, the difficulties reflect very different organizational cultures (Sandfort 1999). The welfare workers are oriented toward applying rules and regulations and uniformly enforcing program requirements. The agencies' staff is oriented toward engaging the clients, offering compassion and providing individualized treatment (Handler and Hasenfeld 1997). As one director expressed it, "Our staff is empowered, they come up with a lot of ideas, we encourage them to think out of the box. But [the welfare department] is just the opposite. Their box is made of steel and they could not get out of it if they wanted to." Others mentioned the culture of sanctions in the welfare department as a stark contrast to the culture of voluntary participation that characterizes the agencies. Similarly, agencies that stress training and education find it difficult to adjust to the work-first approach insisted by the department.

Many of the agencies were particularly disturbed by the difficulty in getting referrals from the welfare department, especially since they were anxious to meet their target caseload (see also Pavetti et al. 2000). Indeed, the agencies have had to resort to what they term "reverse certification." That is, the agencies actively recruit welfare recipients from their own caseloads, through contacts with community groups and presentations at churches and job fairs, and then take the cases to the welfare department to obtain certification. The delays in certification also prevent the agencies from getting the welfare department to approve payment for support services for their clients, such as childcare and transportation. In addition, agencies may also find that recipients lose their certification for reasons unknown to them. The concerns and uncertainties about certification obviously emanate from the agencies' fear of failing to comply with the WtW grant requirements.

Closely related to the certification issue is the dependence on the welfare department to approve allowable services. The welfare workers must approve that the WtW services recipients receive meet their work requirements. This may become a contentious issue. For example, one agency offers a program on basic life skills such as budgeting and introduction to the world of work. However, the welfare department refuses to count the program as an allowable activity.

The considerable discretion welfare workers have in deciding which agencies and services they approve leads to favoritism in which some agencies are preferred over others. Several directors attributed the favoritism to the inevitable competition between the county's own welfare-to-work program and the agencies' WtW programs. These programs are seen as competing for the same participants, as taking over the case management function of the welfare workers, and as challenging the effectiveness of the county's program. As stated by one director, "[welfare] workers have historically been extremely resistant to referring welfare recipients to job training, because they fear that they will lose their jobs when the caseloads decline."

Undoubtedly some of these issues arise from what may be termed "liability of newness" in which both the welfare department and the agencies have had to learn how to collaborate with each other. The agencies engage in a variety of strategies to manage these potentially difficult relations. These strategies revolve around (a) developing and strengthening communication channels with the welfare department, (b) establishing personal relations with key welfare staff; and (c) developing new inter-organizational arrangements. Educating the welfare workers through frequent contacts is a common approach. Personal relations and "selling" the agency to the welfare workers are frequently mentioned as a strategy. Formalizing the relations by creating liaison roles was also mentioned.

Relations with Employers. To be successful, the non-profit agencies must develop relations with potential employers. Only four of the agencies have not had prior contact with employers. The others rely on both existing relations and new ones to find jobs for their WtW participants. Agencies use multiple strategies to locate jobs. As shown in Figure 2, almost half the agencies rely on various mass media tools such as the Internet, newspaper ads, cold calls, or Yellow Pages to solicit jobs. About 20% of the agencies use job developers and/or networking with various employers associations (e.g., Chamber of Commerce). A smaller proportion of the agencies use previous contacts or word of mouth (the various strategies are not mutually exclusive). The heavy reliance on passive strategies (i.e., use of mass media) may not bode well for the agencies; they have to find jobs for hard-to-place recipients who have failed to obtain a job through the county's welfare-to-work program. To place these recipients may require far more intensive contact and pro-active approaches with potential employers, (e.g., through the use of job developers). A study of employers in Minnesota found that they do not respond to mass communication strategies, but do respond to "deliberate and individualized contacts with them," and to offers of concrete support services such as childcare and transportation (Owen 2000).

The importance of pro-active strategies is evident by the comments of the program directors about the difficulties in placing welfare recipients in jobs because of the stigma attached to this population. To quote, "The perception of someone on welfare–that they are lazy, do not want to work, and are not going to show up. But many clients are not like that; they have a good work ethic."

FIGURE 2. Strategies to Recruit Employers

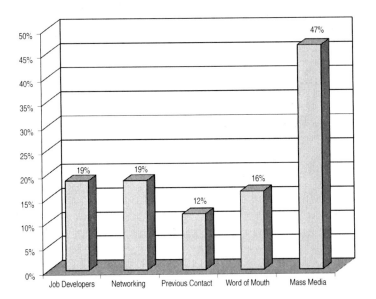

Consequently, several of the agencies do not identify their clients as welfare recipients. Similarly, many directors acknowledged that employers are reluctant to hire welfare recipients or use the Work Opportunity Tax Credit because they fear the added paperwork and the bureaucratic intrusion by government agencies. The directors also recognize the obvious multiple employment barriers of their participants–lack of skills, language barriers, felony record, poor work experience, and lack of childcare. Therefore, the importance of being pro-active and cultivating relations with employers is vital to these agencies, yet a small number of agencies adopt them.

Relations with Other Human Service Agencies. To effectively serve multi-problem recipients may require the agencies to mobilize a wide range of complementary and supportive services from other human service agencies. An important attraction to contract these agencies is the added advantage of capitalizing on their extensive human service network, especially with other non-profit community-based service agencies. In general, the agencies have not sought out many complementary services from other organizations. On average, the directors mentioned only two types of complementary services their programs use. As shown in Figure 3, the complementary service mentioned most often is childcare (44.7%), followed by counseling (32.6%), emergency assistance (28%) and training (28%). Of course, the limited use of the external human service network may be due to the ability to provide many of these services in-house. However, this is not generally the case. As shown later, the WtW programs make moderate use of other services in their own agencies. Hence, the notion that the non-profit agencies have an advantage by being able to use a large human services network may need to be re-examined.

Finally, it is important to note the agencies characterize their employment services network as highly competitive. A majority of the agencies indicated facing competition for WtW funds (72%), and competition for participants (57%). Only for the one-stop centers the competition was less for funding (33%), but more on participants (67%). To compete for funds, the agencies rely on their grantsmanship, reputation, and network and political connections. To compete for participants, the agencies rely mostly on their connections with the welfare department, and by offering services needed by it.

The Role of the WtW Network. To remain competitive, the agencies monitor the employment services network through regular, usually monthly, meetings with the various WtW providers, including the welfare department. The average size of the WtW network is 20, but there is great variation in size ranging from less than 10 to over 100 organizations. In particular, the multi-service and the vocational training agencies tend to affiliate with small networks (average of 10 organizations). It is through the WtW network that the institutional rules of the program are reinforced, issues with the welfare department are

FIGURE 3. Use of Human Service Network

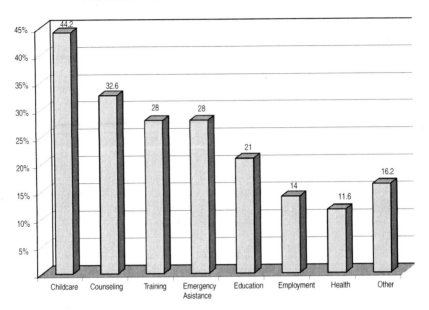

aired, and relations among the various providers are forged. It is also through the network that the various agencies learn about their competitors and the market niches and strategies they employ. The overwhelming majority of the agencies find participation in this network to be very helpful in their ability to manage the WtW environment.

To sum, the task environment in which the non-profit agencies operate sets certain constraints and opportunities: (a) The granting network, through its "work first" policy, which may not be shared by the agencies, sets limits as to the type of participants that can be served, the range of services that can be offered, and the desired outcomes. (b) Because of their high degree of dependence on the welfare department, the agencies must develop complex exchanges that are potentially contentious, especially with regard to referral of recipients, certification of eligibility and allowable activities. (c) Employers play a pivotal role in the ultimate success of these agencies. The agencies must expand considerable energy and resources to recruit them and ensure job placements for their participants. Yet a majority of the agencies adopt passive strategies to mobilize employers. (d) Reliance of the agencies on the human services network for complementary services for their participants is modest at best. (e) While successful in getting WtW grants, the agencies face a highly competitive environment, and they must develop strategies to maintain their competitive edge. In this context, the WtW network is an extremely important inter-organizational tool. It both enforces institutional conformity and structural isomorphism, but also points to niche opportunities and advantageous inter-organizational exchanges.

THE ORGANIZATIONAL FORMS OF THE WtW PROGRAMS

In such an environment, a small number of agencies are able to maintain their competitive edge by the uniqueness of their program. A couple of the agencies specialize in serving refugees. Another agency has the distinction of serving welfare recipients with a history of substance abuse. One agency offers employment services to homeless men and women. Still another offers a program to train truck and bus drivers. Because these agencies have a desirable service and few competitors, they are in a better position of negotiating favorable relations with both the funding agencies and the welfare department.

Most of the other agencies, facing the constraints from the granting environment and the welfare departments, have developed a fairly typical "work first" sequence of services. Unemployed recipients are initially assessed about their work readiness, and are directed to various job search/job club types of activities, or work experience. In addition, they may receive assistance, mostly through referral back to the welfare department, to obtain childcare and transportation subsidies. If the recipients have personal problems such as substance abuse, lack of basic necessities (e.g., food, shelter), or interpersonal difficulties, concomitant support services may be offered either in-house or via referrals. For recipients who are employed or have become employed, the agencies are likely to provide, either directly or via referrals, educational and training opportunities. These may be coupled with additional support services such as counseling and mentoring.

Therefore, to distinguish themselves, a majority of agencies have opted to design what can be best described as a "boutique" case management service technology. In other words, because the agencies are quite constrained as to the type and sequence of services they can provide, they invest and innovate in the area in which they have most discretion–relations with their clients. It is manifested in several ways. First, case management is the core of the WtW program, and most of the agencies have used the grants to invest heavily in case managers. It is also reflected in low caseload sizes. Compared to the average caseload size of 150 participants per case manager in the Los Angeles County Welfare-to-Work program (Weissman 1997), the average caseload size for these agencies is about 29 participants per case manager.[3] Only 14%

of the agencies have caseloads of 75 participants or more. Second, the favorable caseload size is also noted in a much higher cost of service per participant. Using a crude measure–dividing the agency's total WtW grants by its target caseload–the average cost per participant is $10,431. This amount is more than twice of what Los Angeles County's own WtW program spends per participant. Third, the WtW program component is generally small. The typical WtW unit consists of a director, an administrative assistant, and several case managers. Moreover, there is minimal division of labor or specialization among the case managers. In addition to the case managers (or employment counselors), only 37% of the WtW units have job developers, and only 9% have job retention specialists.

Small size, low caseload, high expenditure per participant, and minimal internal specialization are structural features of a service technology whose core activities consist of intensive and frequent interactions between staff and clients. The lack of role specialization also signals a people changing technology that is based on the primacy of interpersonal relations between staff and clients. It is through these intensive relations that the program tries to earn the allegiance of the participants, motivate them to participate, gain their trust and guide them toward job placement and retention. Indeed, the close contact, interpersonal relations, and monitoring of the participants–the hallmark of these programs–makes them stand apart from the county's welfare-to-work program. It is what many of these non-profit agencies do best and is the source of their reputation in the community.

Yet, there is a certain built-in tension in how the agencies view the role of case managers that reflects the internal conflicts in the program as a whole. Recognizing that the case managers have to work with difficult clients, the agencies uniformly identify the most important skills case managers must have as: the ability to motivate and understand their clients, show empathy, and have the capacity to communicate and to engage in counseling and problem solving.

At the same time, these case managers are evaluated on the basis of the number of participants they place in jobs or keep employed and less on their ability to forge close relations with their clients. When asked how case managers are evaluated, one director put it: "Placement numbers: bottom line is did she get a job? Did she stay on it? And how much does she make?" It can be readily seen that the pressure to produce these employment outcomes may conflict with the ability of the case managers to show empathy and patience, and to develop trusting interpersonal relationships that enable individualized counseling and problem solving (Hasenfeld and Weaver 1996). These tensions at the micro level–relations between case mangers and participants–are echoed in the program as a whole. While it targets welfare recipients with multiple employment barriers that require extensive and intensive interventions, the program insists on "work first," and the participants are subject to time limits.

We anticipated that many of the agencies would opt to develop a distinct WtW unit within their agencies in order to conform to the institutional rules of WtW and to buffer their other service units from the tensions and pressures facing this program (Meyer and Rowan 1977). As shown in Figure 4, overall, about half of the agencies have organized a new and distinct WtW work unit, most notably the one-stop centers and the multi-service agencies. While such a strategy enables the agency to cope with the complex WtW task environment, it may also increase the transaction costs of accessing other agency services.

Whether the WtW program is in a separate work unit or not, it seems to be relatively self-contained without making extensive use of other agency services. When asked which other agency services the WtW program relies on the most, on average, the directors mentioned only two other services. About 47% of the programs mentioned the use of education, and 38% mentioned counseling and related services. As expected, only WtW programs in multi-service agencies are more likely to use other in-house services, but even in these agencies the use is not extensive. Of course, the limited use of other services may also reflect their availability in the agency. In any case, the notion

FIGURE 4. Percent New WtW Units by Agency Type

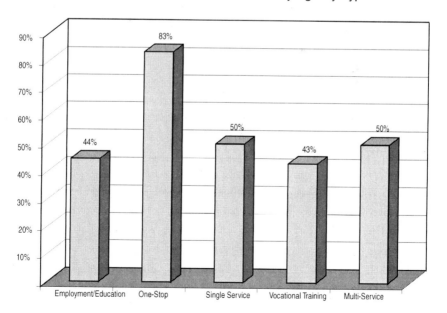

that the advantage of using non-profit agencies is the added value of their other services may be unwarranted.

DISCUSSION

Our findings suggest that the underlying premises of enlisting non-profit agencies to deliver WtW services to hard-to-employ welfare recipients must be seriously re-examined. The non-profit agencies are assumed to have unique organizational and service configurations that give them a particular advantage over public welfare-to-work programs in serving such a population. These include: (a) the ability to provide high quality services tailored to the particular needs of the clients; (b) the capacity to access and mobilize both internal and external resources on behalf of the clients; and (c) the capacity to experiment and develop innovative services as models of "good practices." However, to capitalize on these advantages, the non-profit agencies need to operate in an institutional and political economy environment that supports and reinforces these attributes (Kramer 2000; Schmid 2000).

Our findings suggest that the non-profit agencies contracted to deliver WtW services lack such a supportive environment. The elements in their environment that control their WtW funds and their welfare clients set explicit constraints on who they can serve, what services they can offer and what service outcomes they are expected to attain. In particular, the agencies find that they have to implement a "work-first" program that for many of them stands in conflict with their dominant service ideology. In other words, both the granting organizations and the welfare departments dictate to the agencies a service delivery model that is generally at odds with their own service models. They do so by the evaluation criteria they impose on the agencies, by controlling the flow of clients, and by sanctioning allowable activities.

The conflict between what the agencies can do best and what is expected of them is manifest in their relations with the welfare department. The welfare department operates in an environment that places great emphasis on bureaucratic efficiency–strict enforcement of welfare rules, rapid movement of recipients to work and off the rolls, and the use of sanctions to achieve compliance. The non-profit agencies, serving the same population, attain their legitimacy by emphasizing a professional service model–individualized treatment, and client-worker relations based on trust and compassion (Hasenfeld and Weaver 1996). Although both share a broad goal of self-sufficiency, the welfare department places emphasis on "work-first," while the non-profit agencies have historically emphasized human capital investment, especially training and education coupled with an extensive array of supportive services. Thus, the difficulties with the welfare departments reflect the clash between different institutional frames–regulative, normative, and cognitive–that underlie the survival and growth of each set of organizations. Because of the high degree of dependency of the agencies on the welfare department, they are more likely to develop service delivery models that conform to the institutional frame of the welfare department.

The agencies do not seem to be particularly adept at actively mobilizing either potential employers or other human service agencies in their environment on behalf of their welfare recipients. This may simply reflect the established patterns of the employment service network to which these agencies belong.

The ability of the agencies to innovate is also compromised. Wanting to be players in WtW programs, the agencies find themselves in an environment dominated by the JTPA employment services organizations and their funding agencies. This sector exerts powerful coercive, mimetic and normative forces on the agencies to conform to its institutionalized organizational practices (DiMaggio and Powell 1983; Scott 1995). Therefore, it is not surprising that the organizational forms of the WtW programs are quite similar across the agencies. Moreover, to buffer the rest of the organization from the constraints imposed on the WtW programs, the agencies opt to create a fairly self-contained WtW program within their organization. They do so either by creating a separate work unit, or by limiting the extent to which other programs and services are linked to the WtW service components.

Whatever room and capacity the agencies have to express their distinctiveness and innovation lies in the area over which they have most discretion and control–relations between workers and clients as expressed in their case management practices. Hence, the agencies are able to use the generous grants to invest heavily in case management practices characterized by small caseloads and individualized attention to the participants. Worker-client relations are the core technology used to motivate the participants, to promote trust in the program, and to bring about necessary behavioral changes. These practices are in sharp contrast to the case management practices the participants encounter in the public welfare-to-work programs. In addition, some of the agencies, such as the single-service agencies, can capitalize on their unique expertise in working with certain clients such as the homeless or substance abusers or in offering a special training program (e.g., Alzheimer care workers). It is in these practices that the agencies can demonstrate their advantage.

Still, these case management practices are not insulated from the external exigencies and constraints facing the WtW programs. They are affected by the limits imposed on the participants and the program, and particularly by the available menu of services they can mobilize on behalf of their clients. They also must contend with the expectations that the welfare workers have for their clients. In addition, the WtW evaluation criteria–the number of participants placed in jobs and improvement in wages–put pressures on the case managers that may not be consonant with their own practice ideologies. To accommodate to these pressures and expectations, case managers may have to compromise their own practices and service decisions. However, doing so may erode some of the unique advantages the non-profit agencies have in their service missions and practices.

CONCLUSION

The initial experience of non-profit agencies under government contract to deliver employment and support services to welfare recipients raises anew the policy issue about the proper relationship between the two sectors. Undoubtedly, the reliance of government on non-profit agencies to provide specialized services tailored to the needs of a specific population is a laudable objective. The government affirms its moral responsibility to meet the needs of this population while acknowledging its limited capability to deliver the needed services. Hence, through contracts it mobilizes the moral commitment, organizational resources and expertise of non-profit agencies dedicated to serve that population, in our case, welfare recipients with multiple employment barriers.

However, these contracts locate the non-profit agencies in a task environment that constrains them from achieving the very objectives that they are contracted to fulfill. Funding requirements, performance evaluation criteria, controls over the flow of clients, and normative, coercive and mimetic pressures from their organizational network converge to limit the capability of these agencies to fully exercise their distinct set of values, organizational capabilities, and service practices.

NOTES

1. Excluding one agency with 2000 participants as a target.
2. If the participant loses her job, she is still eligible for post-employment services, but the program must work to place the participant in another employment activity as soon as possible.
3. Excluding one agency with 350 cases per case manager.

REFERENCES

Anderson, K., R. Burkhauser et al. (1993). "The effects of creaming on placement rates under the Job Training Partnership Act." *Industrial and Labor Relations Review* 46: 613-24.
D'Aunno, T., R. I. Sutton et al. (1991). "Isomorphism and External Support in Conflicting Institutional Environments: A Study of Drug Abuse Treatment Units." *Academy of Management Journal* 34: 636-61.

DeVita, C. (1999). Nonprofits and Devolution: What Do We Know? *Nonprofits and Government: Collaboration and Conflict.* E. Steuerle and E. Boris. Washington, DC, The Urban Institute: 213-233.

DiMaggio, P. D., and W. W. Powell (1983). "The iron cage revisited: Institutional isomorphism and collective rationality in organizational fields." *American Sociological Review* 48: 147-60.

Freedman, S., J. T. Knab, et al. (2000). *The Los Angeles Jobs-First GAIN Evaluation: Final Report on a Work First Program in a Major Urban Center.* New York, Manpower Demonstration Research Corporation.

Greenwood, R., and C. R. Hinings (1996). "Understanding radical organizational change: Bringing together the old and the new institutionalism." *Academy of Management Review* 21: 1022-1054.

Gronbjerg, K. A. (1993). *Understanding nonprofit funding: Managing revenues in social services and community development organizations.* San Francisco: Jossey-Bass.

Hagen, J. L., and I. V. Lurie (1994). *Implementing JOBS: Progress and Promise.* Albany, SUNY, The Nelson A. Rockefeller Institute of Government.

Handler, J., and Y. Hasenfeld (1997). *We The Poor People: Work, Poverty and Welfare.* New Haven, Yale University Press.

Hasenfeld, Y., and D. Weaver (1996). "Enforcement, Compliance, and Disputes in Welfare-to-Work Programs." *Social Service Review* 70: 235-56.

Kramer, R. (2000). "A Third Sector in the Third Millennium?" *Voluntas* 11: 1-23.

Kramer, R., and B. Grossman (1987). "Contracting for social services: Process management and resource dependencies." *Social Service Review* 61: 32-55.

Lafer, G. (1994). "The Politics of Job Training: Urban Poverty and the False Promise of JTPA." *Politics & Society* 22: 349-88.

Meyer, J. W., and B. Rowan (1977). "Institutionalized organizations: Formal structure as myth and ceremony." *American Journal of Sociology* 83: 340-63.

Mitchell, J. J., M. L. Chadwin et al. (1979). *Implementing Welfare-Employment Programs: An Institutional Analysis of the Work Incentive (WIN) Program.* Washington, D.C., The Urban Institute.

Nightingale, D. S., J. Trutko et al. (1999). *The Status of the Welfare-to-Work (WtW) Grants Program After One Year.* Washington, DC, The Urban Institute: 1-29.

Oliver, C. (1997). "Sustainable competitive advantage: Combining institutional and resource-based views." *Strategic Management Journal* 18: 697-713.

Owen, G., C. Roy et al. (2000). *How welfare-to-work is working: Welfare reform through the eyes of Minnesota employers, welfare participants, and local community partnerships.* St. Paul, Minnesota, Wilder Research Center: 1-181.

Pavetti, L. et al. (2000). *The Role of Intermediaries in Linking TANF Recipients with Jobs.* Mathematica Policy Research, Inc.

Perez-Johnson, I. (1999). *Early Implementation of the Welfare-to-Work Grants Program: Report to Congress.* Princeton, NJ, Mathematica Policy Research, Inc.: 1-53.

Ruef, M., and W. R. Scott (1998). "A multidimensional model of organizational legitimacy: Hospital survival in changing institutional environments." *Administrative Science Quarterly* 43: 877-904.

Salamon, L. M. (1995). *Partners in public service: Government-nonprofit relations in the modern welfare state.* Baltimore, MD: Johns Hopkins University Press.

Sandfort, J. (1999). "The structural impediments to human service collaboration: Examining welfare reform at the front lines." *Social Service Review* 73(3): 314-39.

Schmid, H. (2000). For-profit and nonprofit human services: A comparative analysis. *Social Security* (Special English Edition) 6: 161-179.

Scott, W. R. (1995). *Institutions and Organizations.* Thousand Oaks, CA, Sage Publications.

Skocpol, T. (1992). *Protecting Soldiers and Mothers.* Cambridge, Harvard University Press.

Smith, S. R. (1999). Government Financing of Nonprofit Activity. *Nonprofits & Government: Collaboration and Conflict.* E. T. Boris and C. E. Steuerle. Washington, DC, The Urban Institute Press.

Smith, S. R., and M. Lipsky (1993). *Nonprofits for Hire: The Welfare State in the Age of Contracting.* Cambridge, MA, Harvard University Press.

Weissman, E. (1997). *Changing to a Work First Strategy: Lessons From the Los Angeles County's GAIN Program for Welfare Recipients.* New York, Manpower Demonstration Research Corporation: 1-89.

Nonprofit Organizations and Welfare-to-Work: Environmental Turbulence and Organizational Change

Elizabeth A. Mulroy, PhD
Melissa Back Tamburo, MSW

SUMMARY. This article analyzes recent empirical studies of welfare-to-work programs implemented by nonprofit organizations as a first step in understanding potential shifts in the political, social, and economic environments of nonprofit organizations in a post-welfare era. Using the political economy as a conceptual framework, the literature review suggests that nonprofits are experiencing organizational change–and frequent turbulence–on four key dimensions: interorganizational relationships, mission and philosophy, resource dependencies, and target populations. The article first analyzes each dimension, then draws implications of the changes for social work managers, practitioners, educators, and researchers. Findings suggest that emergence of new organizational and interorganizational forms may require nonprofit managers to focus

Elizabeth A. Mulroy (E-mail: emulroy@ssw.umaryland.edu) is Professor of Human Services Management and Community Planning, and Melissa Back Tamburo (E-mail: MBTLCSW@aol.com) is a PhD student, School of Social Work, University of Maryland, Baltimore, 525 West Redwood Street, Baltimore, MD 21201.

[Haworth co-indexing entry note]: "Nonprofit Organizations and Welfare-to-Work: Environmental Turbulence and Organizational Change." Mulroy, Elizabeth A., and Melissa Back Tamburo. Co-published simultaneously in *Administration in Social Work* (The Haworth Social Work Practice Press, an imprint of The Haworth Press, Inc.) Vol. 28, No. 3/4, 2004, pp. 111-135; and: *Organizational and Structural Dilemmas in Nonprofit Human Service Organizations* (ed: Hillel Schmid) The Haworth Social Work Practice Press, an imprint of The Haworth Press, Inc., 2004, pp. 111-135. Single or multiple copies of this article are available for a fee from The Haworth Document Delivery Service [1-800-HAWORTH, 9:00 a.m. - 5:00 p.m. (EST). E-mail address: docdelivery@ haworthpress.com].

111

increased attention on external relations in order to build new collaborations and partnerships, and to develop innovative outcome measures as tools to capture program success in complex organizational arrangements. *[Article copies available for a fee from The Haworth Document Delivery Service: 1-800-HAWORTH. E-mail address: <docdelivery@haworthpress.com> Website: <http://www.HaworthPress.com> © 2004 by The Haworth Press, Inc. All rights reserved.]*

KEYWORDS. Nonprofit management, organizational change, welfare-to-work, social policy implementation, social environment

Income security, public assistance, family well-being, and now welfare-to-work are important issues for social policy and central concerns for the practice of social work in nonprofit organizations. This article is about the shifting role of nonprofit human service organizations as implementers of social policy, and the implications for management of nonprofit organizations. Having survived several eras of social policy changes and been progressive leaders in many of them (Fabricant & Fisher, 2002), nonprofits have recently experienced uncharted territory with the Personal Responsibility and Work Opportunity Reconciliation Act of 1996 (PRWORA). It is possible that the current era of welfare reform poses the next critical juncture for the nonprofit organizations struggling with twenty years of neoconservative cuts in social services generally, entitlement programs in particular, and the effects of privatization (Gibelman, 2000; Gibelman & Demone, 2003; Fabricant & Fisher, 2002). The main question is this: To what extent can a nonprofit human service organization play a key role in the implementation of welfare reform, given the current contexts of privatization of human services and the decentralization of federal decision making to states and localities?

This article analyzes recent empirical studies of welfare-to-work programming in order to better understand the conditions under which nonprofits are operating in the post-welfare era. The nonprofit sector is large and diverse. While many nonprofit organizations have struggled, merged, or closed, other nonprofits have adapted and grown under privatization (Gibelman, 2000). What are the emerging issues that impact human service nonprofit organizations as implementers of welfare-to-work? Are these issues driven by external pressures, internal constraints, or both? What should an executive director or program manager in a nonprofit know in order to successfully implement local level welfare-to-work programs in this intergovernmental, multi-sector environment?

Much has been written about the implementation of welfare reform and its impact on public programs (Beckerman & Fontana, 2001; Crowell, 2001;

Faulkner, Cosgrove, Scott, Maier, & Tillman, 2001; Prince & Austin, 2001; Austin, 2003; Carnochan & Austin, 2001). Fewer articles have focused specifically on the impact that welfare reform programming has had on nonprofit organizations. This article begins with an examination of pertinent literature, describes and analyzes findings from the studies reviewed, and then draws implications for nonprofit management and leadership. This article uses a conceptual framework based on the political economy as the lens through which to conduct our analysis. The findings presented suggest nonprofit organizations involved in welfare-to-work programming are experiencing organizational/ environmental turbulence and that impacts are experienced along four dimensions: (1) external and internal organizational relationships; (2) mission and/or philosophy; (3) target populations, and (4) financial constraints and resource dependence.

POLITICAL ECONOMY AS CONCEPTUAL FRAMEWORK

Kramer (2000) identifies three parallel trends that underscore the need for expanding the organization universe in which human service organizations operate. First, there has been exponential growth in the number and types of nonprofit organizations and their rapid and extensive dependence on governmental funding to support their role as implementers of public policy. Second, there is parallel growth in various forms of privatization of many governmental functions, and rapid growth in commercialization and competition in fields formerly dominated by nonprofit organizations. The third trend is one of convergence and blurring of sectoral boundaries that reflect the provision of services by organizations separate from their funding sources.

The primary focus of political economy theory is the examination of the interactions between the organization and its environment and their effects on its internal dynamics (Wamsley & Zald, 1976). This perspective takes into consideration the external and internal political and economic processes that shape the organization's character and influential interest groups (Kramer, 2000). While much has been written about the impact of the environment on organizations (Mintzberg, 1979; Katz & Kahn, 1966; Thompson, 1967), examining the impact of large scale policy implementation with the political-economy perspective allows a close look at how decisions are made that ultimately impact service delivery.

Austin (1988) describes the political economy perspective as one that incorporates a dual focus to include the external societal forces, and the intra-industry factors affected by such forces, which control the processes of organizational legitimation and shape the flow of resources to individual organizations, controlling the continuity of existence for human service organizations (pp. 10-11). Hasenfeld (1992) identifies two fundamental types of resources an organization must secure to survive: (a) legitimacy and power, and (b) economic (production) resources. Legitimacy is achieved by adopting and upholding the moral systems (rules and regulations) that are supported by significant interest groups and organizations, which for human service organizations are state and professional governing bodies. Thus, human service organizations are highly dependent of their institutional environment for legitimacy, which is the key to garner other resources (Hasenfeld, 1992). One of the cornerstones of welfare reform is the shift toward a "work first" philosophy, in which immediate job placement will provide necessary work experience and skill development that will be more effective in moving welfare recipients off the rolls than a more educational model (Mead, as cited in Danziger & Seefeldt, 2000). Legitimacy is gained by instituting programs that meet the requirements for the work first model, which in turn impacts the nonprofit's power, and access to resources.

The political-economy perspective includes examination of the task environment (all stakeholders interests) in which an organization exists and its impact on shaping the organization's service delivery system (Hasenfeld, 1992). Pfeffer and Salancik (1978) identify resource dependence as a way to characterize environmental impact on organizations. They propose that the greater dependence on resources controlled by an external element, the greater the influence of that element on the organization. Aldrich (1979, pp. 63-70) identifies a continuum of six dimensions that distinguish between the nature and distribution of resources in environments that have different impacts on structures and activities of organizations. This continuum includes dimensions of (a) environment capacity (rich/lean); (b) environmental homogeneity-heterogeneity; (c) environmental stability-instability; (d) environmental concentration-dispersion; (e) domain consensus-dissensus; and (f) environmental turbulence. In the end, leaders of nonprofits make strategic choices regarding their response to these environmental factors. Such choices determine organizational activities, change or stability, technology or size of the organization (Aldrich, 1979). The internal changing power and economic relations determines policy development, how service technology is implemented, and how decision-making authority is distributed (Kramer, 2000).

Hasenfeld (1992) also points out that organizations try to manage the external environment through different means, which ultimately influences the service delivery system. How clients are handled within the organization is a strategy to manage external relations through such means as identifying target populations, and choosing outcome indicators that reflect the context in which the organization is embedded.

Nonprofit organizations differ widely in their auspice, size, and purpose which may affect their capability as implementers. Smith and Lipsky (1993) developed a useful typology with three distinct types that may help to inform this discussion. *Type 1* includes large, private service agencies, usually well funded by endowments, and therefore less dependent on the government for funds. This type of nonprofit, typically old, such as traditional family service agencies, often offers many different services, and is less dependent than other agencies on the demand for any single service. *Type 2* is one founded in response to the availability of government funds for specific, categorical programs. Some examples include job training, economic development, pre-natal care, AIDS/HIV detection and treatment, or mental health services. This type of nonprofit derives most revenues from the government, creating clear dependence on the government for its existence. *Type 3* developed in response to unmet neighborhood or community needs. They are typically staffed by volunteers or workers with strong personal commitments to a social movement, cause, or unmet local neighborhood need such as a shelter for victims of domestic violence, advocacy against gang violence, or a settlement house to acculturate newcomer populations. Often this type of agency is a "shoestring operation" operating on shaky financial ground. Since all three types of nonprofits are likely involved in implementing welfare reform programming, it would be of interest to examine changes these organizations experience relative to resource dependence in particular.

MORALITY OF HUMAN SERVICES

The moral judgments and statements about social worth of clients are embedded in human service delivery systems (Hasenfeld, 1983; 1992). He suggests that organizations increase their legitimacy by referencing the institutionalized moral systems in their environment. He suggests that this is done by adopting and upholding the moral systems that are supported by their stakeholders. Brinkley (1998), for example, reminds us that the American welfare state addressed moral issues in terms of the distinctions between the deserving and undeserving poor, issues that were codified in the Social Security Act of 1935.

When President Bill Clinton signed the Personal Responsibility and Work Opportunity Reconciliation Act of 1996 (PRWORA) into law "changing welfare as we know it," the new mandate was intended to decrease the number of welfare recipients by increasing self-sufficiency through work–a responsibility left for the states to implement. The title of the Act itself implies a moral judgment; the Act provides for financial sanctions and time limits to those who do not move into the work force. The use of the work first philosophy is an example of the moral judgments of stakeholders influencing policy and programming. This philosophy values immediate workforce attachment over previous human capital investment strategies.

We wanted to conduct an exploration of the emerging literature on the implementation of welfare to work programs by nonprofit organizations to begin to answer the above questions. The study began by selecting three criteria by which to select articles: They had to be empirically based studies, recently published, that is 2000 or later, that included an examination of the organizational impacts of policy implementation. We began by searching several different databases. The greatest number of articles in all databases were found by using the keywords "welfare reform AND implementation" (N = 194). However, when the search was narrowed to add a fourth criteria–nonprofit organizations–the search produced only one article. The current body of literature was found to focus largely on organizational change in the public sector. Some studies did not perform a sector-specific analysis, so there was no differentiation made in the status of implementing organizations as public, private for-profit, or nonprofit. Authors read the relevant literature on both public sector and non-profit implementation of welfare reform that addressed some aspect of organizational change. The articles described below reveal the research that met the criteria established to conduct our analysis. We recognize there may be other studies that addressed related aspects of welfare-to-work programming that were not included in this search. A broader search that uses additional criteria would be the next step. Also included in this analysis is a study of partnerships among public sector funders and nonprofit organization vendors (Prince & Austin, 2001) that did not specify impacts on nonprofit organizational form per se, but did provide useful information about multi-sector partnership formation.

EFFECTS OF IMPLEMENTING WELFARE TO WORK ON NONPROFITS

Findings suggest that nonprofit organizations did experience organizational/environmental turbulence as Aldrich (1979) predicted, and it occurred along four dimensions: (1) Changes in organizational relationships and arrangements, (2) Changes in mission and/or philosophy, (3) Changes in target populations, and (4) Changes in resource dependence. Each of these dimensions will be analyzed separately. (Refer to Tables 1, 2, 3, and 4 for a summary of the articles' findings on each dimension.)

Organizational Relations and Arrangements

Nonprofit grantees experienced changes in organizational arrangements that impacted the primary relationships between a nonprofit and its environment. These changes had the potential to impact both a nonprofit organization's legitimacy and power, as well as resource dependence. Changes in organizational arrangements included collaboration and shared responsibilities, coordination, conflict, and competition. Table 1 details findings from the literature on these changes.

Collaboration and Shared Responsibilities

Organizations experienced increases in the number of collaborations in which they participated, and shared responsibilities with other organizations as a result of welfare to work programming (Bishoff & Reisch, 2000; Danziger & Seefeldt, 2000; Prince & Austin, 2001). These arrangements allowed organizations to partner with others that had similar functions; they blended funding resources to ultimately meet similar program goals. These were complex arrangements that required flexible organizational structures that were open to considering new arrangements. Cooney and Weaver (2001) note that balancing multiple agendas of an agency required flexibility from staff and an organizational culture that fostered flexibility. Prince and Austin (2001) explained how an Organizational Development specialist was utilized to advantage in order to address the impacts of changes in agency cultures. This permitted the development of interorganizational restructuring, a necessary step that facilitated intra-agency collaboration.

Coordination

With the development of complex collaborations and new interorganizational arrangements came equally complex coordination requirements. Iversen (2000) noted that coordination between and within nonprofits was found to be the most compelling barrier to welfare reform implementation. She sites specific problems with funding coordination that produced administrative strain, and contradictory eligibility criteria and program requirements that impacted participant recruitment and service delivery. The study points to procedural coordination as a cause of organizational delays and strain. In another study Danziger and Seefeldt (2000) found tightened linkages between human service departments and employment and training agencies, with the coordination between the Family Independence Agency and the newly created Workforce Development Boards that work together with all TANF recipients. Coordination of staffing was found to

TABLE 1. Changes in Organizational Arrangements

Article	Purpose of Study	Sample	Findings on New Organizational Arrangements
Bishoff & Reisch (2000)	To obtain preliminary "snapshot" of the extent to which PRWORA affected ability of NPOs to respond to emerging client and community needs; assess the ability of agencies to respond in changing policy and practice environment	In depth interviews with Executive Directors of 42 CBOs providing services in urban neighborhoods in PA, followed up with mailed survey	○ Nearly 50% reported increased inter-organizational collaboration as a way to share scarce resources cited ○ 26% reported increased competition with other organizations for clients ○ 42% reported increase in competition for resources ○ Over 60% reported changes in relationships with Dept. of Public Welfare, most commenting on "adversarial tone" in interactions
Cooney & Weaver (2001)	Examines innovative WtW program model developed by Goodwill Industries of Southern CA	Two focus groups with convenience samples of program participants, interviews with staff (N = 9), observations of on-site work experience sites and quantitative survey of sample of participants	○ Balancing multiple agendas of the agency requires flexibility from staff and an organizational culture the fosters flexibility ○ Changes in staff role requirements, overlaps in staff outcome goals
Danziger & Seefeldt (2000)	Examines how MI implemented its Work First program and examines (1) adequacy of state's mandatory job search program and (2) the needs of clients that may pose barriers and how these are addressed by programming	○ 204 semi-structured interviews with local managers responsible for implementation of both cash assistance and Work First programs and managers of Work First programs ○ 386 in-person interviews with single mothers with children who received cash assistance in an urban county in February 1997	○ Work First program based on labor force attachment model initiated which created new organizational arrangement for welfare agency, with Michigan Jobs Commission leading programming with the charge to improve the state's business climate through a range of initiatives, including workforce development. Workforce Development Boards were created at local levels to allocate resources for Work First programs ○ Family Independence Agency (previously administered all WtW activities) share responsibilities with Workforce Development Boards for TANF recipients

Iversen (2000)	Reports on implementation problems found in WtW programs in Philadelphia area programs	Interviews, observations, and discussions with 30 staff members of 4 area WtW programs	○ Coordination between and within organizations found to be most compelling barrier to implementation
			  • Funding coordination
			  • Procedural coordination
			  • Staffing coordination

| Prince & Austin (2001)

*analyzes public and NPO partnership, does not readily distinguish between programs	Reports on how human service agencies are changing as they transform from eligibility determination to employability enhancement through implementation of WtW programming	19 case studies using interviews with staff and consumers, written documents and literature review relevant to each program	o Enhancement of public/private community partnerships to address needs o Changing agency culture to reflect more collaborative relationships required use of Organizational Development specialist o Merging agencies with overlapping funding and functions o Restructuring programs to foster intra-agency collaboration

be another affected area. Iversen (2000) and Cooney and Weaver (2001) identified changes in staff role requirements and overlaps in staff outcome goals.

Conflict/Competition

While some nonprofits were successful at negotiating new organizational relationships, conflict and competition among agencies was also reported. Bishoff and Reisch (2000) found that 25 percent of respondents experienced increased competition with other organizations for clients, and nearly 42 percent reported increased competition for resources. One in four respondents agreed with the statement "Welfare reform increases conflict and competition between my organization and other organizations." The studies did not differentiate among types of nonprofits according to Smith and Lipsky's typology, so we do not know if agency size mattered on this aspect of this dimension.

Changes in Mission and/or Philosophy

Agencies were found to experience challenges to their mission and/or philosophy as they attempted to implement welfare to work programming. Changes in program mission or philosophy reflected changes in the moral judgments and statements about the social worth of clients. Nonprofits found that they needed to adapt their philosophy to incorporate the work first ideology in order to be perceived as legitimate providers of service and to establish rapid reduction of welfare rolls. Changes were observed in terms of organizational culture, shifts in program goals, and staff commitment (see Table 2).

Cultural Changes in Public Sector

Implementation of welfare reform required state and local public human service agencies to transform themselves from eligibility determination roles to employability enhancement roles (Prince & Austin, 2001). This shift required public agencies to engage in substantial reassessment of mission and organizational structure, changing from hierarchical (characterized by rules, impersonality and accountability) to clan/adhocracy culture (characterized by cohesiveness, participation, flexibility, and creativity) (Cameron & Quinn, as cited in Prince & Austin, 2001). That is, the public sector also experienced major organizational challenges and internal cultural changes themselves. This condition in the major funder would likely contribute to the level and complexity of environmental turbulence nonprofits were experiencing in their task environments (Aldrich, 1979; Hasenfeld, 1983).

TABLE 2. Changes in Mission and/or Philosophy

Article	Purpose of Study	Sample	Findings on Changes in Mission and/or Philosophy
Bishoff & Riesch (2000)	To obtain preliminary "snapshot" of the extent to which PRWORA affected ability of NPOs to respond to emerging client and community needs; assess the ability of agencies to respond in changing policy and practice environment	In depth interviews with Executive Directors of 42 CBOs providing services in urban neighborhoods in PA, followed up with mailed survey	• While agencies remained true to their original missions, they did so by increasing advocacy efforts and implementing additional and/or different operating procedures to satisfy practical survival needs • Nearly 70% reported welfare reform affected changes in program goals
Cooney & Weaver (2001)	Examines innovative WtW program model developed by Goodwill Industries of Southern CA	Two focus groups with convenience samples of program participants, interviews with staff (N = 9), observations of on-site work experience sites and quantitative survey of sample of participants	• Staff members reported that "Work First" focus was limiting to participants, not providing enough educational time
Danziger & Seefeldt (2000)	Examines how MI implemented its Work First program and examines (1) adequacy of state's mandatory job search program and (2) the needs of clients that may pose barriers and how these are addressed by programming	204 semi-structured interviews with local managers responsible for implementation of both cash assistance and Work First programs and managers of Work First programs 386 in-person interviews with single mothers with children who received cash assistance in an urban county in February 1997	• 35% of managers cited Work First as empowering • 25% cited program strength as forcing work and personal responsibility • 42% of managers found Work First did not provide adequate education and training • 35% found support services too limited

TABLE 2 (continued)

Article	Purpose of Study	Sample	Findings on Changes in Mission and/or Philosophy
Prince & Austin (2001) *analyzes public and NPO partnership, does not readily distinguish between programs	Reports on how human service agencies are changing as they transform from eligibility determination to employability enhancement through implementation of WtW programming	19 case studies using interviews with staff and consumers, written documents and literature review relevant to each program	• Substantial reassessment of mission and organizational structure, changing from hierarchical culture to clan/adhocracy culture

Changes in Program Goals

Many nonprofits reported changes in their local-level program goals. At the time of initial interview in Bishoff and Reich's study (2000), for example, nearly 70 percent of respondents reported that welfare reform affected changes in their program goals; in the follow up survey the number had increased to 84 percent. More than half (58%) attributed this to the effects of policy changes on the mission and values of their organizations.

Staff Commitment

Changes in nonprofit mission statements helped to drive the direction of the organization, and staff commitment was important. However, Cooney and Weaver (2001) and Danziger and Seefeldt (2000) reported that staff found the Work First focus limited participants by not providing enough educational time to adequately prepare them for the workforce. Thirty-five percent of managers in the Danziger and Seefeldt study cited Work First as empowering; a quarter of respondents believed that requiring work and personal responsibility was a program strength. This suggests that the managers and front line workers responsible for implementing the programs may have had restrained commitment to the Work First model.

Changes in Resource Dependence

While the studies did not identify the organizations and programs according to the Smith and Lipsky (1993) typology, some information is available to begin to apply the model for limited analysis here. For example, Cooney and Weaver (2001) studied a program developed by Goodwill Industries of Southern California, considered a Type 1 agency, that utilized both public and private funding. The program achieved legitimacy for its public funding in part because of its long and rich history as a private nonprofit organization with demonstrated expertise in blending social services with supervised work experience. It received both a California Governor's 15 percent competitive grant and a U.S. Department of Labor Grant to institute the welfare-to-work program (Cooney & Weaver, 2001). Straatman and Sherraden (2001) described the First Step Fund of Kansas City, a program that used the strategy of micro enterprise to foster economic self-sufficiency through entrepreneurship training, access to capital and ongoing support. Potentially a Type 2 nonprofit, it was created in 1993 with support from a large philanthropic organization and other local institutions to address self-employment as a viable alternative to public assistance or low-paying jobs. Straatman and Sherraden (2001) did not report any changes in resource dependence due to welfare reform essentially because the First Step Fund's mission is in alignment with the goals of welfare reform and the program did not have to make large scale changes in goals. Others, however, reported changes in funding that did impact programming. Changes were found in fund blending and resource sharing, and in the impacts of increased resource dependence (see Table 3).

Blending Funding, Sharing Resources

Some studies identified the blending of funding streams and sharing of resources within agencies and across agency boundaries as ways to meet the policy goals of moving clients from welfare rolls. Danizger and Seefeldt (2000) identified a new organizational arrangement created between local Workforce Development Boards and the Family Independence Agency to share responsibility for TANF recipients. Prince and Austin (2001) found that blended funding streams were important in helping managers design more consumer-responsive programs, as well as responding to the need for interorganizational and organizational restructuring among formerly static boundaries.

Impact of Resource Dependence Changes

Nonprofits experienced a range of funding uncertainties in the welfare to work environment. Nearly half (45%) of respondents in the Bishoff and Reisch (2000) study reported considerable fluctuations in the size of their budgets, with nearly two-thirds indicating the sources of their budget had changed. Many reported increased reliance on private grants or other targeted funds that were viewed as less stable than former funding options. One-quarter of respondents reported greater fiscal instability directly attributed to the onset of welfare reform, and one-fifth noted changes in the internal pattern of resource allocation. Iversen (2000) identified the problem of coordinating diverse funding sources as a barrier to the implementation of welfare reform. While the blending of resource streams had some positive aspects as identified above, some negative aspects were also identified. First, each funding stream came with its own eligibility criteria, and these often conflicted with one another. Second, there were different program requirements with individual sets of goals and expected outcomes that caused administrative strain. These converged to create disconnects among the goals of each of the programs and employer organizations (Iversen, 2000).

TABLE 3. Changes in Resources Dependence for NPOs

Article and Type of NPOs Analyzed	Purpose of Study	Sample	Findings on Budget Changes
Bishoff & Riesch (2000) Mixture of types	To obtain preliminary "snapshot" of the extent to which PRWORA affected ability of NPOs to respond to emerging client and community needs; assess the ability of agencies to respond in changing policy and practice environment	In depth interviews with Executive Directors of 42 CBOs providing services in urban neighborhoods in PA, followed up with mailed survey	• Over 45% reported considerable fluctuations in size of budgets • 1/4 reported greater fiscal instability due to the onset of welfare reform • Nearly 2/3 indicated source of budget had changed • Increased reliance on private grants or other targeted funds • 20% reported changes in internal pattern of resource allocation
Cooney & Weaver (2001) Type 1	Examines innovative WtW program model developed by Goodwill Industries of Southern CA	Two focus groups with convenience samples of program participants, interviews with staff (N = 9), observations of on-site work experience sites and quantitative survey of sample of participants	• Report receiving 2 grants to provide services to disabled welfare recipients, citing long history of Goodwill in providing social services
Danziger & Seefeldt (2000)	Examines how MI implemented its Work First program and examines (1) adequacy of state's mandatory job search program and (2) the needs of clients that may pose barriers and how these are addressed by programming	• 204 semi-structured interviews with local managers responsible for implementation of both cash assistance and Work First programs and managers of Work First programs • 386 in-person interviews with single mothers with children who received cash assistance in an urban county in February 1997	• New organizational arrangement created shared responsibility for TANF recipients between local Workforce Development Boards (provide job search assistance and monitor status) and Family Independence Agency (determines and monitors eligibility)

TABLE 3 (continued)

Article and Type of NPOs Analyzed	Purpose of Study	Sample	Findings on Budget Changes
Iversen (2000)	Reports on implementation problems found in WtW programs in Philadelphia area programs	Interviews, observations and discussions with 30 staff members of 4 area WtW programs	• Multiple funding streams with conflicting eligibility criteria and program requirements caused administrative strain and disconnects between goals of programs and employer organizations
Prince & Austin (2001) *analyzes public and NPO partnership, does not readily distinguish between programs	Reports on how human service agencies are charging as they transform from eligibility determination to employability enhancement through implementation of WtW programming	19 case studies using interviews with staff and consumers, written documents and literature review relevant to each program	• Blending funding streams in order to design more consumer-responsive programs
Straatman & Sherraden (2001) Type 2	Study that examines micro-enterprise as viable option for productive work for those exiting welfare	Data gathered from program records, observation of training, and personal interviews with the Executive Director and the Program Manager	• No changes reported

126

Changes in Target Population

The broad target population included all recipients of public assistance, leaving implementers with the task of identifying more specific target populations for enrollment in their programs. Findings identified a difficulty in reaching the target population and barriers to achieving program goals (see Table 4).

Reaching the Target Population

Changing client demographics influenced an agency's ability to find and serve the targeted beneficiaries. For example, in the study by Bishoff and Reisch (2000), changes were found in four specific areas: (1) An overall increase in demand for services, with nearly half the sample reporting an increase in the number of clients served; (2) A shift in client demographics toward younger clients, increasing numbers of immigrants particularly Latinos, males, grandparent caretakers, and parents working full-time; (3) An increase in client needs with 25 percent reporting an increase in clients with multiple problems and service needs, and (4) Changes in referral sources, with a mix of programs reporting increases in numbers of welfare clients (14%), and others reporting fewer welfare clients (19%). Cooney and Weaver (2001) point to a shift from the original target population of welfare recipients with disabilities who were found difficult to serve, to a new population of monolingual Spanish-speaking clients. This study concluded, however, that when staff viewed the lack of proficiency in English, low education attainment, no Graduate Equivalency Diplomas, and poor employment histories as "disabilities," the original innovation of providing services to the disabled on the welfare rolls remained intact.

Organizational capacity and competence were also found to be factors in reaching and serving target populations. Public sector mis-projections concerning needs of potential clients were problems that required unexpected outreach by staff in order to fill program slots (Iverson, 2000). The mis-projections were based on the Department of Public Welfare (DPW) reliance on estimates of welfare statistics obtained prior to the introduction of time limits. In reality, the state data systems were unable to assess the certainty of these estimates. Iversen cites technological problems that did not allow DPW to identify essential recipient characteristics among those remaining on welfare rolls that was needed by the implementing agencies to match clients with appropriate services.

TABLE 4. Changes in Target Population

Article	Purpose of Study	Sample	Findings on Changes in Target Populations
Bishoff & Riesch (2000)	To obtain preliminary "snapshot" of the extent to which PRWORA affected ability of NPOs to respond to emerging client and community needs; assess the ability of agencies to respond in changing policy and practice environment	In depth interviews with Executive Directors of 42 CBOs providing services in urban neighborhoods in PA, followed up with mailed survey	• Overall demand for services increased • Shift in client demographics • Change in the nature of clients' needs • Changes in source of referrals
Cooney & Weaver (2001)	Examines innovative WtW program model developed by Goodwill Industries of Southern CA	Two focus groups with convenience samples of program participants, interviews with staff (N = 9), observations of on-site work experience sites, and quantitative survey of sample of participants	• Original target population of welfare recipients exempt from time limits due to disability changed due to lack of referrals • Program orientations revealed large numbers of monolingual Spanish-speaking welfare recipients with low education scores, no GEDs, and poor employment histories
Danziger & Seefeldt (2000)	Examines how MI implemented its Work First program and examines (1) adequacy of state's mandatory job search program and (2) the needs of clients that may pose barriers and how these are addressed by programming	204 semi-structured interviews with local managers responsible for implementation of both cash assistance and Work First programs and managers of Work First programs 386 in-person interviews with single mothers with children who received cash assistance in an urban county in February 1997	• Identified "hard to serve" clients as those who have "uncooperative attitudes, child care difficulties, and low education levels" • Underestimation of health problems, mental health problems and transportation barriers

128

Iversen (2000)	Reports on implementation problems found in WtW programs in Philadelphia area programs	Interviews, observations, and discussions with 30 staff members of 4 area WtW programs	• Cites organizational competence as a factor that caused major mis-projections of potential clients that led to start-up delays, program outreach by staff • Cites technological problems that did not allow DPW to identify information needed by implementing agencies to match appropriate services with clients
Prince & Austin (2001) *analyzes public and NPO partnership, does not readily distinguish between programs	Reports on how human service agencies are changing as they transform from eligibility determination to employability enhancement through implementation of WtW programming	19 case studies using interviews with staff and consumers, written documents and literature review relevant to each program	• Lists programs developed to address transportation and child care barriers, health and mental health programs, and rehab services that help increase likelihood of success
Straatman & Sherraden (2001)	Case study that examines micro-enterprise as viable option for productive work for those exiting welfare	Data gathered from program records, observation of training, and personal interviews with the Executive Director and the Program Manager	• Cost of working with former TANF recipients is higher due to higher case management costs • Additional services include case management, alumni group activities, mentoring program, and micro loans

Identifying Barriers to Achieving Program Goals

Specific barriers to successful program completion were found to involve individual, organizational, and community-level issues: client health and mental health problems, differences in prior work experience, transportation issues, and higher case management costs due to increased needs of clients (Danziger & Seefeldt, 2000; Prince & Austin, 2001; & Straatman & Sherraden, 2001). This first cut examination of emerging studies of nonprofit involvement in the implementation of Welfare to Work suggests four areas of interest and concern, a discussion that follows next.

IMPLICATIONS

While these findings can only provide a glimpse into the effects of large scale public welfare policy reform on the nonprofit providers of local-level service, some implications begin to emerge that warrant the attention of social work managers, researchers, practitioners, and educators. New organizational and interorganizational forms are emerging. Skills of nonprofit management are changing as managers' work becomes more external and collaborative. There is a clear and compelling need for nonprofit management and leadership to embrace social policy advocacy as technical and interpersonal skills. Attention must also be given to the innovative construction of outcome measures as tools that capture program success.

New Organizational Forms

The realization that an organization's external boundaries must be open to allow for collaboration and the capability to share resources with other organizations' programs may serve as a model for the future of nonprofit survival. While the problems and complexities of such arrangements are demonstrated by the studies analyzed, the advantages of such reconfigurations are noteworthy. First, expanding the legitimacy and power base of a nonprofit organization through partnerships can serve to buffer the environmental impacts of standing alone. Findings suggest that changes in organizational arrangements had positive influences on nonprofits in many different areas, but not without challenges. Kramer (2000) addressed the need to develop more appropriate analytic paradigms where sectoral lines have less significance. As nonprofits move forward, it will become increasingly necessary for leaders to engage in organizational self-assessments (Drucker, 1999), particularly where the public sector is concerned (Carnochan & Austin, 2001). It is imperative for program managers in particular to understand an organization's capacity and their respective program's role in it–that is, the strengths and weaknesses it brings to the partnership table–in order to craft new organizational forms that work. Findings from organizational self-assessments can be used as a starting point from which to leverage the assets of a nonprofit program or entire organization in future inter-organizational arrangements.

Management and Leadership Requirements

As new organizational forms emerge, the requirements for successful non-profit management and leadership must evolve as well. These changes require managers to develop working relationships with front line workers and staff based on a decentralized model of operation and on an external orientation that keeps track of environmental changes that are predicted to impact the organization. While external forces should be continuously monitored (Schmid, 1992) impacts on internal operations must also be part of the surveillance so that personnel are kept informed and understand diverse stakeholder interests that shape the environment. As the above studies indicated, there is a benefit to congruence between program goals and the Work First philosophy. This raises the issue of staff commitment to immediate work force attachment over human capital development (Bishoff & Reisch, 2000; Cooney & Weaver, 2001; Danziger & Seefeldt, 2000; Prince & Austin, 2001). To the extent that there is dissonance between the policy-level ideology and staff values, there may be administrative delays in putting the policy into practice. Organizations that secure welfare-to-work program funds need to demonstrate outcomes. This suggests managers have leadership and interpersonal skills to identify areas of potential conflict, plan effective ways to resolve these issues, and respectfully manage and support staff who hold diverse points of view and levels of commitment to the range of programs operated by the organization in the long term.

Advocacy Imperative

Managers of nonprofit organizations as social policy implementers are in key positions to let policy makers know what works and what does not work in the field on multiple levels that include client, program, organization, inter-organization, and community factors. For example, in view of shifts in client demographics and changes in the nature of client needs (Bishoff & Reisch, 2000), there may be an underestimation of the impact that health and mental health problems have on program completion and identification of barriers to success (Danizger & Seefeldt, 2000; Prince & Austin, 2001). Such expertise should be shared through oral and written legislative testimony. Managers must determine the most effective way to successfully advocate for programmatic changes while balancing the potential costs to attaining power and resources. One form of advocacy is to use outcome measures in fresh and new ways so they adequately reflect program success based on social work values and are able to pinpoint problem areas that may need a modified approach.

Outcome Measures

The choices involved in adopting and upholding moral systems that are supported by policy stakeholders are manifest in program outcome measures (Hasenfeld, 1992). The studies analyzed identified changes in program missions, goals, resources and organizational arrangements. An important measure of success is client self-sufficiency. Several authors (Cooney & Weaver, 2001; Danziger & Seefeldt, 2000; Straatmann & Sherraden, 2001) report a key problem for real advancement and self-sufficiency was the low level of wages, especially the minimum wage itself. Berlin (2002) found that only those welfare reform programs that included provisions to supplement low earnings, usually by allowing recipients to keep some of their welfare benefits when they took jobs, increased income. This resulted in a reduced level of welfare dollars spent as recipients transitioned to self-sufficiency, yet added to the overall outcome of helping recipients gain success by recognizing that the first jobs obtained will not meet self-sufficiency needs.

Closely tied to self-sufficiency outcomes are the economic and social forces that directly impact client success. Economic growth has slowed precipitously, and the population left on welfare may be less employable and experience more barriers finding and keeping jobs than when welfare reform began in 1996. Employers play a role in making the transition from welfare to work successful. Lane and Stevens (2001) identified different costs associated with hiring and firing workers that were dependent on both the type of worker and the nature of the production process. Some firms deliberately chose high turnover policies which had a disparate impact on low-wage workers who then had a shorter tenure and greater number of job spells than other workers. These employment policies, practices and union issues have enormous impact on the effectiveness of local programs and their client outcomes. If nonprofits seek out suitable local employers for welfare recipients and provide services that enhance employability for these better jobs, the long term impact of the programs will reflect better outcomes with greater levels of self sufficiency, one of the basic values and goals of welfare reform.

CONCLUSION

The political economy perspective provided a framework through which to investigate the interplay of forces found to be operating in the environment of nonprofit organizations as they implemented welfare-to-work programs. The analysis suggests that nonprofits had to make unanticipated, substantive, and often rapid organizational changes during the process of implementation that involved changes in organizational arrangements, mission and philosophy, target populations, and resource dependencies. In light of these changes, the design of new services from a moral agency perspective requires management attention to environmental scanning, internal organizational self-assessment and development, program evaluation, and the negotiation and creation of complex partnerships and interorganizational collaborations. Future research is needed that will examine the impacts of implementation in a sector analysis and using Smith and Lipsky's typology of nonprofit organizations. We need to know more about changes in the nonprofit sector as a whole to determine if certain types of nonprofits, such as small community-based organizations, are more vulnerable or more adept at creating new organizational arrangements than others. Finally, the dissemination of knowledge is needed so that nonprofit managers concerned with welfare-to-work programs in the field can draw lessons learned for their own agency situations, client demographics, and community conditions.

REFERENCES

Aldrich, H. E. (1979). *Organizations and Environments*. Englewood Cliffs, NJ: Prentice-Hall, Inc.

Austin, D. M. (1988). *The Political Economy of Human Service Programs*. Greenwich, CT: JAI Press, Inc.

Austin, M. J. (2003). Managing out: The community practice dimensions of effective agency management. *Journal of Community Practice, 10(4)*, pp. 33-48.

Beckerman, H., and Fontana, L. (2001). The transition from AFDC to PRWORA in Florida: Perceptions of the role of case manager in welfare reform. *Journal of Sociology and Social Welfare, 28(3)*, pp. 29-47.

Bischoff, U. M., and Reisch, M. S. (2000). Welfare reform and community-based organizations: Implications for policy, practice, and education. *Journal of Community Practice, 8(4)*, pp. 69-91.

Brinkley, A. (1998). *Liberalism and its Discontents*. Cambridge, Massachusetts: Harvard University Press.

Carnochan, S., and Austin, M. J. (2001). Implementing welfare reform and guiding organizational change. *Administration in Social Work, 26(1)*, pp. 61-77.

Cooney, K., and Weaver, D. (2001). The implementation of a "Work First" welfare-to-work program in a changing environment. *Journal of Community Practice, 9(3)*, pp. 33-54.

Crowell, L. F. (2001). Welfare reform: Reforming welfare or reforming families? *The Journal of Contemporary Human Services, 82(2)*, pp. 157-164.

Danziger, S. K., and Seefeldt, K. S. (2000). Ending welfare through work first: Manager and client views. *Families in Society: The Journal of Contemporary Human Services, 81(6)*, pp. 593-604.

Drucker, P. F. (1999). *Management Challenges for the 21st Century*. New York: HarperBusiness.

Fabricant, M., and Fisher, R. (2002). *Settlement Houses Under Siege: The Struggle to Sustain Community Organizations in New York City*. New York: Columbia University Press.

Faulkner, A. O.; Cosgrove, M.; Jardine, D. R.; Scott, D.; Maier, M.; and Tillman, L. (2001). Facilitating a TANF passport to enhanced self-sufficiency: The Tarimer County experience with innovation. *Journal of Community Practice, 9(3)*, pp. 15-32.

Gibelman, M., and Demone, H., Jr. (2002). The commercialization of health and human services: National phenomena or cause for concern? *Families in Society, 83(4)*, 387-397.

Gibelman, M. (2000). Structural and fiscal characteristics of social service agencies. In R. Patti, (Ed.), *The Handbook of Social Welfare Administration*. Thousand Oaks: Sage, 113-132.

Hasenfeld, Y. (1983). *Human Service Organizations*. Englewood Cliffs, NJ: Prentice-Hall.

Hasenfeld, Y. (1992). Theoretical approaches to human service organizations. In Hasenfeld, Y. (Ed.), *Human Services as Complex Organizations*. pp. 24-44. Newbury Park: SAGE Publications.

Iversen, R. R. (2000). TANF policy implementation: The invisible barrier. *Journal of Sociology and Social Welfare, 27(2)*, pp. 139-159.

Katz, D., and Kahn, R. L. (2001). Organizations and the system concept. In Shafritz, J. M., and Ott, J. S.(Eds.), *Classics of Organizational Theory* (5th ed.). (pp. 257-267). Fort Worth: Harcourt College Publishers.

Kramer, R. M. (2000). A third sector in the third millennium? Voluntas: *International Journal of Voluntary and Nonprofit Organizations, 11(1)*, 1-23.

Lane, J., and Stevens, D. (2001). Welfare-to-work outcomes: The role of the employer. *Southern Economic Journal, 67(4)*, pp.1010-1032.

Mintzberg, H. (2001). The five basic parts of the organization. In Shafritz, J. M. and Ott, J. S. (Eds.), *Classics of Organizational Theory (5th ed.)*. pp. 222-233. Fort Worth: Harcourt College Publishers.

On the reauthorization of the Temporary Assistance for Needy Families program, Before the U.S. Senate Finance Committee. (2002) (testimony of Gordon L. Berlin).

Pfeffer, J., and Salancik, G. R. (1978). *The external control of organizations: A resource dependence perspective*. New York: Harper & Row.

Prince, J., and Austin, M. (2001). Innovative programs and practices emerging from the implementation of welfare reform: A cross-case analysis. *Journal of Community Practice, 9(3)*, pp. 1-14.

Schmid, H. (1992). Executive leadership in human service organizations. In Hasenfeld, Y. (Ed.), *Human Services as Complex Organizations*. pp. 98-117. Newbury Park: SAGE Publications.

Smith, S. R., and Lipsky, M. (1993). *Nonprofits for Hire: The Welfare State in the Age of Contracting*. Cambridge, MA. Harvard University Press.

Straatman, S., and Sherraden, M. (2001). Welfare to self-employment: A case study of the First Step Fund. *Journal of Community Practice, 9(3)*, pp. 73-94.

Thompson, J. D. (2001). Organizations in action. In Shafritz, J. M., and Ott, J. S., (Eds.) *Classics of Organizational Theory* (5th ed.). pp. 268-281. Fort Worth: Harcourt College Publishers.

Wamsley G. L., and Zald, M. N. (1976). *The political economy of public organizations*. Bloomington: Indiana University Press.

Searching for Utopia:
The Cycles of Service Provider Preferences

Margaret Gibelman, PhD

SUMMARY. A recurrent theme throughout the history of modern social welfare is dissatisfaction with how services are provided and by whom. This article, using media reports, traces the cycles of public sentiment, as expressed through the media, about the capabilities of public, nonprofit, and for-profit human service providers. An enhanced role for each sector is associated with periods of disillusionment with other sectors, stemming from such factors as poor quality performance, management and accountability failures, and outright wrongdoing. Raised expectations, grounded on wishes rather than evidence, it is argued, are likely to result in a cyclical "fall from grace" of each type of service provider. Some of these sector failures in recent years are discussed and their common themes identified. An analysis of thematic patterns reveals that all sectors have been found wanting. Media portrayals reflect perceptions about sector performance "in the moment" and are susceptible to change at the next hint of problems in another sector. Ultimately, access to finances may have more to do with future scenarios than publicity about or the track record of the three sectors. *[Article copies available for a fee from The Haworth Document Delivery Service: 1-800-HAWORTH. E-mail address: <docdelivery@haworthpress.com> Website: <http://www.Haworth Press.com> © 2004 by The Haworth Press, Inc. All rights reserved.]*

Margaret Gibelman is Professor and Director, Doctoral Program, Yeshiva University, Wurzweiler School of Social Work, 2495 Amsterdam Avenue, New York, NY 10033 (E-mail: gibelman@ymail.y.edu).

[Haworth co-indexing entry note]: "Searching for Utopia: The Cycles of Service Provider Preferences." Gibelman, Margaret. Co-published simultaneously in *Administration in Social Work* (The Haworth Social Work Practice Press, an imprint of The Haworth Press, Inc.) Vol. 28, No. 3/4, 2004, pp. 137-159; and: *Organizational and Structural Dilemmas in Nonprofit Human Service Organizations* (ed: Hillel Schmid) The Haworth Social Work Practice Press, an imprint of The Haworth Press, Inc., 2004, pp. 137-159. Single or multiple copies of this article are available for a fee from The Haworth Document Delivery Service [1-800-HAWORTH, 9:00 a.m. - 5:00 p.m. (EST). E-mail address: docdelivery@haworth press.com].

KEYWORDS. Service sectors, service delivery, boundary blurring, media, public perceptions

A recurrent theme throughout the history of modern social welfare is dissatisfaction with how services are provided and by whom. The ramifications of dissatisfaction have taken several forms, including increased accountability demands and the emergence of "watchdog" groups to monitor the nonprofit sector, such as the Better Business Bureau and various voluntary accrediting bodies. Other responses to the perceived failings of human service providers are to reorganize agencies in what has become a pattern of decentralization and then re-centralization and to encourage new types of providers to enter and compete in the human services marketplace.

This article traces the cycle of preferences, as expressed through the media, about public, nonprofit, and for-profit human service providers. An enhanced role for each sector is associated with periods of disillusionment with other sectors, stemming from such factors as poor quality performance, management and accountability failures, and outright wrongdoing. Raised expectations, grounded on wishes rather than evidence, it is argued, are likely to result in a cyclical "fall from grace" of each type of service provider. Some of these sector failures in recent years are discussed and their common themes identified. An analysis of thematic patterns reveals that media portrayals reflect perceptions about sector performance "in the moment" and are susceptible to change at the next hint of problems in another sector.

Although there is a sizable literature concerning individual sector performance and a less substantial literature comparing sector performance, the majority of our professional knowledge is drawn from small samples in regard to such variables as geography, number and types of agencies, labor force characteristics, and specific performance measures, such as outcomes of services (e.g., Bachman, 1996; Barbakow, 1997; Culhane & Hadley, 1992; Gibelman & Demone, 2002; Heinrich, 2000; Hirth, 1999; Kirwin & Kaye, 1993; Schmid, 2001). This article takes a more global view of human service providers, through the lens of the newspaper media, to describe one source of influence in molding public perceptions about sector capability.

Media reports form the basis of this analysis. Newspapers are one form of "watchdog," reporting and commenting on the status of how human service organizations function or, more often, malfunction in pursuit of the public interest. The media functions throughout the world as a forum of communication, with the press assuming the role of "filter"–selecting what is important for us to know and in how much detail (Best, 1995; Chaffee & Frank, 1996; Hiebert, 1999). Such accounts, it should be noted, slant toward the extreme, usually negative; what is newsworthy tends to be the unusual. Nevertheless, press accounts are also a mirror of public concern–either raising public awareness of issues or reflecting existing popular opinion. The power of the newspaper media to shape and create public images and to define what we know is well established (Capella & Jamieson, 1997; Chaffee & Frank, 1996; Cook, 1998; Johnson, Stamm, Lisosky, & James, 1996; Newhagen, 1994).

Articles, drawn from major newspapers with a national readership, such as the *New York Times*, *Washington Post*, and *Boston Globe*, provide the case examples that form the basis of analysis of where the sectors stand, at least as portrayed in the media. These newspapers were selected because they are recognized as the most influential newspapers in the public arena (McDevitt, 1996). Further, the various search engines used to identify articles related to sector performance overwhelmingly produced "hits" from these newspaper sources. Inferences are drawn by identifying themes, patterns, and descriptive language use (Berg, 1995; Rubin & Babbie, 2001). No effort was made to include all articles pertaining to sector performance; rather, the aim was to identify the major themes that emerge and re-emerge over time and to highlight articles which exemplify these themes. The goal was not to find a representative sample amenable to generalization, but to select a wide and diverse universe of cases reflective of media attention (Glaser & Strauss, 1967). Given the sheer volume of media data, there would be no reasonable method to identify a representative sample.

MEDIA PORTRAYAL OF SECTOR CAPABILITY

The media, reflective of or influencing public opinion, is fickle. Government is in. Government is out. Nonprofits are favored. Nonprofits fall into disrepute. For-profits will bring business acumen to the human services and thus instill efficiency and effectiveness. For-profits then fall from grace after a consistent and publicized pattern of ripping off public dollars. A look at this pattern, by sector, reveals the extent of swings in perceptions about sector capability.

The Public Sector

Until the Great Depression, the federal government was not a preferred choice for either the financing or delivery of human services. The New Deal represented a landmark turn-about in traditional attitudes; the federal government had become the only source with the authority and resources to fund and provide services to meet the breadth of need. Although during the 1940s and 1950s there was some retrenchment in the federal role, the notion of public responsibility for the public good established in the Social Security Act of 1935 and its subsequent amendments has remained to this day.

By the 1960s, government's role in initiating and funding human services expanded to an unprecedented level. However, there was general consensus that although government could and should pay the bill, nongovernmental organizations were the preferred vehicle for meeting public purposes (Lynn, 2002). This step was logical, given the emphasis of Economic Opportunity Act programs to mobilize and empower local communities. Social action was best accomplished at the community level and through private sources, even if government was the chief financier of such efforts.

Since the 1960s, the concept and practice of "privatization" has been extended to all sectors of the economy, including the human services. Privatization refers to the divesting of government responsibility for the provision of products or services (Gibelman, 1998). The political ideology favoring the reduced size and power of government has centered not only on anti-government sentiment and intolerance of abuses of the public trust, but also on the belief that the private sector can do a better job (Gibelman, 1998; Morin, 1995; Passell, 1998). The perceived inadequacies of government are matched by a belief that the private sector is capable of resolving the problems of escalating costs and inefficiencies that pervade the health, welfare, and other systems (Savas, 2000).

During the presidential campaign of 2000, George W. Bush made clear his ideological dislike of both central government and public bureaucracy (or "big government"), and his post-election proposals, under the rubric of "compassionate conservativism" suggest a movement to further enhance the private sector role in human services delivery (Bush, 2001).

The Reign of Nonprofits

During the 1960s, government funding to nonprofits increased dramatically under such programs as Model Cities, the Comprehensive Employment and Training Act (CETA), the Older Americans Act, the Community Mental Health Centers Act, and the Economic Opportunity Act (Smith & Lipsky, 1993; Gibelman, 1995; Levine, 1998). The vehicle for this expansion was purchase of service contracts, primarily with nonprofit providers. However, as these contracting arrangements mushroomed, the public sector began to impose its own dysfunctional bureaucratic rules and regulations on its contracted providers, focusing not only on the outcomes of such services, but also on the process used to carry out programs of service (Gibelman, 1998). Nonprofit agencies contracting to do business with government have thus, themselves, taken on many of the bureaucratic features typically associated with the public sector.

In this structural evolution, they, too, have fallen into some measure of disfavor, similar to the government services to which they were earlier perceived to be the solution.

Against the growing concern that nonprofits were increasingly taking on the characteristics of their public funding sources, including their weaknesses, a series of scandals arose which received widespread media attention and heightened disenchantment with this sector (see, for example, Gibelman, Gelman, & Pollack, 1997; Gibelman & Gelman, 2001). Perhaps the most notable of these cases concerned the United Way of America (UWA), one of the nation's largest and most esteemed nonprofit fund raising arms. William Aramony, President of UWA, was accused and found guilty of using charitable donations to finance a lavish life style (Shepard & Miller, 1992; Simross, 1992) and was sentenced to prison (Arenson, 1995). A *Washington Post* editorial cautioned that the UWA debacle should be a "warning to all charitable, civic and other public service organizations to take a hard look at their own oversight . . . the damage done to good causes by bad oversight can be deadly" ("United Way and Mr. Aramony," 1994, p. A14).

For-Profits

The expanding role of for-profits in human services is based on four interrelated factors: (1) the mandate to contain spiraling and, in the opinion of many politicos, uncontrollable health and human service expenditures; (2) the perception that there is money to be made in human services; (3) the growing consensus that a free market approach to service delivery would increase efficiency, reduce costs, and encourage innovation through competition; and (4) changes in state and federal law and/or regulations that opened the door to for-profit providers (Gibelman & Demone, 2002).

For-profits have, with some exceptions, always had the legal authority to enter into the health and human services arenas, but this option was not generally pursued because of the perception that the profit potential was limited. Following enactment, in 1965, of Medicare and Medicaid, utilization rates for health services exploded, with annual increases in excess of two to three times that of the general inflation rate (Mitchell, 1998). It was the for-profits to which government turned in its desire to control costs based on the perception that business could instill the proper level of efficiency (Frumkin, 1999). With some irony, the desire to cost-save created the environment for profit-making opportunities.

The failure, in the 1990s, of Congress and the President to agree upon and pass health care reform allowed the free market embracement of for-profit enterprise to gain further momentum (Sharpe, 1997). With no federal guidance to aid in the search for cost effective options, many states sought their own answers through expanded use of the private market.

The ongoing search to maximize service delivery capability by creating market competition was given significant impetus in the Personal Responsibility and Work Opportunity Reconciliation Act (PRWORA) of 1996. States are specifically authorized to administer and provide family assistance services through contracts or vouchers or certificates that may be redeemed for services at charitable, religious, or private organizations ("Summary of welfare reforms made by Public Law 104-193," p. 6).

This provision came to be known as "charitable choice," in that religious groups and, at the other end of the spectrum, proprietary organizations, were allowed to compete for government contracts. For-profits instantly became eligible for the billions of dollars spent annually for services to children and families, including mental health services such as residential or outpatient care (Bachman, 1996; Schnapp, Bayles, Raffoul, & Schnee, 1999). In the early years of implementation, for-profits have made significant use of the provisions of PRWORA in selected service areas.

Many of the for-profits which entered the competitive human services market already were well-established entities in related areas, such as the manufacturing or distributing of health care products. As business concerns, for-profits have the advantage of expertise in writing and negotiating contracts and grants or quick access to such expertise. Corporations already offering diversified products and services were able to underbid many of the nonprofits.

However, as the for-profits gained dominance in such human service markets as residential treatment centers, substance abuse treatment, home care, prison services, group homes for people with mental retardation and mental illness, and nursing homes, revelations of fraudulent practices began to surface. During the 1990s, for-profit psychiatric hospitals and addiction centers paid over $500 million in federal fines in settlement of profiteering and fraud related to recruiting patients with generous mental health insurance coverage (Sharkey, 1999). Service delivery problems were also revealed. These primarily concerned the money making motive and its impact on the quality of care (Barbakow, 1997; Lown, 1999; Rosenheck, Armstrong, Callahan et al., 1998; Sharfstein, 2001; Sharpe, 1997); cost of services (Kirwin & Kaye, 1993; "Pushing privatization too far," 1995), and the ability of nonprofits to compete (Bloche, 1998; Hirth, 1999).

Disclosures about for-profit business practices in 2001-2002 have centered on the theme of abrogation of the pubic interest, as well as public trust. The outright crimes and their consequences for the U.S. economy of such for-profit corporations such as Enron, Adelphia, Tyco International, ImClone, and WorldCom have exploded upon public conscious to such an extent that for-profit enterprises are, in general, perceived as greed-driven and suspect (Phillips, 2002; "The confidence crisis," 2002). The egregious corporate abuses have tarnished the public image of for-profits and quickly led to widespread support to reign big business in through legislation designed to hold the corporate sector responsible for its foibles (Stevenson & Oppel, 2002). As discussed below, these abuses, albeit on a smaller scale, were also revealed among for-profit human service organizations. In such a climate, the perception that good business sense will lead to more cost-effective and efficient services diminishes.

TRACK RECORD COMPARISONS

A sense of the images of human service providers as portrayed in the media can be distilled from the headlines. Even though the sectors are clearly distinguished, the images are remarkably similar, as illustrated in Table 1.

The details of media stories provide additional fervor to influence public opinion about the performance of human service organizations. In Table 2, some of the recent media exposes of non-profit wrongdoing are illustrated. These cases suggest that for-profits are susceptible to mismanagement and inefficiencies, similar to the accusations long leveled at the nonprofit and public sectors.

The headlines, and the stories behind them, show several common themes, as well as a few distinctive sector characteristics. Press accounts of the follies of for-profit and non-profit managers are remarkably similar in their revelations of greed (see, for example, Billitteri, 1998; Torrey, 1998). The difference lies, generally, in the larger sums of money involved in for-profit sector thievery. Embezzlement is an ongoing theme among nonprofits, but is not unknown in the public or for-profit sectors. For example, a former senior Fairfax County (VA) financial manager pleaded guilty, in 2002, to embezzling more than $1 million from government employees' retirement funds over a period of years (Glod, 2002).

Ineptitude is another pervasive theme. In the public sector, it is bureaucratic structure that is at the heart of most of the allegations made against it–weak management; failure to initiate reforms; children, people with chronic mental illness, the homeless lost in the system or harmed while under the care of the agencies charged to protect them (Kaufman, 2002; Larrubia, 2002; Pear, 2002). In Los Angeles, Anita Bock, who was hired with the charge to reform the Los Angeles County Department of Child and Family Services, was ousted two years after her hiring (Larrubia, 2002). That the job was impossible; that resources were lacking to do the job and predecessors–in L.A. and throughout

TABLE 1. The Track Record of Service Providers: Clues from the Headlines

Headline	Year	Auspice
Charities use for-profit units to avoid disclosing finances [a]	1998	For-profit
Study: For-profit hospitals drive up overall med care spending [b]	1999	For-profit
Nonprofit groups accused of bilking lunch programs [c]	1999	Nonprofit
For-profit care's morbid results [d]	1999	For-profit
The perils of for-profit care [e]	2000	For-profit
U.S. asks judge to hold Red Cross in contempt [f]	2001	Nonprofit
City says inmate care fails in most contract categories [g]	2001	For-profit
Children suffer as Florida agency struggles [h]	2002	Public
Officials overlooked dire signs at charity [i]	2002	Nonprofit
A Study finds children's aid goes to adults. [j]	2002	Public
Audit finds lapses in Maryland child care [k]	2002	Public
Charity overwhelmed in bid to meet attack victims' bills [l]	2002	Nonprofit
FEMA's pace on 9/11 aid is criticized [m]	2002	Public
Marketing patriotism, companies blur lines of charity and profit [n]	2002	For-profit
Seen as safety net, 9/11 program is anything but [o]	2002	Public
Ex-Official guilty of embezzling [p]	2002	Public
Growing concerns on the health of HealthSouth [q]	2002	For-profit
9/11 Fund Cheating Victims, Firm Says [r]	2002	Public
Red Cross to Open its Books on Aid After September 11 [s]	2002	Nonprofit
Charity criticized for withholding excessive funds [t]	2002	Nonprofit
Supervisors force out child welfare director [u]	2002	Public
State is failing mentally ill, study says [v]	2002	For-profit
City to pay millions to homeless forced to sleep in an office [w]	2002	Public

[a] Abelson, 1998; [b] Webster, 1999, [c] Pear, 1999; [d] Lown, 1999; [e] "The perils of for-profit care," 2000; [f] Flaherty & Gaul, 2001; [g] Finkelstein, 2001; [h] Canedy, 2002b; [i] Bernstein, 2002; [j] Pear, 2002; [k] Mosk, 2002; [l] Henriques, 2002; [m] Hernandez, 2002; [n] Barstow & Henriques, 2002; [o] Chen, 2002; [p] Glod, 2002; [q] Freudenheim & Abelson, 2002; [r] Associated Press, 2002; [s] Strom, 2002; [t] Whoriskey & Salmon, 2002; [u] Larrubia, 2002; [v] Levy, 2002b; [w] Kaufman, 2002.

the U.S.–had similarly failed in efforts to reform public systems was seemingly irrelevant.

At the federal level, the Bush administration improperly allowed some states to use federal funds targeted for the Children's Health Insurance Program on programs for childless adults (Pear, 2002). This misuse of funds has its counterpart in the nonprofit sector. The Red Cross' Liberty Fund was heavily criticized

TABLE 2. Recent Examples of Accountability Failures, by Sector

Year	Organization	Sector	Wrongdoing
1991-2002	Brooklyn Manor (New York) [a]	For-profit	Inaccurate, incomplete, or non-existent records; embezzling residents' retirement benefits; mishandling or misappropriating residents' money; poor conditions
1998-2002	Leben Home for Adults (NY) [b]	For-profit	Misappropriation of residents' funds; subjecting residents to unnecessary surgery
1998	Goodwill Industries of Santa Clara Cty, CA [c]	Nonprofit	Embezzlement, money laundering ($15m +)
1999	Cambridge Credit Counseling Corp [d]	For-profit	Profiteering; frivolous lawsuits
1999	United Way, CA [e]	Nonprofit	Financial improprieties
1999	Columbia/HCA HealthCare Corp. [f]	For-profit	Fraud ($1.7m +); bogus expense claims
1999	Charter Behavioral Health Systems [g]	For-profit	Falsification of records, injuries, suspicious deaths
2000	Helpline Soul Rescue Ministry [h]	Nonprofit, Sectarian	Mortgage Fraud ($2.3m)
2000	Toys for Tots [i]	Nonprofit	Theft (Founder, CEO)
2000	Catholic Charities of San Francisco (CA) [j]	Nonprofit, Sectarian	Misappropriation of Funds ($73,000)
2001	Greater Ministries International [k]	Nonprofit, Sectarian	Pyramid Scheme (448m)
2001	New Hope Guild Centers (NY) [l]	Nonprofit	Expanded services without approval, lied to cover up violations; billed Medicaid for unauthorized services. Charged with defrauding Medicaid of $9m
2001	Harvard Pilgrim Health Care [m]	For-profit	Fraud based on company profits to the company's chief psychiatrist, fined $100,000
2001	Prison Health Services [n]	For-profit	Inadequate services; poor quality care
2001	Project Social Care [o]	Nonprofit	Bogus enterprise (Diversion of $325,000)
2001-2002	Ocean House (NY) [p]	Nonprofit	CEO siphoned millions through improper mortgage transactions; improper Medicaid claims

TABLE 2 (continued)

Year	Organization	Sector	Wrongdoing
2002	Benevolence International Foundation [q]	Nonprofit,Sectarian	Defrauding donors by secretly siphoning funds to al Qaeda
2002	HealthSouth Corp. [r]	For-profit	Inadequate/inappropriate service quality; faulty business practices
2002	Hale House (NY) [s]	Nonprofit	Embezzlement; diversion of more than $1m.
2002	United Way–Washington D.C. area [t]	Nonprofit	Inflating accounts, excessive overhead, withholding money earmarked for charity, conflict of interest (withheld $1m from charities)
2002	University Forest Nursing Care Center [u]	For-Profit	Misappropriation of patient funds
2002	National D-Day Memorial Foundation[v]	Nonprofit	Falsely stated pledges to get a $1.2 bank loan and manipulating statements to gain state matching funds (left agency $7m in debt)
2002	Northwestern Human Services (PA) [w]	Nonprofit	Fraud through filing false Medicare and Medicaid bills; $7.8m fine

[a] Levy, 2002a; [b] Levy, 2002a; [c] Billitteri, 1998; [d] Fickenscher, 1999; [e] Hall & Sommerfeld, 1999; [f] Eichenwald, 1999; [g] Kong, 1999; [h] Pristin, 2000; [i] "Charity ex-chief admits to stealing"; [j]Associated Press, 2000; [k] "5 guilty in bilking based on a ministry", 2001; [l] Levy, 2002a; [m] Scharfstein, 2001; [n] Finkelstein; [o] Lambert, 2001; [p] Levy, 2002b; [q] Mintz, 2002; [r] Freudenheim & Abelson, 2002; [s] Bernstein, 2002; [t] Salmon, 2002c; Whoriskey & Salmon, 2002; [u] Young, 2002; [v] Jenkins, 2002; [w] Vigoda, 2002

for using some of the money raised to create a permanent fund for use in the event of a future terrorist attack. This decision was reversed when New York's attorney general threatened the Red Cross with legal action unless all dollars contributed for the Liberty Fund were used as promised for needs resulting from the September 11th disaster (Williams, 2001).

Many of the misdeeds revealed by the press are long-term in nature. In the Fairfax County case, cited earlier, the financial manager stole retirement funds over a period of four years by falsifying paperwork so that money was diverted into his own account (Glod, 2002). In New York, the operator of Brooklyn Manor, a for-profit adult home for the mentally ill, was charged with stealing residents' money. Throughout the early 1990s, state inspectors cited the operator for mishandling or misappropriating residents' money. The facility was also cited for its poor conditions and overall lack of resident supervision (Levy, 2002a). The State Department of Social Services moved to revoke the owner's license, but the decision was reversed, perhaps because the owner-operator was married to a state senator. The home remains open and, in 2001, the Health Department cited it for many violations, including inaccurate, incomplete, or absent records. Also in New York, the State Department of Health was aware, as far back as 1998, that residents of the Leben Home for Adults were subjected to unnecessary surgery to take advantage of Medicaid or Medicare payments. But the same oversight department did not increase its supervision of the Leben Home and the unnecessary prostate and eye surgeries continued to be inflicted upon residences until the *New York Times* blew the whistle (Levy, 2002a; 2002b).

The government agencies paying the bills knew and did not act upon these cases of fraud. The for-profits were given license to continue fraudulent behaviors that put the mentally ill residents at risk. No significant action was taken in regard to these several New York State for-profit residential home owner/operators until the press began an investigative report. The majority of agencies identified by the *New York Times* were already known to the supervising public agency, but action had been postponed, reversed, or ignored. At the same time, the state, which pays the for-profit providers, has failed to protect the residents from poor service. An investigation of these same care facilities by the *New York Times* led to the conclusion that these ". . . for-profit residences have become magnets for schemes that exploit the mentally ill" (Levy, 2002a). The failure of federal or state officials to act quickly to remedy flaws, deficiencies, and outright illegal acts among service providers is characterized by the press as "ineptitude" in performing its oversight and monitoring function (Pear, 1999).

For-profits, more than the other two sectors, get in trouble for providing poor quality services. HealthSouth Corporation, the largest chain of rehabilitation hospitals in the U.S., came into the news for using unlicenced care providers. The company also faces questions about its financial practices, inside stock sales, conflict of interest among board members, and business dealings, including improperly billing Medicare by seeking payment for services provided by unlicenced therapists (Abelson, 2002b; Freudenheim & Abelson, 2002).

Cost-cutting measures to maximize profits is a pattern of organizational behavior frequently cited in relation to for-profits. Examples generally focus on neglectful and inadequate services and their consequences for the clients served (Demone & Gibelman, 2002). In Massachusetts, for-profit managed care companies were accused by the state of spending only $4 to $5 per person per month for psychiatric services while being reimbursed $22 per person per month. A managed behavioral health care company in Iowa was accused of earning $880 in "commission" for each adult who applied for but was denied admission to a psychiatric unit (Torrey, 1998). They apologized and promised to be better. Marjorie Kelly, editor of *Business Ethics*, lamented that the quest for profits tends to trump the ideals of social responsibility and that the system is designed to serve certain people and not others (as cited in Carlson, 2002).

Although each revelation of fraud, embezzlement, theft, and/or malfeasance is met with media attention that fuels public outrage, the outcry is particularly potent in regard to the nonprofit sector. The funds that support this sector, after all, come largely out of the pockets of citizens through their charitable contributions or, indirectly, through their tax dollars in the form of special IRS status. Although the absolute dollars are relatively insignificant in comparison to the wrongdoings of the for-profit sector, the fallout is, perhaps, greater. This is because of the vaulted position of nonprofits in American society and the degree of trust placed in them to serve the public interest. The image emphasized in press accounts is that these wrongdoings boil down to stealing food out of the mouths of children or leaving adults with mental retardation or mental illness without supervision or needed medication. These images are potent, long-lasting, and offensive.

Nonprofits may have played an unwitting role in the expansion of for-profit human services by not addressing some of the sector's identified weaknesses. Examples abound. In 1999, the United Way of Santa Clara County (CA) found itself on the verge of financial collapse after years of spending more than it raised and using up all of its reserve funds (Hall & Sommerfeld, 1999). The blame was placed largely on the CEO for failing to keep the board informed of the true financial situation. In 2002, the United Way of the National Capital Area repeatedly made front-page headlines when it stood accused of withholding more than $1 million from hundreds of charities by questionable bookkeeping practices (Whoriskey & Salmon, 2002a). Shortly thereafter, the UWA affiliate's CEO resigned on the heels of a board-approved plan to radically transform the charity. This transformation is to include budget slashing and overhauling how it spends, distributes, and accounts for distributions (Whoriskey & Salmon, 2002b). In a move remarkably similar to the national UWA scandal in the 1990s, the board of the D.C. affiliate was negotiating to provide a "large settlement package" to the departed CEO, Norman O. Taylor. Media revelations of this intention prompted Sen. Charles E. Grassley, the ranking Republican on the Senate Finance Committee which oversees tax-exempt organizations, to write a letter to the acting president of the UWA of the National Capital Area questioning the wisdom of a settlement before the results of several probes of the organization's finances and management were known. The affiliate agreed to hold off on a settlement (Salmon, 2002d).

Organizations that rely on public goodwill to achieve their missions have few assets more precious than a positive public image. In the aftermath of media disclosure of nonprofit wrongdoing, blame has often been assigned to the board of directors, with admonishments that they must clean up their act. But the same admonishments have also been leveled at the for-profit sector. In the business world, it is similarly believed that boards should oversee their corporations with knowledge, honesty, and integrity. A *New York Times* editorial echoed the view of corporate board responsibility: "One of the most important lessons of Enron is the havoc that can result when oversight by corporate boards of directors breaks down" ("Cleaning up the boardroom," 2002).

ACCELERATING CYCLES

The cyclical nature of sector preferences, as reflected in the media, is perhaps best illustrated in regard to the terrorist attacks of September 11, 2001, and their aftermath. Suddenly, government was back in favor. Airport security was placed under federal government control (Alvarez, 2001; Bumiller, 2001). A special federal government appropriation was earmarked to compensate victims of the terrorist attacks (Associated Press, 2002). The promises made during the Bush campaign to ensure a small government and fiscal conservatism gave way to a White House budget proposal that increased spending by 9 percent, did away with the goal to maintain budget surpluses, and abandoned the pledge to reduce the national debt (Stevenson, 2002). The objective became that of protecting the U.S. from terrorism, rebuilding–spiritually, psychologically, and structurally–from the devastation of 9/11, and helping the economy recover.

This activism on behalf of the public interest was widely heralded. The proportion of Americans who voiced trust in the federal government doubled from 30 percent in 2000 to 64 percent in the weeks following September 11, 2001. Surveys consistently showed that Americans were feeling more religious, more patriotic, and more charitable (Morin, 2001; Morin & Deane, 2001). Patriotism translated to a form of public mandate for the federal government to take action, the net result of which was to expand its role.

But the permissive environment for government expansion and the implied faith that it would do so in the public interest was short lived. Problems in mounting a huge relief effort with no planning time surfaced. An October 1, 2001, *New York Times* headline proclaimed: "Fund for victims' families already a sore point" (Henriques & Barstow, 2001). Canter Fitzgerald, the brokerage firm that lost 658 employees in the World Trade Center attack, charged that the federal victims compensation funds was biased and basing awards illegally on after-tax income (Associated Press, 2002).

The proposal to create an Office of Homeland Security received mixed reviews, with critics charging that the creation of a new mega bureaucracy would accelerate rather than resolve government unresponsiveness. Also casting doubt on the enhanced government role was the gradual revelation of massive bureaucratic bungling among the agencies charged with national security and law enforcement. These federal agencies, it is charged, failed to detect or mishandled the warning signs of terrorism ("The past as prelude," 2002). With accountability for these intelligence failures now squarely on the shoulders of the federal government, it is not surprising that faith in the ability of the same government to ensure the safety of Americans, no less attend to their needs in the aftermath of tragedy, was met with skepticism. The public sector quickly cycled out of public favor; the image of government ineptitude had been reinforced.

In the days following September 11th, charitable nonprofits also played a major role. Individuals quickly donated more than $2 billion to charitable causes, mostly related directly to disaster relief and channeled to both existing and new charities (Salmon, 2002a). The Red Cross and Salvation Army were among the key beneficiaries of public largess. These nonprofits were held in high public esteem, at least for a while. First, it was revealed that the American Red Cross had used some of the 9/11 restricted donations for other causes. Then came repeated press accounts about administrative chaos in channeling funds to the survivors and families of 9/11 victims. Headlines again suggest the changing climate. For example, the Salvation Army, which raised over $60 million to help September 11th victims, sought to provide immediate help by paying the household bills of families affected by the disaster. But it was then overwhelmed with requests—more than 30,000 bills from about 8,000 families. The Salvation Army lacked the administrative capability to respond and, in some cases, the submitted bills were never paid at all (Henriques, 2002). The performance of the American Red Cross in the aftermath of September 11th was also questioned, leading to demands for fuller disclosure of its finances and enforcement of more stringent monitoring of its disaster relief operations (Strom, 2002).

In sum, within months, the outpouring of positivism toward government and nonprofits had dissipated. Trust in the federal government, which had doubled to its highest point in almost four decades, returned, one year later, to a level not much above that of year 2000, according to a poll conducted by the *Washington Post* (Deane, 2002; Morin & Deane, 2002). At the same time, surveys conducted by the Brookings Institution and the Independent Sector revealed that, since July 2001, the percentage of people indicating that they have no confidence in charitable organizations doubled, a phenomenon attributed largely to the way nonprofits handled donations and program operations following September 11th (Gose, 2002; Salmon, 2002b). Conversely, those indicating that they have "a lot" of trust in charities dropped from one in four in July, 2001, to less than one in five a year later (Salmon, 2002b). A survey conducted by the *Chronicle of Philanthropy* a few months after the Brookings and Independent Sector surveys revealed further erosion in public confidence, with 42% of the sample saying that relief efforts had damaged their faith in nonprofit groups (Gose, 2002).

Sector capability was tested to the extreme in the days, weeks and months following September 11th and the scope of need seems to have outmatched the ability of public and nonprofits to meet the challenge. For-profits, by and large, were not major players in the human services response to September 11th since they were ineligible to raise or receive charitable funds. Further, the type of social services for which for-profits are best known—residential care, day care, home care—are not suitable venues for the provision of emergency relief services. Ironically, the exclusion of for-profits from the response network of public and non-profit providers may have worked to their public image benefit, as they avoided the tarnish of the cycle of accolades and then condemnation that befell their public and nonprofit counterparts.

PROGNOSES FOR THE FUTURE

When the track record of the three sectors is examined, all are found wanting. With each disappointment, newspaper stories and editorials promote the virtue of another sector. Management lapses, if not downright incompetence, have been a major and consistent theme for all sectors providing human services. First, it was the nonprofits as an alternative to the public sector. Then, when the nonprofits failed to live up to the expectations set for them and evidenced their own brand of management and accountability problems, attention turned to the potential of for-profits based on their perceived business acumen. Predictably, high expectations of any sector are likely to prove, at minimum, overly optimistic, or at worst, totally unfounded.

Newspaper accounts of the foibles of human service providers may offer a skewed picture of their track record, since exposés that explore violations of public trust, consumer fraud, and other associated misdeeds tend to be of greater interest than stories about successes and achievements, although the latter are by no means excluded as occasional human interest stories. There are, of course, many legitimate service providers. However, newspaper accounts, backed by selective scholarly studies, do suggest that there is some legitimacy to concerns raised about how human services are provided. Even if the cases of wrongdoing represent only a very small proportion of service providers, the incidents call into question whether and to what extent accountability mechanisms work to protect the public interest. Changing perspectives about the strengths and weaknesses of each sector may reflect the salience of media messages to politicians, public administrators, and the general public. Lacking a receptive audience, newspapers would turn to other topics. Continued reporting, then, of human service sector misdeeds suggests an attuned readership receptive to the message and influenced by its direction (Neuman, Just, & Crigler, 1992; Chaffee & Frank, 1996).

Mediating Influences

Ultimately, the financial bottom line may have more to do with future scenarios than publicity about the track record of the three sectors. Here, for-profits may have the advantage. The growth of a huge for-profit healthcare industry is evidenced in stock trends which defy the overall market. For example, shares of Triad Hospitals gained 33 percent by mid-2002, compared with a 25 percent decline for the market as a whole (Abelson, 2002a). Admissions to the growing number of for-profit hospitals, a substantial proportion of which converted from nonprofit status, is attributed to the aging of the baby boomers and the easing-up of managed care restrictions on hospital stays. But as admissions have increased, for-profit hospitals have also begun to charge more for services, a move made possible by their dominance in some markets (Abelson, 2002a).

Thus, market strength and viability leads to the exercise of considerable for-profit influence on who gets what, when, how, by whom, and at what cost.

Future for-profit market strength is also evident in proposals emanating from Washington. In early 2003, President Bush proposed comprehensive prescription drug coverage for the elderly under Medicare, but with the proviso that enrollees switch to subsidized private insurance plans, a metaphor for managed care (Pear & Toner, 2003). The driving force behind this proposal is the belief that free-market competition will offer more choices and better benefits. Those who opt to stay in traditional Medicare would receive far more modest prescription benefits. Perhaps as a precursor of further cycles of provider preferences, the *New York Times* issued a caution: These private plans may not perform as well as hoped ("A Bad Prescription," 2003).

In the shorter term, economic forces, backed by political preferences, may well be decisive in regard to the relative dominance of the sectors. The realities of glaring federal and state budget deficits, a war with Iraq and the costs therein, and federal spending priorities favoring defense, emergency response efforts, bio-terrorism research, and the like suggest a bleak scenario for human service organizations dependent on government funds–largely public and nonprofit agencies. President Bush has recommended sharp cuts in domestic programs, including social services, as a trade-off for the growth in military spending and the cost of domestic security (Planin, 2002). In other times of federal government cutbacks, states have been able to assume some additional costs. This is not a likely occurrence now, given the budget-strapped condition of the majority of states. Similarly, with the significant market downturn, corporate and foundation contributions are constrained (Anft & Wilhelm, 2002; Lipman, 2002). Corporate downsizing affects the pocketbook of individual citizens, who may have fewer dollars to give in the form of charitable donations. Nonprofits are already dipping into their reserves, when they have such, to make up for lost grants and donations. This depletion of assets cannot continue for long without jeopardizing the continued viability of these nonprofits. For those without assets, the options will seem to lie in merger or dissolution.

In the longer term, if effectiveness is to be a more potent influence on decisions regarding provider choice, then perhaps we need to define or clarify what constitutes "effective" when the product is the human condition. The few empirical studies which have compared the sectors in regard to outcomes suggest that, on this dimension, there are questions about the performance of both nonprofits and for-profits (see, for example, Heinrich, 2000), as the cases described herein indicate. As Schmid (2001) concluded in his comparative study of nonprofit and for-profit providers of home care services in Israel, perhaps the more germane question of concern is not who provides services but how and with what outcome.

REFERENCES

"A bad prescription." (2003, March 5). Editorial. *New York Times*. Retrieved March 6, 2003 from <http://nytimes.com/2003/03/05/opinion/05WED.html>.

Abelson, R. (1998, February 9). Charities use for-profit units to avoid disclosing finances. *New York Times*, p. A1.

Abelson, R. (2002a, August 4). Hospitals strut in a lurching market. *New York Times*. Retrieved August 4, 2002 from: http://nytimes.com/2002/08/04/business/yourmoney/04HOSP.html.

Abelson, R. (2002b, September 30). HealthSouth tries to regain its credibility with investors. *New York Times*. Retrieved October 3, 2002 from: http://www.nytimes.com/2002/09/30/business/30PLAC.html.

Alvarez, L. (2001, October 26). Bush supports House bill on airport screeners. *New York Times*. Retrieved October 26, 2001 from: http://www.ntimes.com/2001/10/26/national/26AIR.html.

Anft, M., & Wilhelm, I. (2002, August 8). Off the charts: As the stock market gyrates, charities face tough times. *Chronicle of Philanthropy*, p. 25, 27-28.

Arenson, K.W. (1995, April 4). Former United Way chief guilty in theft of more than $600,000. *New York Times*, pp. A1, A22.

Associated Press. (2000, June 23). Charity paid for CEO's hair removal. *The Record*, p. A17.

Associated Press. (2002, September 17). 9/11 fund cheating victims, firm says: Brokerage faults formula used for compensating families. *Washington Post*, p. A7.

Bachman, S.S. (1996). Why do states privatize mental health services? Six state experiences. *Journal of Health Politics, Policy and Law*, *21*(4), 807-824.

Barbakow, J.C. (1997). Point-counterpoint. Not-for-profits vs. for-profits: Is one better patient care? *Health Systems Leadership*, *4*(8), 16-17.

Barstow, D., & Henriques, D.B. (2002, February 2). Marketing patriotism, companies blur lines of charity and profit. *New York Times*. Retrieved February 3, 2002 from: http://www.nytimes.com/2002/02/02/nyregion/02CHAR.html.

Berg, B. (1995). *Qualitative research methods for the social sciences*. Needham Heights, MA: Allyn & Bacon.

Bernstein, N. (2002, February 7). Officials overlooked dire signs at charity. *New York Times*, p. B1.

Best, J. (Ed.). (1995). *Images of issues*. New York: Aldine de Gruyter.

Billitteri, T.J. (1998, February 12). Goodwill looting: California scam yields lessons for charity managers. *Chronicle of Philanthropy*, p. 39.

Bloche, M.G. (1998). Should government intervene to protect nonprofits? *Health Affairs* (Millwood), *17*(5), 7-25.

Bumiller, E. (2001, September 28). Bush to increase federal role in security at airports. *New York Times*. Retrieved September 28, 2001 from: http://www.nytimes.com/2001/09/28/national/28BUSH.html.

Bush, G.W. (2001, May 26). *Rallying the armies of compassion*. Retrieved September 8, 2001 from: http://www.whitehouse.gov/news/reports/text/faith-based.html.

Candy, D. (2002, July 1). Children suffer as Florida agency struggles. *New York Times*. Retrieved July 5, 2002 from: http://www.nytimes.com/2002/07/01/national/01GIRL.html.

Capella, J.N., & Jamieson, K.H. (1997). *Spirals of cynicism: The press and the public good*. New York: Cambridge University Press.

Chaffee, S., & Frank, S. (1996). How Americans get political information: Print versus broadcast news. *The Annals of the American Academy of Political and Social Science*, *546*, 48-58.

"Charity ex-chief admits to stealing." (2000, April 6). *Chronicle of Philanthropy*, p. 29.

Chen, D.W. (2002, September 28). Seen as safety net, 9/11 program is anything but. *New York Times*. Retrieved September 29, 2002 from: http://www.nytimes.com/2002/09/28/nyregion/28GRAN.html.

"Cleaning up the boardroom." (2002, March 8). Editorial. *New York Times*. Retrieved March 8, 2002 from: http://www.nytimes.com/2002/03/08/opinion/08FRI1.html.

Cook, T. (1998). *Governing with the news*. Chicago: University of Chicago Press.

Culhane, D.P., & Hadley, T.R. (1992). The discriminating characteristics of for-profit versus not-for-profit free standing psychiatric inpatient facilities. *Health Services Research, 27*(2), 177-194.

Deane, C. (2002, May 31). Trust in government declines. *Washington Post*, p. A29.

Eichenwald, K. (1999, July 3). Two found guilty of hospital fraud. *New York Times*. Retrieved August 4, 1999 from: http://www.nytimes.com/1999/07/03/news/financial/healthcare-fraud.html.

Fickenscher, L. (1999, June 25). Debate brews over for-profit credit counseling. *American Banker, 164* (121), 1.

Finkelstein, K.E. (2001, July 19). City says inmate care fails in most contract categories. *New York Times*. Retrieved July 23, 2001 from: http://www.nytimes.com/2001/07/19/nyregoin/19PRIS.html.

"5 guilty in bilking based on a ministry." (2001a, March 14). *New York Times*, p. A12.

Flaherty, M.P., & Gaul, G.M. (2001, December 14). U.S. asks judge to hold Red Cross in contempt. *Washington Post*, p. A4.

Freudenheim, M., & Abelson, R. (2002, September 19). Growing concerns on the health of HealthSouth. *New York Times*. Retrieved September 19, 2002 from: http://www.nytimes.com/2002/09/19/business/19PLAC.html.

Frumkin, P. (1999). The rise of the corporate social worker. *Society, 36*(6), 46-57.

Gibelman, M. (1995). Purchasing social services. In R.L. Edwards (Ed.-in-Chief), *Encyclopedia of social work* (19th ed., Vol. 3, pp. 1998-2007). Washington, DC: NASW Press.

Gibelman, M. (1998). Theory, practice, and experience in the purchase of services. In M. Gibelman, & H.W. Demone, Jr. (eds.). *The privatization of human services: Policy and practice issues*, (Vol. 1, pp. 1-51). New York: Springer.

Gibelman, M., & Demone, H.W., Jr. (2002). The commercialization of health and human services: Neutral phenomenon or cause for concern? *Families in Society: The Journal of Contemporary Human Services, 83*(4), 387-397.

Gibelman, M., & Gelman, S.R. (2001). Very public scandals: An analysis of how and why nongovernmental organizations get in trouble. *Voluntas, 12*(1), 49-66.

Gibelman, M., Gelman, S.R., & Pollack, D. (1997). The credibility of nonprofit boards: A view from the 1990s. *Administration in Social Work, 21*(2) 29-40.

Glaser, B., & Strauss, A. (1967). *The discovery of grounded theory: Strategies for qualitative research*. New York: Aldine de Gruyter.

Glod, M. (2002, September 17). Ex-official guilty of embezzling. *Washington Post*, p. A31.

Gose, B. (2002, September 5). 42% of Americans say relief effort damaged faith in nonprofit groups. *Chronicle of Philanthropy*, p. 12.

Hall, H., & Sommerfeld, M. (1999, May 20). Cal. United Way dismisses CEO amid charges of financial wrongdoing. *Chronicle of Philanthropy*, p. 35.

Heinrich, C.J. (2000). Organizational form and performance: An empirical investigation of nonprofit and for-profit job-training service providers. *Journal of Policy Analysis and Management, 19*(2), 233-261.

Henriques, D.B. (2002, January 5). Charity overwhelmed in bid to meet attack victims' bills. *New York Times*. Retrieved January 15, 2002 from: http://www.nytimes.com/2002/01/05/nyregion/05SALV.html.

Henriques, D.B., & Barstow, D. (2001, October 1). Fund for victims' families already proves sore point. *New York Times.* Retrieved October 1, 2001 from: http://www. nytimes.com/2001/10/01/nyregion/01FUND.html.

Hernandez, R. (2002, June 14). FEMA's pace on 9/11 aid is criticized. *New York Times.* Retrieved June 14, 2002 from: http://www.nytimes.com/2002/06/14/nyregion/ 14FEMA.html.

Hierbert, R.E. (1999). The growing power of mass media. In R.E. Hiebert (Ed.). *Impact of Mass Media: Current Issues* (4th ed., pp. 3-15). New York: Addison Wesley Longman.

Hirth, R.A. (1999). Consumer information and competition between nonprofit and profit nursing homes. *Journal of Health Economics, 18*(2), 219-240.

Jenkins, C.L. (2002, June 22). D-Day fund's former chief is accused of fraud. *Washington Post,* p. B1.

Johnson, M., Stamm, K., Lisosky, J., & James, J. (1996). Differences among newspapers in contributions to knowledge of national public affairs. *Newspaper Research Journal,* Winter, 1-8.

Kaufman, L. (2002, September 20). City to pay millions to homeless forced to sleep in an office. New York Times. Retrieved September 22, 2002 from: http://www. nytimes.com/2002/09/20/nyregion/20HOME.html.

Kirwin, P.M., & Kaye, L.W. (1993). A comparative cost analysis of alternative models of adult day care. *Administration in Social Work, 17*(2), 105-122.

Kong, D. (1999, April 21). TV magazine spotlights Mass. psychiatric units. *Boston Globe.* p. B3.

Lambert, B. (2001, October 1). 2 Rabbis plead guilty in conspiracy to divert federal money. *New York Times,* p. B2.

Larrubia, E. (2002, July 4). Supervisors force out child welfare director. *Los Angeles Times,* p. A1.

Levine, E.M. (1998). Church, state, and social welfare: Purchase of service and the sectarian agency. In M. Gibelman, & H.R. Demone, Jr. (Eds.). *The privatization of human services: Policy and practice issues* (pp. 117-153). New York: Springer.

Levy, C.J. (2002a, April 30). Voiceless, defenseless, and a source of cash. New York Times. Retrieved April 30, 2002 from: http://www.nytimes.com/2002.04/30/ nyregion/30HOME.html.

Levy, C.J. (2002b, September 15). State is failing mentally ill, study says. New York Times. Retrieved September 16, 2002 from: http://www.nytimes.com/2002/09/15/ nyregion/15MENT.html.

Lipman, H. (2002, November 14). Survey identifies troubling trends for nonprofit organizations. *Chronicle of Philanthropy,* p. 13.

Lown, B. (1999, August 1). For-profit care's morbid results. *Boston Globe,* pp. E1, E5.

Lynn, L.E., Jr. (2002). Social services and the state: The public appropriation of private charity. *Social Service Review, 76*(1), 58-82.

McDermitt, S. (1996). The impact of news media on child abuse reporting. *Child Abuse and Neglect, 20*(4), 261-274.

Mintz, J. (2002, October 10). Muslim charity leader indicted. *Washington Post,* p. A14.

Mitchell, C.G. (1998). Perceptions of empathy and client satisfaction with managed behavioral health care. *Social Work, 43*(5), 404-411.

Morin, R. (1995, October 11). A united opinion: Government doesn't go a good job. *Washington Post*, p. A12.

Morin, R. (2001, October 29-November 4). United States of mind. *Washington Post National Weekly Edition*, p. 35.

Morin, R., & Deane, C. (2001, September 28). Poll: Americans' trust in government grows. *Washington Post*, p. A3.

Morin, R., & Deane, C. (2002, September 16-22). From crisis, growth and change. *Washington Post National Weekly Edition*, p. 34.

Mosk, M. (2002, August 22). Audit finds lapses in Maryland child care. *Washington Post*, p. A1.

Neuman, R., Just, M., & Crigler, A. (1992). *Common knowledge: News and the construction of political meaning*. Chicago: University of Chicago Press.

Newhagen, J. (1994). Self-efficacy and media uses as predictors of current events knowledge. *Journalism Educator*, Autumn, 27-32.

Passell, P. (1998, January 5). Doing the American-opposition-to-big-government 2-step. *New York Times*, p. D10.

Pear, R. (1999, October 3). Nonprofit groups accused of bilking lunch program. *New York Times*, pp. A1, A34.

Pear, R. (2002, August 8). A study finds children's aid goes to adults. *New York Times*. Retrieved August 9, 2002 from: http://www.nytimes.com/2002/08/08/politics/08CHIL.html.

Pear, R., & Toner, R. (2003, March 5). Bush medicare proposal urges switch to private insurers. New York Times. Retrieved March 6, 2003 from http://www.nytimes.com/2003/03/05/politics/05MEDI.html.

Phillips, K. (2002, July 17). The cycles of financial scandal. *New York Times*. Retrieved July 17, 2002 from: http://www.nytimes.com/2002/07/17/opinion.17PHIL.html.

Planin, E. (2002, February 3). Bush to seek deep cuts in domestic programs. *Washington Post*, p. A1.

Pristin, T. (2000, November, 29). Suit alleges major housing fraud against U.S. by Brooklyn charity. *New York Times*, pp. B1, B10.

"Pushing privatization too far." (1995, January 27). *Boston Globe*, p. 16.

Rosenheck, R., Armstrong, M., Callahan, D., Dea, R., Del Vecchio, P., Flynn, L., Fox, R.C., Goldman, H.H., Horvath, T., & Munoz, R. (1998). Obligation to the least well off in setting mental health service priorities: A consensus statement. *Psychiatric Services*, *49*(10), 1273-1274, 1290.

Rubin, A., & Babbie, E. (2001). *Research methods for social work*, 4th ed. Belmont, CA: Wadsworth.

Salmon, J.L. (2002a, September 9). Nonprofits show losses in the public's trust. *Washington Post*, p. A2.

Salmon, J.L. (2002b, September 16-22). For charities, a loss of trust. *Washington Post National Weekly Edition*, p. 10.

Salmon, J.L. (2002c, September 21). United Way could lose major drive. *Washington Post*, p. B1.

Salmon, J.L. (2002d, September 28). United Way to delay severance deal. *Washington Post*, p. B1.

Savas, E.S. (2000). *Privatization and public-private partnerships.* New York: Chatham House.

Scharfstein, J. (2001). Unhealthy partnership: How Massachusetts and its managed care contractor shortchange troubled children. *Health Letter, 17*(2), 1-4.

Schmid, H. (2001). Nonprofit organizations and for-profit organizations providing home care services for the Israeli frail elderly: A comparative analysis. *International Journal of Public Administration, 24*(11), 1233-1265.

Schnapp, W.B., Bayles, S., Raffoul, P.R., & Schnee, S.B. (1999). Privatization and the rise and fall of the public mental health safety net. *Administration and Policy in Mental Health, 26*(3), 221-225.

Sharkey, J. (1999, June 6). Mental illness hits the money trail. *New York Times.* Retrieved June 7, 1999 from: http://www.nytimes.com/library/review/060699mental-healthcare-review.html.

Sharpe, A. (1997, January 24). Psyched up: More states turn over mental-health care to the private sector. *Wall Street Journal,* p. A1.

Shepard, C.E., & Miller, B. (1994, September 14). Former United Way chief is indicted in fund misuse. *Washington Post,* pp. A1, A8.

Simross, L. (1992, April 28). Charities in a bind. *Washington Post,* p. C5.

Smith, S.R., & Lipsky, M. (1993). *Nonprofits for hire: The welfare state in the age of contracting.* Cambridge, MA: Harvard University Press.

Stevenson, R.W. (2002, January 28). In a sign of changing times, Bush calls for more spending. *New York Times.* Retrieved February 3, 2002 from: http://www.nytimes.com/2002/01/28/politics/28BUDG.html.

Stevenson, R.W., & Eppel, R.A., Jr. (2002, July 17). Fed chief blames corporate greed as house revises fraud bill. *New York Times.* Retrieved August 2, 2002 from: http://www.nytimes.com/2002/07/17/business/17CONG.html.

Strom, S. (2002, June 5). Red Cross to open its books on aid after Sept. 11. *New York Times.* Retrieved June 7, 2002 from: http://www.nytimes.com/2002/06/05/nyregion/05CROS.html.

"Summary of Welfare Reforms Made by Public Law 104-193." (2001). Ways and Means Committee Print WMCP: 104-15. U.S. Government Printing Office. Retrieved November 19, 2001 from: http://www.access.gpo.gov/congress/wm015.txt.

"The confidence crisis." (2002, July 21). Editorial. New York Times. Retrieved July 22, 2002 from: http://www.nytimes.com/2002/07/21/opinion/21SUN1.html.

"The past as prelude." (2002, May 26). Editorial. *New York Times.* Available: http://www.NYTimes.com/2002/05/26/opinion/26SUN1.html.

"The perils of for-profit care." (2000, January 15). *Boston Globe,* p. A14.

Torrey, E. F. (1998). Is for-profit managed care an oxymoron? *Psychiatric Services, 49*(4), 415.

"United Way and Mr. Aramony." (1994, September 17). Editorial. *Washington Post,* p. A14.

Vigoda, R. (2002, May 30). Montgomery County, PA, Health company settles false-billing case. *Knight Ridder Tribune Business News,* p. 1.

Webster, K. (1999, August 4).Study: For-profit hospitals drive up overall med care spending. *Boston Globe.* Retrieved September 2, 1999 from: http://www.boston.com/news/daily/04/profithospitals.htm.

Whoriskey, P. & Salmon, J.L. (2002a, June 14). Charity criticized for withholding excessive funds. *Washington Post*, p. B1.

Whoriskey, P., & Salmon, J.L. (2002b, September 6). United Way CEO quits as charity is recast. *Washington Post*, p. A1.

Williams, G. (2001, November 1). Turmoil at the Red Cross. *Chronicle of Philanthropy*, p. 1.

Young, V. (2002, January 29). Authorities may close U. city nursing home; funds are unaccounted for, but operators dispute audit. *St. Louis-Post Dispatch*, p. B1.

Flameout at the Top–
Executive Calamity in the Nonprofit Sector:
Its Precursors and Sequelae

John E. Tropman, PhD
H. Luke Shaefer, PhD

SUMMARY. This paper deals with the issue of nonprofit executive problematics, which can be defined as behaviors that executives engage in that cause harm to themselves and their organizations such as inappropriate personal use of agency resources, embezzlement, and sexual acting out. It expands the study of "derailment" by exploring cases where through their misbehavior executives do extensive damage to themselves, their families, and their agencies. The paper will explore contributing personal causes as well as those inherent in both the formal and informal organizational structures of nonprofit organizations, and identify possible solutions. In many cases, such causes stem from an executive's strengths that become weaknesses when over applied, especially in conditions where the executive is used to success (hence a predisposition to continue using the strength), has no observing ego (and hence is

---

John E. Tropman is Professor, Management of Human Services Sequences, University of Michigan School of Social Work, and Adjunct Professor of Organizational Behavior and Human Resources Development, University of Michigan Business School. H. Luke Shaefer is completing his PhD at the School of Social Service Administration, University of Chicago.

[Haworth co-indexing entry note]: "Flameout at the Top–Executive Calamity in the Nonprofit Sector: Its Precursors and Sequelae." Tropman. John E., and H. Luke Shaefer. Co-published simultaneously in *Administration in Social Work* (The Haworth Social Work Practice Press, an imprint of The Haworth Press, Inc.) Vol. 28, No. 3/4, 2004, pp. 161-182; and: *Organizational and Structural Dilemmas in Nonprofit Human Service Organizations* (ed: Hillel Schmid) The Haworth Social Work Practice Press, an imprint of The Haworth Press, Inc., 2004, pp. 161-182. Single or multiple copies of this article are available for a fee from The Haworth Document Delivery Service [1-800-HAWORTH, 9:00 a.m. - 5:00 p.m. (EST). E-mail address: docdelivery@haworthpress.com].

http://www.haworthpress.com/web/ASW
Digital Object Identifier: 10.1300/J147v28n03_08

poor at self control), and controls a weak board (hence external controls are limited). The study of executive problematics, especially the most egregious cases, is of the utmost importance because in the nonprofit sector, when a chief executive engages in any form of problematic behavior, it reflects badly not only upon his or her own organization, but upon the sector and even to the philanthropic and social service world as a whole. *[Article copies available for a fee from The Haworth Document Delivery Service: 1-800-HAWORTH. E-mail address: <docdelivery@haworth press.com> Website: <http://www.HaworthPress.com> © 2004 by The Haworth Press, Inc. All rights reserved.]*

KEYWORDS. Executive directors, nonprofit sector, executive derailment, governance

INTRODUCTION

This special volume considers organizational and structural dilemmas of nonprofit human service organizations. This paper deals with the issue of executive problematics, which can be defined as behaviors that executives engage in that cause harm to themselves and their organizations. Such problematics take a wide variety of forms and include mismanagement; inappropriate personal use of agency resources; and more harmful activities like verbal or physical abuse of staff, embezzlement, and, commonly, sexual acting out. A good deal of scholarly work has been undertaken to examine these problems in both the governmental and for-profit sectors, but less attention has been paid to these issues in nonprofit human services organizations. Such study is of the utmost importance because in the nonprofit sector, when a chief executive engages in any form of problematic behavior, it reflects badly not only upon his or her own organization, but on the movement or field in which he or she is engaged as a whole. This paper explores executive problematics, which can be categorized into four major types or stages: detours; periderailment; derailment; and the most harmful, flameout/calamities. Because they are by far the most harmful, the most attention will be paid to flameout/calamities.

We proceed within a framework of understanding that, while there may be some exceptions, most CEOs of charitable organizations come to their positions with good intentions and a desire to benefit their organization and constituents. Therefore, although personal faults play some part, there must also be some external causes that lead to these problematics. This paper will explore contributing personal causes as well as those inherent in both the formal and informal organizational structures of nonprofit organizations, and identify possible solutions. Furthermore, we argue that these structural causes make nonprofit human service organizations at least as likely to suffer from serious executive problematics including flameout/calamity as their counterparts in the governmental and for-profit sectors. This is a serious problem that must be addressed by human services organizations, and the field as a whole.

SOURCES AND METHOD

As we have already stressed, this particular field is new to research, and so the purpose of this paper is to open a dialogue on the subject and expand the field of "derailment" research. Among other valuable references, we will draw on two important works. The first is Van Velsor and Leslie's seminal work on executive derailment, "Why executives derail: Perspectives across time and cultures" in the *Academy of Management Executives* (1995). We will draw heavily on their work in our discussion of that topic and adapt it to the nonprofit sector. Also important is John Glasser's authoritative account of the well-known United Way of America scandal that ended in the firing and imprisonment of William Aramony (Glaser, 1994).[1] That work provides many insights into the flawed structural causes that allowed that particular scandal to "flameout" in such a spectacular and public manner. In this paper, as we examine other such incidents in similar organizations, it becomes apparent that these causes are indicative and suggestive of the field of causes.

Finally, over the past several years–beginning in 1993–the senior author has collected articles from the *New York Times*, the *Wall Street Journal*, and other papers that detail the stories of executives who have "flamed out." It is a purposive sample. This is certainly not a comprehensive list of "calamatarians" (by any means). In fact, as the authors have discussed this subject with colleagues and students, it seems almost everyone has an example–often several examples–to share of such an incident. This particular sample includes over 75 incidents, and of them, eight are from the nonprofit sector (social agencies, churches, schools, etc.) and illustrate the issues. The list is displayed in Figure A and includes synopses of the original articles.

EXECUTIVE PROBLEMATICS

Executive problematics is our phrase for troubling, difficult, harmful, inappropriate behavior on the part of the CEO of an agency or members of her or his top team. It includes executive detours, periderailment, derailment, and flameout. While problematics include a wide variety of specific behaviors

FIGURE A. Executive Calamities

Name	Initial Year of Issue	Position Held	What Happened?	What Was the Outcome?	Sources
Bill Aramony	April, 1995	President, United Way	Bill Aramony resigned from United Way of America (UWA) under allegations that he conspired to defraud UWA.	On April 3, 1995, Mr. Aramony was convicted in the U.S. District Court for the Eastern District of Virginia on 25 counts, including: conspiracy, fraud, and filling false tax returns. He was sentenced to 84 months in prison and fined $300,000.	(Glasser, 1994)
Vincent Buccirosso	August, 1996	President, Washtenaw County United Way	Vincent Buccirosso was accused of misappropriating funds.	Buccirosso voluntarily resigned from his position and the Ann Arbor police then launched an investigation into alleged financial irregularities at the Washtenaw United Way.	(George1996), (Opal, 1996, 1997a,b,c,d)
Edward Crouch	December 1, 1993	President of Sheet Metal Workers Union	Crouch abused his power, developed a drug problem, and was accused of lavish spending and abuse of union tab.	Crouch was forced to resign from his position after a three-day internal trial found that "he had used the union's $27 million coffers, generated by the highest dues in the building trades, to create a personal fief for lavish living at a time when unemployment among members of his union had hit a staggering 25%." The internal committee also had an additional 82 charges mostly focusing on Mr. Crouch unauthorized use of the union credit card. Following his resignation, the Union is now under new leadership that is trying to cut spending. All spending over $100,000 had to be approved by the council.	(Salwen, 1993)
Ellen Cook	April 11, 1997	Executive Director of United Way Pottawatomie, Oklahoma	Cook accused of misappropriations of United Way funds.	Ellen Cook was fired from her position. George Cook, President of the United Way stated that "We know that the campaign pledges that we publicized the past four years were exaggerated," and the United Way has been allocating more money that it has actually received. The FBI got involved and is researching the misapplication of the agency's funds.	(Billington, 1997)
Frank Hudson	August, 2000	Catholic Charities Chief	Frank Hudson used charity money to pay for expensive meals and cosmetic procedures.	Frank Hudson resigned as chief executive office of Catholic Charities of San Francisco after the board condemned him for his extravagant spending in restaurants and on cosmetic surgery. He spent close to $73,000 of the charity's money on personal expenses.	(Zoellner, 2000)
Lewis Hickson	June 15, 2001	Executive Director of Capuchin Soup Kitchen, Detroit, MI	Lewis Hickson was accused of embezzlement from the charity.	Hickson, the ex-Soup Kitchen Chief Executive, received 14 months in prison and had to repay hundreds of thousands of dollars he stole from the charity.	(Audi, 2001)

Louis Spisto	July 25, 2001	Director of the American Ballet Theatre	Louis Spisto resigned after high staff turnovers, hostile work environment, and financial troubles.	Spisto was hired in October 2002 as Executive Director of The Globes Theatre in San Diego, CA. The American Ballet Theater hired Wallace Chappell to be its next Executive Director in October 2001, although as of August 2002 a new Executive Director was hired: Elizabeth Kehler.	(Carvajal, 2001), (Riedel, 2001)
Norman Taylor	September 1, 2002	Chief Executive of United Way, National Capital Area	Accused of financial mismanagement, excessive compensations, and impeding oversight that were threatening to hurt the organization's beneficiaries.	Taylor resigned after the United Way's board of directors approved a complete transformation of the charity, cutting its budget and staff, and revamping all of its financial systems including completing an audit of the organization and eliminating staff perks such as cell phones and credit cards.	(Whoriskey & Salmon, 2002) (Strom, Senator Questions Finances of United Way, 2002), (Strom, Washington United Way to Select New Board, 2002) (Salmon, 2002) (Johnson, 2002)

165

(substance abuse and criminal activities such as embezzlement, physical acting out, sexual harassment, etc.), one important attribute they all share is that they always stem from a point of cause; these incidents "don't just happen." The cause may be a particular event, but more likely includes a set of factors that leads up to the state in which the executive engages in harmful behavior. This is why Figure B shows all stages of problematic coming from that point. Later on, we will discuss what comes *before* that point, but for now we concentrate on the *after*. It is also important to note that the four stages of problematics can develop from one another, until they reach the most harmful, flameout/calamity.

One important goal of human services organizations' governance is to recognize lower-stage problematics and prevent escalation and the eventual total unraveling of the executive, which we call flameout (or, in mental health parlance, executive decompensation). An obvious example of this might be a board member who becomes aware that the CEO has developed a drinking problem and wants the CEO to seek treatment. But as a group, the board engages in "defensive routines" and chooses not to say anything (and not to say anything about not saying anything) because the board feels that the executive brings great worth to the organization. So, in spite of the inappropriate behavior, the board allows the problem to escalate to a potentially more public and harmful crisis situation later on. Figure B shows the stages in such an escalation.

DETOURS AND PERIDERAILMENT

Executives and CEOs in organizations lose their way all the time. Many who lose their way remain busy but not in strategic ways. Some executives spend endless amounts of time on their in-box. One executive we have worked with communicates with his staff only by re-sending e-mail messages he re-

FIGURE B. Stages of Executive Problematics

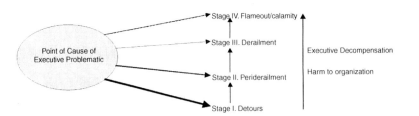

ceives from official sources. Others occupy themselves with meaningless meetings, called "rearranging deck chairs on the titanic." Still others travel constantly, and are seemingly never "there." They are called MIAs (Missing in Action!). We classify executives engaged in these types of behaviors as "detourees" and they are in stage I of executive decompensation. They are going somewhere but know not where.

Many executives take detours at some point during their tenure, but find their course again after a short period. Others fail to find their course and continue with detours for extended periods of time. As a result, they cause increasing harm to their agency and find themselves in stage II, called periderailment. Unfortunately, as with minor detours, organizations and especially boards find it hard to identify periderailment because executives have latitude in how they do their job, and so many times it is unclear whether they are on course or not. For that reason, lost executives in this stage can be, and frequently are, promoted. However, even when boards are aware of the problematic, many times they fail to act in the agency's best interest for a variety of reasons we will discuss later on. In these cases, the problematic executive is usually just passed over for promotion, and remains in the job for as long as allowed. Such inappropriate retention can prove very costly and damaging to the organization.

DERAILMENT

Sometimes organizations do confront problematic executives. Often when there is a significant change in board leadership, the executive is finally fired or reprimanded. This is called derailment and is stage III in executive decompensation. Usually, derailed executives are shocked. As one consultant the senior author knows says, "Most of the people going into the bosses' office to be fired think that they are being promoted!"

A good amount of scholarly work has been done on derailment and the reasons for it. The most extensive work was done by Van Velsor and Leslie (1995). They explored a range of causes of executive derailment, and we have organized them into two groups: precipitating/catalytic and predisposing/ antecedent.

Precipitating/catalytic causes are publicly obvious problems and have something to do with a specific personal behavior of the derailed executive. They can include ethical breeches, betrayals of trust, and specific behavioral issues such as substance abuse or sexual acting out. In many instances, these breeches were "tolerated" by the organization because the "perp" was powerful and often clever at covering his tracks until something changed in the environment around him that brought more attention to the behavior. A "catalytic agent" is sometimes needed to crystallize the precipitating event(s). For example, a new employee who is not co-opted by norms of "toleration" "blows the whistle." In some cases, detailed allegations of executive misbehavior are sent to the press, and the resulting publicity forces a previously reluctant board to act. Another example is an executive's failure to adapt to a new boss's approach and style. This difficulty can be "exasperated" (as one of my students put it) if the new CEO got a job that one or more of the remaining subordinates expected to and or hoped to get.

Predisposing causes are a bit more complex. They include organizational, interpersonal, and intrapersonal elements. Organizational ones include failure to build a team and delegate, failure to think strategically, over-reliance on a narrow circle of advisors, and failure to know the business and deliver results. Interpersonal ones include abrasive style, which is problematic in and of itself, and drives away employees and others with information to share. Intrapersonal ones include low emotional intelligence quotient and thus a failure to manage one's own emotions.[2] Not infrequently executives here are "burned out" or "burning out." It is important to intervene while their burnout is "mild" and they have not "ignited" others around them. More often than not, such intervention does not occur.[3]

Derailed executives often wind up losing their jobs, and while bad, losing the job at this point can often be a wake-up call, sort of like a "mild" heart attack. Derailment happens before any major, lasting damage has been done to the executive and organization. And as bad as the problems of derailment are, they pale in comparison to flameout/calamity.

FLAMEOUT/CALAMITY

Flameout/calamity is more flagrant, more public, and more costly than derailment over a range of dimensions and venues to the agency, and hence is a special, post derailment stage. It refers to a destructive episode in which a senior executive loses, or almost loses, his position in a spectacular way that includes but greatly exceeds self-harm. It usually occurs because derailment did not occur, and the executive is permitted to act in ways that produces a conflagration that consumes both him and others. (Baumeister, 1997). Such occurrences generate very harmful or fatal effects for the individual, his family, his coworkers, the agency, and even the movement of which the agency is a part.[4]

The "flameout" part refers to the personal condition of the executive that allows him to engage in self-destructive behaviors that any rational person would know were extremely inappropriate. The "calamity" part addresses the issues of fallout, "blast impact," occurring at the time of the implosion and down the line. It means that the correlative costs are huge to all those around the flame, and many far away from it as well. It is the fourth and final stage of executive decompensation.

There are many well-known examples of this most harmful stage. They include President Clinton's impeachment scandal, the current crisis in the Catholic Church, where arguably both the perpetrating priests and the Church hierarchy have "flamed out," and the demise of Enron, a firm that will always be remembered as a temple for executive enrichment at the expense of shareholders, employees, and the country at large. (One could add from the for-profit sector Global Crossing and Health South.) A recent screaming headline "Chief Justice's Daughter Lands in Hot Seat" provides one good example (Lueck, 2002). In her position as Inspector General of the Department of Human Services, Janet Rehnquist (daughter of Supreme Court Chief Justice William Rehnquist) exhibits executive behavior that is deeply problematic, including a volatile management style. Many civil servants in her office have left precipitously–"People have been asked to leave . . . with little or no notice." She once called from a local airport and yelled at a secretary because her ticket had no seat assignment. She kept an unloaded gun in her office and hung a target on the wall. Her behavior has gone on so long (without derailment) that she now faces a possible Congressional hearing initiated by Senator Charles Grassley (R. Iowa). She recently resigned to spend more time with her family.

While these are a few national examples, for each one of them, there are numerous local example in all fields, such as the legislators in Wisconsin who are being indicted for fraud as discussed by Michael Feldman (2002) in "Clean State, Dirty Politicians."

EXECUTIVE FLAMEOUT/CALAMITY IN THE NONPROFIT HUMAN SERVICE SECTOR

In the nonprofit sector, there are far too many examples of executive flameout/calamity. Probably the best documented example is William Aramony of the United Way of America, who was forced to leave his position after the *Washington Post* printed an article that detailed his $463,000 compensation package and other personal benefits, and he was eventually imprisoned. In San Francisco, Frank Hudson, the chief executive officer of Catholic Charities, was forced to resign after it was found that he had spent close to $73,000 of the charity's money on personal expenses, including cosmetic surgery (Zoellner, 2000). And for a final example, there is Edward Carlough, former president of the Sheet Metal Workers Union, who developed a drug problem and spent an exorbitant amount of money on personal expenses while unemployment among members of his union was at 25 percent (Salwen, 1993). All of these examples illustrate the disastrous nature of executive flameout/calamity. The dire consequences of such crises, for all parties involved, make obvious the need for further study into the causes of such incidents, and possible methods of prevention.

CAUSES OF EXECUTIVE FLAMEOUT/CALAMITY

With a definition of executive flameout/calamity and an understanding of its serious consequences, we turn to the obvious question: What could cause individuals to act in such ways? In many cases the picture is not an unvarnished one at all. For the most part, when dealing with this final stage of executive decompensation, we are not talking about "loser" executives who make no contribution; rather we are looking at people of talent who somehow go "astray." Many times, as with William Aramony, these individuals are considered by those around them to be "great leaders" before they flameout. Indeed, many, as was the case with Aramony, *are* great leaders. They just have a "dark side." Great leaders, when they go askew, do great damage.

As stated earlier in this paper, obviously personal choice and personal responsibility on the part of the executive plays some part. In "My Fair Lady," a musical from the mid 1950s, there is a song about "temptation." "When temptation comes I'll give right in" is a refrain that seems to resonate well today. At the beginning of the 21st century, many important senior managers of organizations seem to have done just that.

However, the incidents of executive flameout/calamity are myriad, and personal faults can only account for so much. In the human services sector, there is even more reason to look for other explanations, given that nonprofit executives might be considered less prone to act out inappropriately than their counterparts in other sectors.

With that in mind, we turn to the causes inherent within the formal and informal organizational structures of nonprofit human service agencies. To identify these causes, it proves helpful to use as a framework the *Five C Theory of Organizational Analysis* (Tropman, 1998)–Characteristics, Competencies, Conditions, Contexts, and Change. This perspective, developed by the senior author (Tropman & Morningstar, 1989; Tropman, 1998) helps to organize the various categories of factors that affect executives. As exhibited in Figure C, the Five C's can all contribute to executive problematics, and within each of these categories, we will explore the specific role that organizational structures plays.

FIGURE C. Causes of and Stages of Executive Problematics

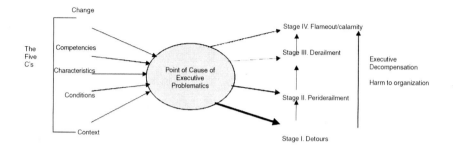

Conditions refers to the substructure and subculture of the agency itself. Context refers to the structures and cultures outside of the agency–in the industry, community and/or society. Characteristics refers to the personal attributes and temperament of the executive. Competencies refers to the skill sets that the executive brings to his job. Obviously, both characteristics and competencies are primarily aspects of the individual. However, we list them here in an effort to emphasize the organizational structure's components that can have an effect on these two "C's," i.e., nonprofits (along with organizations in other fields) tend to hire executives with certain characteristics and competencies, and the characteristics that executives take on as a result of the type of work they do. These structural aspects within the "C's" in turn play an important role in executive problematics. And the final C is Change, which refers to the inevitable process of alterations and transformations that executives and agencies need to go through over time.

CONDITIONS AND CONTEXT

Two elements that prove extremely important in understanding executive problematics are the substructure and subculture of the organization, referred to in the Five Cs as conditions; and the dominant culture and structure outside the organization in the movement or field, referred to as context. The two are undeniably linked to each other, and are both essential to truly understand the causes of problematics.

Conditions–Organizational Substructure: The substructure of the organization refers, in this case, to the control structures that can operate to rein in an executive. Such behaviors refer to things like expenditure limits (how much the executive can spend on his own authority) and other limits on executive behavior such as accessorizing, office décor, travel, etc. For the most part, where there is a problem of executive excess, there is a problem of inadequate organizational control and CEO governance. Sometimes the executive has co-opted the board though a process of "appointments management" over the years (Waldo, 1986). Nonprofit executives do not have the largess of contracts and other perks that are available to corporate executives, but there can still be a process of co-optation.

A very good example of "conditions" as a primary cause of flameout/calamity is the hiring, and later firing, of Norman Taylor as chief executive of the United Way of the National Capitol Area. A large article on the calamity appeared in the *New York Times* on September 3, 2002. The article reported that the appointment of Mr. Taylor, who had been relieved of a similar job in Baltimore in 1995, was "orchestrated" by his predecessor, who then was awarded a consulting contract (Johnson, 2002). This incident shows that the board was problematic in hiring an improperly vetted executive. Furthermore, while in office, Mr. Taylor forced several of his critics off the board and was never held accountable. Both these conditional elements opened the door for Mr. Taylor's problematic behavior while in the position. As another *New York Times* article reports, that United Way is currently under investigation for serious financial irregularities.

Another "condition" element in executive problematics has been the structural changes in the titles of the executives, and more subtly, the expectations that go along with them. For many years, "executive director" was the respected title of the boss of a nonprofit human service organization. That title was itself an elevation from the historic "executive secretary" or "general secretary." But then there was some status envy we think, in comparison with the corporate sector. While corporate executives were envious of the compensation of movie stars and sports figures, nonprofit executives became envious of the rapidly rising situation of their corporate compeers. They argued that since they mainly interacted with "other presidents" they themselves should have the title of president. That trend is well under way, and will, we think, continue. Presented as a "nominal shift," this change in nomenclature in fact carried with it subtle, but real, expectations of "presidential treatment." These expectations, while somewhat undefined, were nonetheless much grander than that which would be accorded an "executive director."

Context–Organizational and Movement Subculture: Organizations vary in the extent to which their values permit executives to live large or live modestly (Malloy & Agarwal, 2001). Nonprofit organizations generally have a penurious and impecunious mindset. Their notion is that they are service organizations, custodians of the public trust. Executives want to do good rather than do well and their employees are similar. However, over time, those norms have become altered. For one thing, as corporate and governmental compensation increased, to a degree it has also pulled up nonprofit executive compensation. The general fear of boards was that the sector could not get too far behind or they would lose good people. And not only did salaries increase, but you began to see nonprofit CEOs in Jaguars (after all, it is a "Ford"). The boards, mostly businesspeople themselves, were apparently not deeply troubled by this trend. And of course the board is the group that hired the problematic executive in the first place. In the Washington case above, raising a question would be, of course, raising a question about their own judgment. Naturally that acts to forestall calling problematic executive behavior to account, and explains why, in many cases, boards stonewall for a while before being almost literally forced, through massive public disclosure, to "fess up." In an example local to the authors, the local paper, the *Ann Arbor News*, had received letters alleging executive wrongdoing in the local United Way chapter in the spring. It repeatedly tried to get information from the board, which stonewalled until fall, when the News published an "expose" on the front page. Still, after that, the board was unwilling to engage the issue publicly until the pressure became too intense (George, 1996).

Another "context" element that can lead to executive problematics in human services agencies is the very difficulty of their mission as well as knotty complexity of the issues with which they deal. Indeed, one might expect that nonprofits would be more likely to experience flameouts. Rittel and Webber (1973) address this issue, calling the tremendously complex problems that these organizations face "wicked problems," which include poverty, drug abuse, crime, domestic violence, sexual abuse, and a myriad of other terrible issues. Each of these and others point to a set of difficulties that are especially unique to a particular package of problems. The senior author discusses them in detail in *Policy Management in the Human Services* (Tropman, 1984, p. 32-33). If executives deal with wicked problems all day long, one might expect detours, periderailment, derailment, and calamity. A few elements are as follows:

1. There is no definitive formulation of a wicked problem, so it can be very hard to understand;
2. Wicked problems have no stopping rule;
3. Solutions to wicked problems are not true or false, but good or bad;
4. There is no immediate and no ultimate test of a solution to a wicked problem;
5. Every solution to a wicked problem is a "one-shot operation," because there is no opportunity to learn by trial and error, every attempt counts significantly (and sometimes your first error can be your last trial!);

6. Wicked problems have an innumerable (rather than exhaustible and describable) set of potential solutions; there is not a well-described set of permissible operations that may be incorporated into the plan;
7. Every wicked problem is essentially unique;
8. Every wicked problem can be considered a symptom of another problem;
9. The existence of a discrepancy representing a wicked problem can be explained in numerous ways. The choice of explanation determines the nature of the problem's resolution;
10. The planner (we would say executive) has no right to be wrong; and
11. The constant pressure of human problems and the limited ability to be as helpful as one would like are factors as well.

Adding to this set of pressures, however, there is the presence of "higher expectations" of nonprofit executives, relating to the service purpose of their mission. The "higher purpose" or "civic purpose" of organizations–nonprofit social service agencies, churches, philanthropies, etc., may create a stress of its own. Somehow one hopes that organizations established to serve the community and help others, organizations set up to offer religious services, and so on would hold to a higher standard. These higher expectations are problematic in their own right, and, in addition, may add even more problems because their stakeholders, tending to think of nonprofits and their staff as "more pure" than corporate executives, are less vulnerable to the range of human venalities available. It is likely that nonprofit executives and boards have this view of themselves. If so, the staff and governance structure may be less robust and have fewer social/organizational controls which need, apparently, to be always in place and always working. Hence, when it comes to the context elements, human service organizations may well have more difficulties, higher pressures of expectations, and fewer social controls than either governmental or corporate America.

CHARACTERISTICS

People who get to the top of organizations, whatever the organization is, have needs for power and control. This is not a bad thing. These needs drive and motivate each of us to some degree. Success, however, brings its own problems. One of these problems is the pressure to repeat the success, and to have even more success. Some examples specific to nonprofits include the need for more public personal recognition and bigger programs (many times at the expense of other initiatives). For some executives the very achievement of success taints it. Accomplishment provides no satisfaction. Groucho Marx once said that he would not like to be a member of any club that would accept him. No matter how much one achieves, it is never enough. For these individuals, and individuals like them, the continual push for more can lead to flameout. There are a number of specific ways that executives' problematic behaviors grow as a result of success and the need for success.

From Self Confidence to Overconfidence: Successful executives believe in themselves, tend not to listen to others, push their own agenda, can convince others to join them, and are behavioral trendsetters rather than followers. They are ambitious, enjoy power, and like to run things. All of the "flameout" executives used as examples so far in this paper share a majority of these traits. The problem is that getting to the top, and being at the top, are not the same job. The characteristics that help one get to the top may, at the top, become dysfunctional. Overbelief in self, not listening, pushing personal agendas, ambition for self, and power absorption all need an "off switch" at the top. If all of them are running, the executive becomes isolated, ill informed, and increasingly likely to act problematically. One illustration of this is an organization that had a phrase called "LSD" as part of its argot. It came from the fact that there was an executive named "Larry" and LSD meant "Larry Says Do it."

From Challenge to Stroking: We all need reassurance (stroking) that we are "doing a good job." The riskier and the lonelier the job, and the greater need for success, the more reassurance people need. Up to the top job, reassurance comes from moving up the ladder. At the top, uncertainty increases and reassurance becomes even more rare. The ratio of challenge to ideas and reassurance about those idea shifts to reassurance. The top staff soothes rather than criticizes. Executives also may resort to reassuring themselves through substance abuse (drinking, drugging), financial abuse (the reassurance of big bucks; "if I am rich I must be good"), and sexual abuse (the aphrodisiac of power is exchanged for sexual access/favors). In one example of this, an organization the senior author knows, was looking always for the "Low Cost Alternative" or LCO. However, it had an executive named "Olsen" who was at the same time making substantial compensation. LCO came to mean "Let's Compensate Olsen."

From Side Kick to Sycophant: Related to the point on reassurance, many executives have a "sidekick"–someone with whom they were very close, who could make them listen. That could be a spouse or partner, or someone at the office. The sidekick position is a perilous one, because she or he not only needs to be honest with yet wary of the boss, but others in the organization resent her or his access, and may try to socially undermine the sidekick. For one reason or another they often leave the organization, and the last voice of restraint is cut. They are replaced with "clones," individuals just like the executive. Even worse is "sycophantic cloning," in which the associates are not only like the executive, but groveling, supportive, and complimentary as well. If you come into your agency and say good morning, and the reply is "Good point!" you know you are in trouble.

From We to Me: Working in organizations requires working through others, and with others. The higher you go, the more you may experience a diminishment of the "we" and the enhancement of the "me." These are called attribution problems; self-attribution becomes more important than ever. You may feel that you are making all the key decisions and everyone else is just a peon. There is a story about an organizational researcher who did a study of an organization of many levels. This researcher asked one question, "If there were really no technical problems with technology, at what point do you think that this firm could be completely automated and computerized?" The answer, from all levels, was the same: "Below me." Narcissism may also be a characteristic. Perhaps there really is no "we to me"; it may have always been about me. (Readers may recall the joke about the narcissist talking with an acquaintance: "Well, enough about me; what do you think about me?") Executives who flame out may always have been heavily self-interested but concealed it or worked with it until they became the top person.

From Observing Ego to Feedback Deafness: People at the top often come to have inflated and skewed ideas about their own prowess and importance. The observing ego is that part of our ego that watches our own behavior and makes appropriate adjustments to keep ourselves on a more or less steady path. Think of driving as an example. As we drive, we are constantly alert for other drivers, pedestrians, animals, weather, etc., and adjusting our driving behavior. Someone who does not do these things, who bulldozes ahead regardless, is a great danger on the road, and in the organization. They experience a sense that it is "my way or the highway." Virtuoso performance becomes solo performance.

From Substance to Substance Abuse: In many cases these executives–persons of substance to be sure–became substance abusers. Excessive use of substances–alcohol and drugs–is something that one sees in many cases. All to often, "persons of substance" become "persons full of a substance." There are of course issues here about executive lifestyle and the difficulties of controlling diet, getting adequate rest, and working out regularly, etc., when one moves through the day from power breakfasts to power dinners.

From Need to Greed: Individuals in the nonprofit sector are not rewarded with the handsome financial packages of the for-profit sector. Yet within the sector boundaries, greed takes over in some cases. The Enron example is one from the corporate world, and there are hundreds of others.

From At the Top to Over the Top: The problems executives face when they get to the top (or very near the top within their respective divisions) is that they move from the skein of control that limited their behavior to minimal control.

Indeed, the path to the top of the organization is one of decreasing external and increasing internal controls. At the CEO level, there is the board of directors, but we have seen (and we will discuss) the fact that boards seem to be unable to develop a *modus operandi* to deal with the executives. For-profit boards have both inside and outside directors, making board control of the executive even more difficult since the "controlees" are on the board themselves. Nonprofits have outside directors only, although there is a movement to have the CEO be a member of the board, a trend that we would see as continuing and expanding. Executives thus become, effectively, the only controller of their own behavior until something really awful happens. It is at this point that some at the top go over the top.

COMPETENCIES

Oddly–or perhaps not so oddly–some of the very competency traits that make an executive successful become slightly altered at the top, leading to problems. They are good at convincing others; they are good at getting their way; they are good at organizing (Light, 2002). These competencies are fantastic when turned toward the success of one's family, community, and organization. When turned toward self-aggrandizement, these selfsame skills have the ability to enrich the self and avoid or deal with challenge to their behavior. The skills make detection difficult, confrontation problematic, and control truly daunting. These skills "gone wrong" or "applied inappropriately" are one of the precursors to flameout.

CHANGE

Change is a process that goes on all the time. Some change is rapid while some is slow. Each kind of change can impact the executive. Fast change may mean that the competencies that worked "only yesterday" are no longer viable, or as viable. Slow change means that differences in context sneak up on the executive, as no day of change is "enough" to take any decisive action.

STEPS TO PREVENTION

The incidents we have examined seem to be a combination of each of the C's. Executives who flame out have temperaments that embrace risk and grandiosity, and these temperaments most likely helped them get to the top.

Their skills both allow them to engage in problematic behavior and protect them from the consequences. The culture of the organizations both supports and perhaps encourages such behavior to a degree and the structure of the organization has insufficient social controls in place to prevent it until it is too late. No single factor seems plausibly responsible. Hence, a multifactor approach to change is appropriate. Thinking about two categories of intervention–Executive Responsibilities and Board Responsibilities–is a good way to go.

EXECUTIVE RESPONSIBILITIES

Executives need to take some personal responsibility for themselves and their potential for flameout. Much as a boxer must be aware that his hands are lethal weapons, the executive needs to realize that the very characteristics and competencies that lead him or her to be successful can also lead to destruction. Also, we all have a "dark side"–resentments, hurts, people we want to "get," and when power allows us to do that, who among us can say that we would turn the other cheek?

These potentials require personal reflection and self-examination, to be sure. But it also means that in leadership training centers, programs, and seminars the issues of derailment and flameout should be part of the curriculum. With the exception of the Center for Creative Leadership that explicitly deals with issues of derailment, and the Menninger Clinic that treats executives with issues, the area of executive problematics is very much unaddressed. Executives need to be provided with the tools for self-reflection (Denhardt, Denhardt, & Aristigueta, 2002). We suspect that the popularity of the field of "emotional intelligence" was developed in part because of this lacuna. Notwithstanding, executive training programs of most sorts are out of the reach of many, if not most, of the executives from the nonprofit world.[5]

However, that said, we are also aware of the limitations of self-awareness, however well resourced. No doubt those who need it most are among the least likely to apply self-reflection. Associates and small groups must play a role as well. A similar problem faced those involved in drinking and driving safety some years back. Readers will recall that there was a slogan something like "If you drink, don't drive." It seemed sensible, except that by the time drinkers got to the point where the slogan should apply, they were too drunk to notice. While it still is appropriate to have that admonition out there, other measures are needed. In the drinking driver case, changing the norms and empowering the drinker's network seemed to be the key. Hence, we now have the phrase "Friends don't let friends drive drunk." We think a similar empowerment of the executive's network is needed in this case. Partners, board members, associates, and those who interact regularly with executives should be culturally empowered to speak up and address the issues of self-derailment and flameout behavior. We must not wait for the crash.

BOARD RESPONSIBILITIES

At the structural level, boards need to be continually alert to the signs of derailment and flameout, and each board needs to set up a plan for executive review that includes derailment and flameout monitoring. This process should begin through boards training themselves in board responsibilities and procedures (Tropman & Tropman, 1999). Board training sessions need to address these issues, along with programs on how to read a financial statement. Our recommendation is that the large national agencies set up a Director Certification Program (sort of like the life saving program developed by the Red Cross). This program would define and assess qualifications for directorship, and within a period of years, perhaps five, all agencies would have to have individuals with this certification as their directors. In our professional opinion, we have long past the "citizen-board member" period, where "good citizens" "do good" by volunteering on the board, even though they really have no idea what they are to do. Nonprofit agencies were often started to do good; now they must do it well and do it right.

In particular, such training should stress the regular evaluation of the CEO. Many CEOs with whom the senior author has worked, in periderailment situations, have either had no yearly evaluation, or only one of the most perfunctory sort.

Nonprofit boards typically do not have audit committees (though their presence has not done much for many of the failed commercial organizations). It may be time to consider that agencies need such a board committee.

CONCLUSION

We all desire success, for ourselves and our organizations. Senior managers of nonprofit organizations are pushed to succeed, and are rewarded for succeeding. However success has its costs and one of them is exposure to derailment and flameout. Flameout especially is destructive for the person, his or her family, and for the agency and the industry.

Now we must continue to strive for success, but in this case, success also means being alert for signs of an impending calamity, and moving proactively to prevent such destruction. It means developing norms for executive self-regulation and board action that hold even the most energetic and inspiring nonprofit leaders accountable to their organizations long before they "flame out." This may prove just as hard as creating innovative programs or growing organizations because it goes against the very organizational structure that makes up most human services agencies, and more deeply, against our desires to trust charismatic leaders of social movements and view them as "more than human."

To be successful in this new endeavor we will need detailed research on the causes and patterns of calamity and flameout. Good theory and a rich understanding of causal dynamics always precede good intervention. While this paper provides a starting point, there is much more to do. And so we call for more research to build on the work done here and examine the causes of "flameout" and nonprofit executive problematics, and develop means of preventing such behaviors. The academic portion of this research should be done collaboratively, undertaken in concert with associations of executives and CEOs. This approach will yield both a deeper understanding of the problems as well as practical approaches to addressing them. Only through this research can we protect the missions of our organizations, the good work that so many nonprofit leaders have done, and most importantly, the individuals and families we serve.

NOTES

1. United Way of America is the "national" organization that supports "local" United Ways.

2. Emotional Intelligence is a growing concept pioneered by Daniel Goleman. For more, visit the Consortium for Research on Emotional Intelligence in Organizations at www.eiconsortium.org, and other sources online.

3. The "intervention" can be the reestablishment of "self-control" or the arrival of control by others.

4. Former President Clinton, for example, did not lose his job but caused great harm to his family and community, and to the Democratic party.

5. The nonprofit world is really two countries: rich countries like the University of Michigan, big foundations, big orchestras and museums, etc., and the remaining "smallish fry" like most human service organizations and thousands of others.

REFERENCES

Audi, T. (2002, October 25). Ex-soup kitchen chief gets jailed. *Detroit Free Press*, p. A01.

Baumeister, R. (1997). Esteem threat, self regulatory breakdown, and emotional distress as factors in self-defeating behavior. *Review of General Psychology*, 1 (2), 145-74.

Billington, J. (1997, April 11). United Way director fired: Allocations reduced. *Shawnee News-Star*

Carvajal, D. (2001, April 11). High staff turnover underlines offstage turmoil at ballet theater. *New York Times*, p. B1.

Denhardt, R. B., Denhardt J. V., & Aristigueta, M. P. (2002). *Managing human behavior in public and nonprofit organizations*. Thousand Oaks, CA: Sage Publications.

Feldman, M. (2002, October 24). Clean state, dirty politicians. *New York Times*, p. A31.

Feinberg, M., & Tarrant, J. J. (1995). *Why smart people do dumb things*. New York: Fireside.

George, M. (1996, August 31). United Way official quits Washtenaw: Faces money questions. *Detroit Free Press*, p. 3A.

Glasser, J. S. (1994). *An insider's account of the United Way scandal: What went wrong and why*. New York: John Wiley & Sons Inc.

Ingrassia, P., & Sterz, B. A. (1990, September 17). Mea culpa; With Chrysler ailing, Lee Iacocca concedes mistakes in managing; . . . I'm confessing my sins here. *Wall Street Journal*.

Johnson, D. (2002). United Way official knew about abuses, memo says. *New York Times*, p. A10.

Kets de Vries, M. (1988). *Unstable at the top*. New York: New American Library.

Light, P. C. (2002). *Pathways to nonprofit excellence*. Washington, D.C.: Brookings Institute.

Lueck, S. (2002, November 11). Chief justice's daughter lands in hot seat. *Wall Street Journal*, p. A4.

Malloy, D. C., & Agarwal, J. (2001). Ethical climate in nonprofit organizations: Propositions and implications. *Nonprofit Management and Leadership*, 12 p. 39-54.

Oppat, S. (1996, November 20). United Way officials embrace suggestions: Board members confident changes will be made to regain public confidence and strengthen organization. *Ann Arbor News*, p. A1.

Oppat, S. (1997a, February 28). Al Buccirosso will face three charges of fraud. *Ann Arbor News*, p. A1.

Oppat, S. (1997b, March 21). United Way looks for new president. *Ann Arbor News*, p. C1.

Oppat, S. (1997c, April 12). United Way allocation policy may change. *Ann Arbor News*, p. A5.

Oppat, S. (1997d, May 3). United Way auditors recommend improvements. *Ann Arbor News*, p. A1.

Strom, S. (2002, August 22). Senator questions finances of United Way. *New York Times*, p. A20.

Strom, S. (2002, October 4). Washington United Way to select new board. *New York Times*, p. A18.

Riedel, M. (2001, July 26). Ballet big in deep tutu quits. *New York Post*, p. 002.

Rittel, H., & Webber, M. (1973). Dilemmas in a general theory of planning. *Policy Sciences*, (July), 4 (2), 155-169.

Salmon, J. (2002, October 19). Nominees sought for all-new United Way board; In wake of scandals, panel hoping to make 'clean sweep.' *Washington Post*, p. B01.

Salwen, K. (1993, December 1). The fast lane how lavish spending brought down head of sheet metal union. *Wall Street Journal*, p. 1.

Tropman, J. (1984). *Policy management in the human services*. New York: Columbia University Press.

Tropman, J., & Tropman, E. (1999). *Nonprofit boards: What to do and how to do it.* Washington Child Welfare League of America.

Tropman, J., & Morningstar, G. (1989). *Entrepreneurial systems for the 1990s.* Westport, CT: Quorum.

Tropman, J. (1998). *The management of ideas in the creating organization.* Westport, CT: Quorum.

Van Velsor, E., & Leslie, J. (1995). Why executives derail: Perspectives across time and cultures. *Academy of Management Executive*, 9, 4 (November).

Waldo, C. (1986). *A working guide for directors of not-for-profit organizations.* New York: Quorum Books.

Whoriskey, P., & Salmon, J. (2002, September 6). United Way CEO quits as charity is recast; Directors slash budgets, staff as part of overhaul. *The Washington Post*, p. A1.

Zoellner, T. (2000, August 11). Catholic charities chief forced out: Lavish spending berated–donations are off. *The San Francisco Chronicle*, A1.

Ownership and Age in Nonprofit and For-Profit Home Care Organizations: What Makes the Difference?

Hillel Schmid, PhD
Ronit Nirel, PhD

SUMMARY. The article examines the question: What makes the difference between nonprofit organizations and for-profit organizations providing home care services? The organizational properties examined are type of ownership and age of the organization. Multiple regression analysis was conducted in order to examine the relationships between these properties and process variables such as training workers, growth of clientele, and increase in income and expenses. The results reveal that structural properties such as age indeed affect the difference between nonprofit and for-profit home care organizations. Findings also indicate that type of ownership generates the differences between the organizations as well as the dynamics between them. *Article copies available for a fee from The Haworth Document Delivery Service: 1-800-HAWORTH. E-mail address: <docdelivery@haworth press.com> Website: <http://www.Haworth Press.com> © 2004 by The Haworth Press, Inc. All rights reserved.]*

Hillel Schmid (E-mail: mshsmid@mscc.huji.ac.il) and Ronit Nirel are affiliated with The Paul Baerwald School of Social Work, The Hebrew University of Jerusalem, Mt. Scopus 91905, Jerusalem, Israel.

[Haworth co-indexing entry note]: "Ownership and Age in Nonprofit and For-Profit Home Care Organizations: What Makes the Difference?" Schmid. Hillel, and Ronit Nirel. Co-published simultaneously in *Administration in Social Work* (The Haworth Social Work Practice Press, an imprint of The Haworth Press, Inc.) Vol. 28, No. 3/4, 2004, pp. 183-200; and: *Organizational and Structural Dilemmas in Nonprofit Human Service Organizations* (ed: Hillel Schmid) The Haworth Social Work Practice Press, an imprint of The Haworth Press, Inc., 2004, pp. 183-200. Single or multiple copies of this article are available for a fee from The Haworth Document Delivery Service [1-800-HAWORTH, 9:00 a.m. - 5:00 p.m. (EST). E-mail address: docdelivery@haworthpress.com].

KEYWORDS. Nonprofit organizations, for-profit organizations, ownership, age of organization

The article seeks to examine the question: What makes the difference between nonprofit organizations (NPOs) and for-profit organizations (FPOs) providing home care services? The issue at hand is whether the differences between organizations in the two sectors derive from type of ownership and legal status, or from structural properties that influence their functioning or from both of them.

The question is examined through a presentation of the results of a study conducted in organizations providing home care services to frail elderly people in Israel, in accordance with the Israeli Long-Term Care Insurance Law (1988). Before the law was enacted, home care services were provided through various administrative arrangements. Services were usually delivered by the Personal and Social Services Bureau of the Ministry of Labor and Social Affairs, and by voluntary organizations. The recipient population was very limited, since eligibility was based on a means test.

The need to organize these services developed as the number and proportion of elderly persons in the Israeli population increased. Israelis over age 65 currently represent 10% of the population, compared with 4% in 1948, when the state was established. The rapid growth of the elderly population, which exceeds the growth rate of the general population, is particularly evident in the 75+ age bracket. This group comprised 28% of all elderly Israelis (about 108,000 persons) in 1980, and reached about 40% (215,000 persons) in 1995 (Brodsky & Habib, 1997). Increased life expectancy has also affected Israel's elderly, especially at age 65. Specifically, the average life expectancy at age 65 is 8.15 years for men and 9.17 for women. Thus, over the past decades, life expectancy at age 65 has increased by an average of 19% for both men and women. Another factor that has influenced the aging of Israeli society is the influx of immigrants from Ethiopia and the Former Soviet Union in the early 1990s, unparalleled in Western countries (Litwin & Lightman, 1996). These developments highlight the urgent need to find appropriate and rapid solutions for care of the elderly, and provide the background for the enactment of the Long-Term Care Insurance Law (LTCI).

The law essentially sought to provide long-term care benefits as a matter of right or entitlement, based on clearly defined eligibility criteria. The primary purpose of the LTCI Law was to benefit chronically and severely disabled elderly living in the community by providing personal care, companionship, and domestic services such as shopping, house cleaning, hot meals, and other household assistance. In addition, the LTCI Law sought to complement rather than replace the existing limited system of service provision, and to substantially expand the overall scope of services. The LTCI Law sought to relieve the burden of care for family members of the frail elderly by providing services in home and community-based settings. In this way, it also aimed to reduce the demand for institutional placement. According to the law, home care is no longer a service provided through the state budget. Thus, unlike other government-funded services, home care is not subject to changes in government or priorities that affect eligibility. The law gives priority to benefits in kind, i.e., direct services for the elderly such as personal care and help with household chores. These benefits can only be exchanged for a monetary allowance if the necessary services are not available. The law guarantees home care services for all eligible applicants according to uniform, equal criteria defined in legal regulations. The criteria for eligibility are based on evaluations of Activities of Daily Living (ADL). Eligibility for benefits begins at age 60 for women and age 65 for men. The law provides for two levels of benefits, depending on the severity of the person's functional disability: (1) benefits amounting to a full (100%) disability allowance for those who are highly dependent on help from others to carry out most daily activities; and (2) benefits amounting to 150% of a full disability allowance for those who are completely dependent on others to carry out daily activities.

As a means of providing the required services, the government chose the strategy of contracting out to non-governmental organizations, i.e., voluntary nonprofit organizations (VNPOs) and private for-profit organizations (FPOs). This policy was intended to encourage competition and disperse the risks of relying on one source of providers, and possibly contribute toward improvement of service quality. The field of home care services, which had been dominated by VNPOs prior to the enactment of the law, significantly changed as a result of the entry of FPOs into the field and growing competition for government resources (Cohen, 1988). According to new policy, the government assumed responsibility for policy-making and finances, as well as for determining care plans, scope of services, and standards of quality and monitoring of services. The organizations contracted by the government are responsible for providing the services, training home care workers, and professional supervision.

During the first decade of the law's implementation, a new ecological niche of human services was established in Israel, and the amount of funding at its disposal reached two billion dollars. Seventy-five percent of the income of the organizations in both sectors derives from funds mandated by the law. Initially, about 7,000 elderly clients were entitled to home care services, compared with 103,000 today.

The article begins with a review of previous studies that have compared the organizational behavior of for-profit and nonprofit organizations over the past two decades. The review presents the main findings of relevant studies on the topic, and discusses the similarities and differences between NPOs and FPOs in this regard. The literature review is followed by a presentation of this study's conceptual framework, which also serves as the basis for the research questions. The next sections describe the research methodology and the results, including findings on the structural properties examined in the study. The Discussion and Conclusions sections offer explanations that may shed light on directions for future research in this field.

LITERATURE REVIEW

Several theories have been put forth in an attempt to explain the similarities and differences between NPOs and FPOs. These theories include institutional theory (DiMaggio & Powell, 1983; Meyer & Rowan, 1977; Meyer & Scott, 1983); competitive forces (Porter, 1980, 1991); population ecology (Hannan & Freeman, 1977, 1989); resource dependency (Pfeffer & Salancik, 1978), and the stakeholder perspective (Abzug & Webb, 1999; Schlesinger, 1998). The settings that have been studied most extensively are health care services (Bargthold, Estes, Hanes, & Swan, 1988; Gray, 1986; Marmor, Schlesinger, & Smithey, 1986; Wolf & Schlesinger, 1998); residential child care services (Knapp, 1986, 1989; Knapp & Fenyo, 1987; Krashinsky, 1998; Mauser, 1998); prisons (O'Brien, 1993); legal services (Mansneurus, 1993); home care services (Midwinter, 1988; Schmid, 1993, 1998; Schmid & Nirel, 1995); nursery schools (Badelt & Weiss, 1990); nursing homes (Bradley & Walker, 1998); elementary and secondary schools (Downes, 1992; James, 1987); and residential boarding schools (Schmid & Bar-Nir, 2001). Almost all of the studies have examined similarities and differences between organizations according to type of ownership, i.e., nonprofit and for-profit. Within these settings, several important issues have been investigated, including the ideology and espoused goals of the organizations (Lewis, 1989; Mauser, 1998) and the types of client populations receiving services (Abzug & Webb, 1996; Badelt & Weiss, 1990; Gibelman, 1989; Gray, 1997; Karoly, 1993; Kegan, 1991; Weisbrod, 1997, 1998). Other relevant topics include analyses of the organizational strategies adopted by organizations (Badelt & Weiss, 1990; Bargthold, Estes, Hanes, & Swan, 1988; Salvatore, 1985; Schmid & Hasenfeld, 1993), as well as aspects of human resource management such as training and development of professional staff (Mauser, 1998) and wages and employment conditions (Kegan, 1991; Tuominen, 1991; Whitebook, Howes, & Phillips, 1990).

Various aspects related to cost of operation have also been investigated. In this regard, some findings have revealed certain advantages for NPOs

(Bradley & Walker, 1998; Weisbrod, 1998), while others have revealed advantages for FPOs (Judge, Knapp, & Smith, 1986; Knapp, 1989). The conclusions depend on several factors, including clients' personality attributes such as age, level of dependence on assistance from others, level of disability, rate of occupancy at institutions, settings in which services are provided, and size of the organization (Knapp, 1988). Bradley and Walker (1998) argue that although studies vary in the reported magnitude of cost differences, the data suggest that the average cost of for-profit facilities ranges from 5% to 15% lower than the cost of nonprofit facilities, even after controlling for patient service and facility characteristics.

In addition, research has dealt with quality of services (Aaronson, Zinn, & Rosko, 1994; Kisker, 1991; Krashinsky, 1998; Mauser, 1998; Preston, 1989, 1993; Roomkin & Weisbrod, 1995; Rose-Ackerman, 1996; Weisbrod, 1997; Weisbrod & Schlesinger, 1986). Although it is common belief that NPOs have a qualitative advantage over FPOs under conditions of information asymmetry because for-profit organizations tend to skimp on undetectable quality in order to enhance profit margins, comparative data on quality of services in both sectors are inconclusive (Bradley & Walker, 1998).

Finally, studies of client satisfaction indicate that high levels of satisfaction exist in both sectors, with a slight advantage for NPOs (Riportella-Muller & Slesinger, 1982; Schmid, 1993; Weisbrod, 1996). These studies indicate that analysis of similarities and differences between organizations based on ownership yields inconclusive results owing, among other factors, to the heterogeneity of funding sources, disparate organizational goals, and varied constituencies. Moreover, researchers have argued that it is difficult to identify general differences between the organizations based solely on their ownership. For any given variable, differences within sectors are often greater than between sectors, and conclusions reached for one industry or country may not be applicable in other contexts (Abzug & Webb, 1999; DiMaggio & Anheier, 1990; Knapp, Kendall, & Forder, 1999; Knapp, Robertson, & Thomason, 1990; Krashinsky, 1998; Patel, Needleman, & Zeckhauser, 1993; Weisbrod, 1997; Young & Steinberg, 1995). Other researchers have claimed that the distinctions between sectors are becoming blurred. Public and private suppliers of human and social services are subject to the same regulations, utilize the same service technologies, employ the same type of staff, and have become increasingly bureaucratic, professionalized, political, and entrepreneurial (Billis, 1993; Billis & Harris, 1992; Bozeman, 1987; Douglas, 1987; Langton, 1987; Ostrander, 1987). Weisbrod (1997) claims that it is increasingly difficult to evaluate the social contribution of NPOs in the modern world, where barriers between nonprofit organizations and for-profit firms are crumbling. According to Weisbrod, the increased fuzziness of boundaries between nonprofit and for-profit organizations is not accidental, i.e., the process involves forces that break down the borders.

Indeed, scholars in the field have begun to pursue different directions in the study of organizations, which consider variables that may have a greater impact than ownership, such as organizational size, age, diversification of services, and geographical distribution (Judge et al., 1986; Knapp, 1989; Knapp & Missiakoulis, 1982) or the external environment (Schlesinger, 1998). Consistent with this perspective, the article attempts to examine which variables have a greater impact on differences between the organizations that provide home care services: ownership, organizational properties, or a combination of the two?

This question is examined on the basis of a study conducted in 1998, which investigated the functioning of nonprofit and for-profit home-care organizations (HCOs) that provide services for the frail elderly.

CONCEPTUAL FRAMEWORK

The conceptual framework of the study and the selection of research variables are based on the government's decision to establish a committee of experts consisting of a representative of the National Insurance Institute, a social worker from the local welfare services, and a public health nurse. According to the decision, the committee assumes responsibility for referring elderly clients to the provider organizations, in addition to transferring funds, which constitute about 75% of their revenue. The criteria guiding the committee's decisions provide the basis for selecting the research variables. Thus, for example, type of ownership and age influence the committee's decisions regarding placement of elderly clients. Since the government decided to encourage competition between provider-organizations, it enabled the entry of for-profit organizations into the niche of home care services which was dominated by nonprofit organizations. Age is associated with the extent to which the organization establishes itself in the market, as well as with the existence of a suitable professional and organizational infrastructure that will enable effective coping with service provision. Since older organizations (mainly nonprofits) operate side by side with younger organizations (mainly for-profits), it is important to understand how they are distinguished on the basis of their functions.

The other variables, which are mainly process variables, were found to have a strong impact on the delivery system in this kind of service market, where the labor force consists mainly of unskilled, non-nursing, female workers. Hence, training workers at all levels substantially affects their professional level and can ensure delivery of high-quality services that satisfy the needs of the elderly clients. As far as marketing is concerned, the government examines the ability of organizations to develop marketing mechanisms that expose clients to the organizations and to the kinds of services they provide. Such mechanisms can even be used as a basis for expanding sources of income beyond governmental funding. In addition, diversification of the services offered by the organization constitutes a criterion for allocating clients among them. The greater the diversity of services offered by the organizations–particularly innovative services, and services that go beyond those mandated in the law–the better their chances of attracting a large number of clients.

The other criteria are related to outcome variables selected by the committee, which represent the organization's activities and its ability to respond to the needs of the elderly clients. Notably, growth in the number of clients reflects the provider organization's capacity, capabilities, and developed structural mechanisms. In addition, the committee also examines the extent to which organizations invest in developing services, initiating new programs and increasing their geographical distribution by establishing new branches and improving accessibility of services to the elderly clients. All of these activities are reflected in the organization's expenses, which also constitute a criterion for evaluation of the organization's effectiveness.

Consistent with the goals and the conceptual framework of the study, the article aims to examine what factors influence the differences between organizations: ownership, structural properties such as age, process variables, or a combination of these variables?

It was hypothesized that differences between these organizations would be influenced more by structural properties such as age than by type of ownership. An attempt is also made to examine whether other structural properties deriving from the conceptual framework generate differences between organizations, or whether the differences between organizations are affected by a combination of ownership and age of the organization.

Specifically, the article examines the effect of age and ownership on process and performance variables as represented by:

1. Training (home care workers, social workers, and controllers).
2. Marketing of services.
3. Diversification of services.
4. Growth in clientele.
5. Increased income.
6. Increased expenses.

METHODS

Sample

The population consisted of all 150 provider organizations in the country that provide home care services, which were stratified by ownership (NPOs and FPOs), age categories, and size categories. A sample of 54 organizations was drawn from that population. The final sample consisted of 24 NPOs and 25 FPOs. Five FPOs were not investigated, either because they refused to co-operate or due to technical difficulties.

Measures

The primary research instrument was a questionnaire with open-ended and closed questions. Responses were confirmed through supplementary sources such as activity reports, salary reports and scales, written material published by the organizations, and statistical data published by the National Insurance Institute.

Response and Explanatory Variables

The variables chosen to represent the response (or dependent) variables relate to the functioning of the providers, the unique characteristics of home care organizations, and the services they provide. These include training effectiveness (home care workers, social workers, and controllers), marketing effectiveness, diversification of services, and growth in clientele. For the FPOs alone, increase in income and expenses were measured.

The variables chosen to represent the explanatory (or independent) variables relate to ownership and age of the organization. Ownership is defined as either for-profit or nonprofit (for a detailed description of the variables see the Appendix).

Statistical Analysis

Multiple regression analysis was carried out for the dependent variables. When appropriate, logarithmic transformations were performed in order to linearize the relationship between the explanatory and response variables. For each response variable, a stepwise algorithm selected a subset of covariates that best explain the response variance, using a p-value of 0.15 for entry into the model. Since the subset of variables chosen by a stepwise algorithm need not have the largest R^2 among all subsets of the same size, the optimality of all resulting models was verified by an all-subsets analysis (Weisberg, 1980). In order to determine whether differences in functioning derive from age of the organization, ownership, or a combination of the two, both main effects and their interaction were considered for inclusion in the final model.

RESULTS

Table 1 displays means, standard error of the means (StdErr = Std/sqrt(n)), minimum, and maximum values of the response and explanatory variables by ownership. For-profit organizations scored higher on effectiveness of home care workers' training and marketing, as well as for diversification of services. However, NPOs scored higher on effectiveness of training for social workers and controllers, as well as in growth of clientele. Variability of the response variables was similar for both types of organizations–except for growth of clientele, where the variability was higher in NPOs compared with FPOs (Std = 236.18 and 108.00, respectively). None of the differences in means was statistically significant.

Table 2 presents the results of the multiple regression analyses. The salient findings of the table are: Effectiveness of social workers' training correlates with age in NPOs ($r = 0.65$, $p < 0.01$), but not in FPOs. The linear model indicates that for new FPOs, the effectiveness of social workers' training was higher than for NPOs. However, for FPOs the level of effectiveness remained constant as the organization grew older, whereas effectiveness increased with age in NPOs, i.e., the older the NPO, the more effective the training of social workers ($R^2 = 0.26$).

Effectiveness of controllers' training correlates significantly with age in NPOs only. The regression analysis identifies dependence on ownership, age, and the interaction between the two. The relationship with age differs by ownership, as follows. The indicated model for NPOs is:

(1)   Effectiveness = 2.247 + 0.048 (age);

and the model for FPOs is:

(2)   Effectiveness = 4.454   0.142 (age).

That is, effectiveness of controllers' training is higher for new FPOs than for new NPOs. However, the model indicates that effectiveness decreases with age for FPOs and increases for NPOs. Thus, according to the model, NPOs and FPOs are expected to have the same levels of effectiveness for controllers'

TABLE 1. Mean, Standard Error (SdErr), Minimum, and Maximum Values of Response and Explanatory Variables, by Ownership

| | | FPOs | | | | | NPOs | | | |
	N	Mean	StdErr	Min	Max	N	Mean	StdErr	Min	Max
Response Variables										
Effectiveness of home care workers' training*	25	3.78	0.16	2.17	5.00	24	3.56	0.13	2.50	4.50
Effectiveness of social workers' training*	24	2.97	0.21	1.00	5.00	23	3.10	0.27	1.00	5.00
Effectiveness of controllers' training*	21	3.04	0.26	1.00	5.00	22	3.16	0.26	1.00	4.75
Effectiveness of marketing*	25	2.26	0.19	0.67	4.50	24	1.91	0.15	0.67	3.25
Diversification of services*	20	3.13	0.21	1.00	5.00	22	2.88	0.20	1.33	4.67
Growth in clientele**	21	58.54	23.56	0.00	500.00	24	100.80	48.21	0.00	11.50
Increased income**	19	75.76	26.69	3.50	500.00	0	-	-	-	-
Increased expenses**	20	108.10	34.80	3.80	600.00	0	-	-	-	-

*   Index of 1 to 5 measures, where 1 = low and 5 = high.
** In percents, measured for FPOs only.

training at the age of 11.6 years (the point of intersection of the respective lines). The percent of explained variance for this model is 25%.

Regarding growth in clientele, the linearizing transformation is $\log(x + 2)$. A significant negative correlation of similar magnitude was found for NPOs and FPOs ($r = -0.59$ and -0.51). The regression model indicates that as organizations' age increases, the growth in their clientele declines. However, the decline in NPOs is more moderate (slope -0.056) than in FPOs (slope -0.140).

The revenue variables were measured for FPOs only. The increase in income (in log scale) correlates negatively with age ($r = -0.61$, $p < 0.01$). According to the model, the increase in income diminishes as the organization grows older ($p = 0.01$). The percent of explained variance for this model is 38%.

The increase in expenses (log scale) also correlates negatively with age ($R^2 = 0.29$). The variability in the effectiveness of home care workers' training, effectiveness of marketing, and diversification of services was not significantly explained by the combination of ownership and age.

DISCUSSION

The article deals with the variables that distinguish between for-profit and nonprofit organizations in terms of type of ownership and age of organiza-

TABLE 2. Results of Regression Analysis*

	Effectiveness of Social Worker Training	Effectiveness of Controller Training	Growth in Clientele	Increased Income[1]	Increased Expenses[1]
	47	43	45	19	21
Transformation	-	-	log(x + 2)	log(x)	log(x)
R^2	0.26	0.25	0.24	0.38	0.29
n	42	39	41	17	18
p	0.003	0.015	0.006	0.007	0.018
Intercept	3.029	4.454	4.556	6.013	6.313
	(< 0.001)	(< 0.001)	(< 0.001)	(< 0.001)	(< 0.001)
Ownership	0.964	−2.207			
(n = 49)	(0.029)	(0.020)			
Age of		−0.142	−0.140	−0.239	−0.238
organization		(0.094)	(0.007)	(0.007)	(0.018)
(n = 45)					
Age ×	0.057	0.190	0.084		
ownership	(< 0.001)	(0.030)	(0.048)		

*R^2 denotes percent of explained variance
n indicates the number of cases
p denotes the model p-value
[1] Measured for FPOs only

tions, and the interaction between those two dimensions. The results of multiple regression analysis presented in the article indicate that indeed, age affects the differences between nonprofit and for-profit organizations. However, its impact is not critical since type of ownership also generates differences between the organizations. Thus ownership, age, and the interaction between them affect the differences between the organizations.

Table 1 indicates certain differences between the organizations in terms of type of ownership–although the differences are minor and, in some cases, insignificant. Thus, the distinctions between organizations have become blurred over time. Several explanations for this trend are put forth, which relate to three main processes of organizational isomorphism: coercive, mimetic, and normative. Owing to the high dependence of organizations on governmental funding, the government has the coercive power to dictate the care programs to be included as services offered to the frail elderly. In addition, the government sets standards for implementation, control, and supervision of home care workers as well as for quality of services. Thus, organizations that seek to ensure a steady flow of resources tend to conform with government policy stipulations and develop similar organizational and procedural patterns. Undoubtedly the organizations also tend to imitate each other, and often adopt similar service technologies and management techniques since they operate in an established environment of service providers and recipients. These similarities can also be attributed to the fact that professional and therapeutic staff members receive similar training and role socialization, which they transmit to other organizations. Consequently, if there are any differences between organizations by type of ownership, they are minor.

Analysis of the findings in Table 2 reveals a positive correlation between training of social workers and age in nonprofit organizations. However, the level of effectiveness in training social workers was higher in young for-profit organizations than in nonprofits. Clearly, the findings indicate that age has an impact on effectiveness of training in nonprofit organizations. Notably, nonprofit organizations are older, and have more experience in training workers and in developing professional, skilled workers. Young private for-profit organizations are now required to make a greater effort to train workers, both because the government requires them to do so, and due to competition with the nonprofit organizations.

A similar finding was obtained for training of controllers. Young private organizations in the for-profit sector make more efforts to provide training for their workers as required by the government in order to ensure service quality. Concomitantly, the results indicate that effectiveness of training controllers, like training of social workers, is higher on the average in nonprofit organizations. It should be emphasized, however, that the differences are negligible.

Regarding growth in clientele, the findings revealed that the growth rate declines in older organizations, albeit to a lesser extent in NPOs than in FPOs. The reduced growth rate can be attributed to the fact that older organizations stop growing at a certain stage of their lives, when their client population stabilizes. The organization's ability to provide services to a very large number of clients is limited in terms of available staff and in terms of the organization's structural and professional infrastructure—in addition to other factors that prevent the organization from continuing to expand once it has reached a certain size. On the whole, the differences between NPOs and FPOs in this area are not substantial, and support the explanation presented here, i.e., that organizations stop expanding their clientele because they are afraid that their staff and their organizational and structural infrastructure are not sufficient to provide high quality services.

As far as revenue and expenses are concerned, the findings revealed that a decline with age occurs in FPOs. Accordingly, older organizations stabilize when their income and expenditures reach a certain level. In this process, the organizations learn to stabilize their fixed and changing expenses in accordance with the scope of their activities and revenue.

In conclusion, the findings of this study clearly indicate that the functioning and effectiveness of home care organizations are influenced by the interrelationships between ownership and age. The contribution of the study lies in its multivariate consideration of factors related to both dimensions. Despite the basic assumption that under conditions of competition structural properties play a relatively significant role, ownership, and legal status cannot be disregarded in the analysis of differences between the organizations. Specifically, type of ownership affects organizational behavior because organizations in each sector have distinct organizational identities and goals as well as different organizational cultures, values, and norms. All of these variables affect the organization's orientation toward provision of services, quality of services, and relations with clients. At the same time, however, close examination of the differences indicates that besides ownership, there are organizational and process variables that distinguish the behavior of the organizations in each sector. Each of these variables was examined independently and in relation to type of ownership. Although the findings indicated that age of the organization affects differences in organizational behavior, it may vary for organizations with different types of ownership. Therefore, notwithstanding the relevance of this conclusion to the context of home care organizations examined in this study, it would be worthwhile to conduct further research in other organizational settings. Notably, numerous researchers claim that the distinctions between organizations are becoming blurred as a result of various processes such as institutional isomorphism through acculturation, assimilation, or imitation. In a similar vein, it has been argued that all organizations, regardless of their ownership, are subject to changes in their internal or external environments that might influence the blurring of distinctions between them (Brody, 1996). The findings of this study contradict some of these arguments by pointing to the intricate system of interrelationships that distinguish between the organizations examined.

REFERENCES

Aaronson, W., Zinn, J., & Rosko, M. (1994). Do for-profit and not-for-profit nursing homes behave differently? *The Gerontologist, 34,* 775-786.

Abzug, R., & Webb, N.J. (1996). Another role for nonprofits: The case of mop-ups and nursemaids resulting from privatization in emerging economies. *Nonprofit and Voluntary Sector Quarterly, 25(2),* 156-173.

Abzug, R., & Webb, N.J. (1999). Relationships between nonprofit and for-profit organizations: A stakeholder perspective. *Nonprofit and Voluntary Sector Quarterly, 28(4),* 416-431.

Badelt, C., & Weiss, P. (1990). Nonprofit, for-profit and government organizations in social service provision: Comparison of behavioral patterns for Austria. *Voluntas, 1*, 77-96.

Bargthold, L.A., Estes, C.L., Hanes, P., & Swan, J.H. (1988). Running as fast as they can: Organizational changes in home health care. In C. Estes et al. (Eds.), *Organizational and community responses to Medicare policy*. San Francisco, CA: University of California Institute for Health and Aging.

Billis, D. (1993). Sector blurring and nonprofit centers: The case of the United Kingdom. *Nonprofit and Voluntary Sector Quarterly, 22(3)*, 241-257.

Billis, D., & Harris, M. (1992). Taking the strain of change: UK voluntary agencies in the post-Thatcher period. *Nonprofit and Voluntary Sector Quarterly, 21(3)*, 211-225.

Bozeman, B. (1987). *All organizations are public: Bridging public and private organizational theories*. San Francisco, CA: Jossey-Bass.

Bradley, E.H., & Walker, L.C. (1998). Education and advance care planning in nursing homes: The impact of ownership type. *Nonprofit and Voluntary Sector Quarterly, 27(3)*, 339-357.

Brodsky, J., & Habib, J. (1997). New developments and issues in home care policies. *Health Provision, Disability and Rehabilitation Journal, 18(4)*, 150-154.

Brody, E. (1996). Institutional dissonance in the nonprofit sector. *Villanova Law Review, 41*, 493-504.

Cohen, S. (1988). The Long-Term Care Insurance Law: Background, principles and organization toward implementation. *Social Security: Journal of Welfare and Social Security, June* (Special English edition), 4-22.

DiMaggio, P.D., & Anheier, H.K. (1990). The sociology of nonprofit organizations and sectors. *Annual Review of Sociology, 16*, 137-159.

DiMaggio, P.D., & Powell, W.W. (1983). The iron cage revisited: Institutional isomorphism and collective rationality in organizational fields. *American Sociological Review, 48*, 147-160.

Douglas, J. (1987). Political theories of nonprofit organizations. In W.W. Powell (Ed.), *The nonprofit sector: A research handbook* (pp. 43-54). New Haven, CT: Yale University Press.

Downes, T.A. (1992). Evaluating the impact of school finance reform on the provision of public education: The California case. *National Tax Journal, 45*, 405-419.

Gibelman, M. (1989). Private market strategy for social service provision: An empirical investigation. In H.W. Demone, & M. Gibelman (Eds.), *Services for sale, purchasing health and human services*. New Brunswick & London: Rutgers University Press.

Gray, B.H. (Ed.). (1986). For-profit enterprise in health care. Committee on implications for for-profit enterprise in health care. Division of Health Care Services, Institute of Medicine, Washington, D.C.: National Academy of Sciences Press.

Gray, B.H. (1997). Conversion of HMO's and hospitals: What's at stake? *Health Affairs, 16(2)*, 29-47.

Hannan, M., & Freeman, J. (1977). The population ecology of organizations. *American Journal of Sociology, 82*, 929-964.

Hannan, M., & Freeman, J. (1989). *Organizational ecology.* Cambridge, MA: Harvard University Press.

James, E. (1987). The public/private division of responsibility for education: An international comparison. *Economics of Education Review, 6,* 1-14.

Judge, K., Knapp, M., & Smith, J. (1986). The comparative costs of public and private residential homes for the elderly. In K. Judge, & I. Sinclair (Eds.), *Residential care for elderly people.* London: Her Majesty's Stationery Office.

Karoly, L.A. (1993). The trend in inequality among families, individuals and workers in the United States: A twenty-five year perspective. In P. Gotschalk, & S. Danziger (Eds.), *Uneven tides: Rising inequality in America* (pp. 71-87). New York: Russell Sage Foundation.

Kegan, S.L. (1991). Examining profit and nonprofit child care: An odyssey of quality and auspices. *Journal of Social Issues, 47(3),* 87-104.

Kisker, E.E. (1991). *A profile of child care settings: Early education and child care in 1990.* Princeton, NJ: Mathematical Policy Research.

Knapp, M.R.J. (1986). The relative cost-effectiveness of public, voluntary and private providers of residential child care. In A. Culyer, & B. Jönsson (Eds.), *Public and private health services.* London: Blackwell.

Knapp, M.R.J. (1988). Private and voluntary welfare. PSSRU Discussion Paper 596. University of Kent at Canterbury.

Knapp, M.R.J. (1989). Intersectoral differences in cost effectiveness: Residential child care in England and Wales. In E. James (Ed.), *The nonprofit sector in international perspective* (pp. 193-216). New York: Oxford University Press.

Knapp, M.R.J., & Fenyo, A. (1987). Fee and utilization variations within the voluntary residential child care sector. Discussion Paper 378/3 PSSRU, University of Kent at Canterbury.

Knapp, M.R.J., & Missiakoulis, S. (1982). Inter-sectoral comparisons: Day care for the elderly. *Journal of Social Policy, 11,* 335-354.

Knapp, M.R.J., Kendall, J., & Forder, J. (1999). Is the independent sector important in social care? *PSSRU Bulletin, 11 (February),* 14-17.

Knapp, M.R.J., Robertson, E., & Thomason, C. (1990). Public money, voluntary action: Whose welfare? In H. Anheier, & W. Seibel (Eds.), *The Third Sector* (pp. 183-248). Berlin: DeGruyter.

Krashinsky, M. (1998). Does auspice matter? The case of day care for children in Canada. In: W.W. Powell, & E.S. Clemens (Eds.), *Private action and the public good* (pp. 114-123). New Haven, CT: Yale University Press.

Langton, S. (1987). ENVOI: Developing nonprofit theory. *Journal of Voluntary Action Research, 16(1/2),* 134-148.

Lewis, H. (1989). Ethics and the private non-profit human service organization. *Administration in Social Work, 13(2),* 1-14.

Litwin, H., & Lightman, E. (1996). The development of community care policy for the elderly: A comparative perspective. *International Journal of Health Services, 26(4),* 691-708.

Mansneurus, L. (1993). Bar groups are happy to find you a lawyer. *New York Times,* February 27, 1993, A-30.

Marmor, T.R., Schlesinger, M., & Smithey, R.W. (1986). A new look at nonprofits: Health care policy in a competition age. *Yale Journal Regul.*, 3(2), 313-349.

Mauser, E. (1998). The importance of organizational form: Parent perceptions versus reality in the day care industry. In: W.W. Powell, & E.S. Clemens (Eds.), *Private action and the public good* (pp. 124-133). New Haven, CT: Yale University Press.

Meyer, J.W., & Rowan, B. (1977). Institutionalized organizations: Formal structure as myth and ceremony. *American Journal of Sociology*, *83*, 340-363.

Meyer, J.W., & Scott, W.R. (Eds.). (1983). *Organizational environments: Ritual and rationality*. Beverly Hills, CA: Sage.

Midwinter, E. (1988). *Caring for cash: The issue of private domiciliary care*. CPA Reports. Washington, D.C.: Center for Policy and Aging.

O'Brien, T.L. (1993). Private prison market attracts more and more firms. *Wall Street Journal*, June 10, 1993, B2.

Ostrander, S.A. (1987). Introduction to the special issue. *Journal of Voluntary Action Research*, *16(1/2)*, 7-11.

Patel, J., Needleman, J., & Zeckhauser, R. (1993). Who cares? Hospital ownership and uncompensated care. Working Paper, John F. Kennedy School of Government, Harvard University.

Pfeffer, J., & Salancik, G. (1978). *The external control of organizations: A resource dependence perspective*. New York: Harper & Row.

Porter, M.E. (1980). *Competitive strategy*. New York: Free Press.

Porter, M.E. (1991). Towards a dynamic theory of strategy. *Strategic Management Journal*, *12*, 95-117.

Preston, A. (1989). The nonprofit worker in a for-profit world. *Journal of Labor Economics*, *7(4)*, 438-463.

Preston, A. (1993). Efficiency, quality, and social externalities in the provision of day care. Comparisons of nonprofits and for-profit firms. *Journal of Productivity Analysis*, *4*, 165-182.

Riportella-Muller, R., & Slesinger, D.P. (1982). The relationship of ownership and size to quality of care in Wisconsin nursing homes. *The Gerontologist*, *21*, 429-434.

Roomkin, M.J., & Weisbrod, B.A. (1995). Managerial compensation in for-profit, nonprofit, and government hospitals. Working Paper, Northwestern University Center for Urban Affairs and Policy Research.

Rose-Ackerman, S.R. (1996). Altruism, nonprofits and economic theory. *Journal of Economic Literature*, *34*, 701-728.

Salvatore, T. (1985). Organizational adaptation in the VNA: Paradigm change in the voluntary sector. *Home Health Care Services Quarterly*, *6(2)*, 19-31.

Schlesinger, M. (1998). Mismeasuring the consequences of ownership: External influences and comparative performance of public, for-profit, and private nonprofit organizations. In W.W. Powell, & E.S. Clemens (Eds.), *Private action and public good* (pp. 85-113). New Haven, CT: Yale University Press.

Schmid, H. (1993). Nonprofit and for-profit home care in Israel: Clients' assessments. *Journal of Aging and Social Policy*, *5(3)*, 95-115.

Schmid, H., & Bar-Nir, D. (2001). The relationship between organizational properties and service effectiveness in residential boarding schools. *Children and Youth Services Review*, *24(3)*, 243-271.

Schmid, H., & Hasenfeld, Y. (1993). Organizational dilemmas in the provision of home care services. *Social Service Review, 67(1)*, 40-54.

Schmid, H., & Nirel, R. (1995). Relationships between organizational properties and service effectiveness in home care organizations. *Journal of Social Service Research, 20(3/4)*, 71-92.

Tuominen, M. (1991). Caring for profit: The social, economic, and political significance of for-profit child care. *Social Service Review, 65(3)*, 450-467.

Weisberg, S. (1980). *Applied linear regression* (pp. 190-199). New York: Wiley.

Weisbrod, B.A. (1996). Does institutional form matter? Comparing behavior of private firms, church-related nonprofits and other nonprofits. Northwestern University, Center for Urban Affairs and Policy Research.

Weisbrod, B.A. (1997). The future of the nonprofit sector: Its entwining with private enterprise and government. *Journal of Policy Analysis and Management, 16(4)*, 541-555.

Weisbrod, B.A. (1998). Institutional form and organizational behavior. In W.W. Powell, & E.S. Clemens (Eds.). *Private action and the public good* (pp. 69-84). New Haven, CT: Yale University Press.

Weisbrod, B.A., & Schlesinger, M. (1986). Public, private, nonprofit ownership and the response to asymmetric information: The case of nursing homes. In S.R. Rose-Ackerman (Ed.), *The economics of nonprofit institutions*. London: Oxford University Press.

Whitebook, M., Howes, C., & Phillips, D. (1990). *Who cares? Child care teachers and the quality of care in America*. Oakland, CA: Child Care Employee Project.

Wolf, N., & Schlesinger, M. (1998). Access, hospital ownership and competition between for-profit and nonprofit institutions. *Nonprofit and Voluntary Sector Quarterly, 27(2)*, 203-236.

Young, D.R., & Steinberg, R. (1995). *Economics for nonprofit managers*. New York: The Foundation Center.

APPENDIX 1: DEFINITION OF VARIABLES

Explanatory variables:

Ownership/Type of organization: FPO, NPO
Age: Number of years since the organization's establishment, as calculated in 1998.

Response Variables

Home care workers' training: Reflects discussions, written material and individual supervision, frequency of group and individual training by a senior worker, professional training, day seminars, workshops and courses.
Social workers' training: The extent to which the organization provides professional, personal and group training to social workers.
Controllers' training: The extent to which the organization provides professional, personal and group training to controllers and participation in workshops and courses.
Effectiveness of marketing: Reflects the usage of advertisements, gifts and bonuses; the relative expenditure for marketing, and use of marketing surveys.
Diversification of services: The extent to which the organization offers a variety of service programs to clients.
Growth in clientele: Mean of the percent of growth in clientele under the long-term insurance law, and other elderly clients that are not eligible according to the law.

Increased income over the past five years: Expressed as the percentage of growth in revenue.

Increased expenses over the past five years: Expressed as the percentage of various expenses incurred by the organization.

Social Work Graduates
and Welfare Economy Sector Preferences:
A Cross-National Perspective

Idit Weiss, PhD
John Gal, PhD

SUMMARY. Upon completion of their studies social work graduates are faced with a choice of employment in various sectors of the welfare economy. This article looks at the preferences of graduates in seven different countries, representing various types of welfare economies. The findings indicate that the private non-profit sector is that most preferred by graduates in most countries while for-profit employment was not the most preferred in any of them. Two different explanations, one focusing upon employment opportunities and the other upon the congruence between

Idit Weiss is affiliated with the Bob Shapell School of Social Work, Tel Aviv University, Ramat Aviv, Israel (E-mail: iditweis@post.tau.ac.il). John Gal is affiliated with the Paul Baerwald School of Social Work, Hebrew University of Jerusalem, Mt Scopus, Jerusalem, Israel (E-mail: msjgsw@mscc.huji.ac.il).

The authors would like to gratefully acknowledge the contribution of John Dixon and country researchers Cecilia L.W. Chan, David Cox, Agnes Darvas, Bill Healy, Gabor Hegyesi, Bernd Kolleck, David Kramer, C.W. Lam, Rolf Landwehr, Tim Reutebuch, Johanna Woodcock, and Charles Zastrow to this project.

[Haworth co-indexing entry note]: "Social Work Graduates and Welfare Economy Sector Preferences: A Cross-National Perspective." Weiss, Idit, and John Gal. Co-published simultaneously in *Administration in Social Work* (The Haworth Social Work Practice Press, an imprint of The Haworth Press, Inc.) Vol. 28, No. 3/4, 2004, pp. 201-216; and: *Organizational and Structural Dilemmas in Nonprofit Human Service Organizations* (ed: Hillel Schmid) The Haworth Social Work Practice Press, an imprint of The Haworth Press, Inc., 2004, pp. 201-216. Single or multiple copies of this article are available for a fee from The Haworth Document Delivery Service [1-800-HAWORTH, 9:00 a.m. - 5:00 p.m. (EST). E-mail address: docdelivery@haworthpress.com].

201

social work values and types of sectors, are employed in order to interpret these results. *[Article copies available for a fee from The Haworth Document Delivery Service: 1-800-HAWORTH. E-mail address: <docdelivery@haworth press.com> Website: <http://www.HaworthPress.com> © 2004 by The Haworth Press, Inc. All rights reserved.]*

KEYWORDS. Sectors, social work graduates, preferences, welfare economy, non-profit

INTRODUCTION

Social work graduates on the very threshold of their professional careers can, theoretically at least, chose to seek employment in one or more of four potential types of employment. They can opt to work in a social service agency within the public governmental sector or they can choose to work in a third sector voluntary organization. In addition, they can seek employment in a for-profit enterprise that provides services to individuals for a fee or as part of a contracted-out service funded by the state, or they can establish their own private practice. Obviously the imperatives of a rapidly changing welfare economy and the impact of market-driven demands in an age of welfare-to-work reforms upon both state and private non-profit agencies have tended to blur the differences between the various sectors (Dixon & Hyde, 2002; Hasenfeld, 2000; Lymbery, 2001). This process has been augmented by growing pressure for partnerships between state and private non-profit or for-profit agencies (Prince & Austin, 2001). Nevertheless, all of the sectors still retain specific identifiable characteristics, goals and values that have obvious implications for both clients and social worker employees (Burke & Rafferty, 1994; Krashinsky, 1998; Schmid, 1993; Weisbrod, 1997). Clearly there is great significance for the profession and for social services in a better understanding of student perceptions of the sectors within the welfare economy, as these will have an impact upon trends within social work in the years to come.

Discussions of student preferences for welfare sectors have focused primarily on the legitimacy of for-profit employment within social work and its congruence with the ideals and goals, of the profession and its members (Butler, 1992), generally ignoring other sectors of the welfare economy, such as the voluntary sector. Supporters of for-profit employment, particularly private practice, laud the benefits of private practice for those who engage in it and argue for the legitimacy of social workers seeking increased earnings, status, and greater professional autonomy. They underscore the benefits of private practice for the client observing that it is as legitimate to work on behalf of persons who are "psychologically deprived" as for those whose deprivation is social and economic (Masi, 1992; Wakefield, 1992). Opponents of this type of social work employment (e.g., Chung, Fitzpatrick, & Pardeck, 1995; Reisch, 1992; Specht & Courtney, 1994) claim that the profit motive may undermine social workers' commitment to their needy clients, decrease their ability to provide assistance to the deprived, and reduce their willingness to stand up for social justice. In short, they point to a fundamental conflict between social work for profit and the profession's mission to work on behalf of the oppressed. The findings in the literature as to the affinity between students' professional preferences and social work's mission and values are mixed and not conclusive (Aviram & Katan, 1991; Perry, 2001). However, if students are motivated by social work values in their career choices (Bogo et al., 1993), then debates on the congruence between various sectors within the welfare economy and these values will be reflected in their preferences.

While student preferences for various sectors may reflect their stands on the values linked to this debate, they may also be indicative of additional influences over choices. One of these influences may be the perceived employment possibility open to graduates as a consequence of specific institutional settings, such as the structure of the welfare economy (McDonald, Harris, & Wintersteen, 2003). Indeed an examination of the employment structure within the welfare economy throughout the world reveals a stunning degree of diversity. This is true not only of differences between developed and less-developed countries but also of divergences between various welfare states.

In the study described in this article four types of welfare economies (though clearly others can be identified) are included. The first is the "state-dominant type," in which most social services are provided by the state, through national- or local-level agencies. Great Britain and Australia are the exemplars of this type of structure (Ife, 1997; Martin, 1996; Payne, 1997). A second type is the "non-profit type," represented here by Germany and Hong Kong, in which non-profit agencies play a very major role in social service provision. In the German case this a legacy of a traditional "subsidiary" approach to welfare by which the state funds services provided by voluntary organizations (Klug, 2001; Kramer, Landweher, & Kolleck, in press), while in Hong Kong this reflects a long-term colonial reluctance to provide state social services and the increasing role of externally-run agencies (Lam & Chan, in press; Lee, 1992). A third type of welfare economy is represented in this study by Hungary. It is described here as a "transitional type" not only because it is one of the transitional economies of Eastern Europe but primarily due to the ongoing process of transformation of the social services in this country from a state-dominated system to one growingly characterized by non-profit agencies (Darvas & Hegyesi, in press; Kuti, 1997). A final fourth type of welfare economy is that existing in the United States and Israel, in which public, governmental and non-governmental, agencies exist alongside for-profit agencies, either firms or the private practices of social workers (Leighninger & Midgley, 1997; Spiro, Sherer, Korin-Langer, & Weiss, 1997). Despite the major differences between these two countries in various aspects of their welfare provision, they are similar in that different types of sectors both provide social services and offer employment to social workers. As such, we have termed this a "multiple-sector type" of welfare economy.

If student preferences are influenced by employment options within specific national settings, we will expect the preferences of the students to be distributed roughly according to the contours of the various welfare economies sketched above. Thus, for example, graduates in state-dominant type countries will presumably prefer employment within the state sector while students in countries in which non-profits are the dominant sector will opt for them.

Given the importance of a better understanding of social work graduates' employment preferences, it is surprising that very few scholars have examined student preferences as to the sector in which they would like to work after graduation. Most have focused on the interest of American MSW students in working in private practice (Abell & McDonell, 1990; Butler, 1990, 1992; Rubin & Johnson, 1984; Rubin et al., 1986). The findings show mixed results. Three studies show high percentages of students, ranging from 63% (Butler, 1990) to 86% (Rubin & Johnson, 1984), wanting to engage in private practice either alone or in combination with agency work. One study, however, reports that only 17% of the students in its sample expressed an interest in entering private practice (2% alone, 15% in combination) upon completion of studies, while 20% indicated that they would be interested in full time private practice five years later (Abell & McDonell, 1990). The authors offer no explanation for the very different findings they obtained. MSW students requested by Canadian researchers (Bogo et al., 1993; Bogo et al., 1995) to rate the degree to which they wanted to work in private practice on a 16 point scale registered a mean of 8 at the beginning of their studies and 7.1 at the end. These findings were interpreted as showing the students' "neutrality" towards the matter.

The limitations of these studies are that, first, they focus on private practice and do not examine in detail students' interest in working in other sectors. While Rubin and colleagues (1984, 1986) and Bogo and colleagues (1993, 1995) ignore additional sectors completely, Abell and McDonell (1990) investigate students' interest in working for agencies under either public or private auspices–thereby missing the important for-profit/non-profit distinction. Without direct examination we cannot know whether students are, in fact, reluctant to work in the governmental sector or how interested they are in working in the other two non-governmental sectors. Second, these studies lack any international comparative perspective. This makes it impossible to determine the extent to which the findings are country-specific. The studies do not reveal whether the appeal of private practice and the distancing from the public sector found among social worker students in the United States characterizes the social work profession elsewhere. Although the Canadian findings suggest that social work students in Canada are less interested in working in private practice than their American counterparts, comparison is problematic because the Canadian studies inquire about degree while the American studies pose dichotomous question and report percentages. An initial attempt to overcome this lack of an international comparative perspective was undertaken by Weiss, Gal, and Cnaan (in press); however, this study focused only on graduates in the two "multiple-sector type" countries, the United States and Israel.

The present cross-sectional survey seeks to overcome these limitations through a comparative investigation of seven countries representing different types of welfare economies: Australia, Britain, Germany, Hong Kong, Hungary, Israel, and the United States. It offers findings from a cross-national research project that examined various aspects of the professional preferences and ideologies of graduating social work students in different countries (Weiss, Gal, & Dixon, in press). While it is not claimed that these students comprise a representative sample of social work graduates in all these countries, the findings do provide a unique opportunity to examine the views of social work graduates in a wide variety of national settings. The article compares the degree of interest among graduating social work students in these countries in working in the four sectors in which social workers may be employed: the governmental sector, the voluntary non-profit sector, the for-profit sector, and private practice. More precisely, it conducts two comparisons: the first aims at determining the hierarchy of preferences of students in each of the cohorts, the second at gauging the similarities and differences in the preferences of students in the different countries. This article then seeks to contribute to a better understanding of the preferences of social work graduates with regard to the sectors in which they seek employment by employing a unique cross-national comparative perspective. Through this study of the preferences of social work graduates in a number of countries representing various welfare economies, we seek to identify the differences and similarities in the preferences of the graduates across the world. This type of examination should provide a wider perspective of this issue and offer a better understanding of influences upon the occupational choices of the next generation of social workers in specific national settings.

METHOD

Sample

The sample consists of 594 graduating BSW students from seven countries[1]: Australia (n = 62), Britain (n = 64), Germany (n = 141), Hungary (n = 101), Hong Kong (n = 41), Israel (n = 138), and the United States (n = 78). Although social work training programs obviously differ substantially between countries, all the students in the study were graduates of programs towards a degree that enables them to become social workers. In each of the countries, the research team contacted social work scholars who distributed the study questionnaire among all the graduating students in their respective schools of social work. In Hungary three schools were sampled; in the remaining countries, samples were obtained from a single school. The response rates were: Australia–42%, Britain–94%, Germany–41%, Hungary–80%, Hong Kong–60%, Israel–83%, United States–77%. The relatively low response rate in Australia probably stemmed from the fact that the students filled out the questionnaires outside class and returned them by mail. The low response rates in Germany stems from the fact that not all classes were in session when the questionnaire was administered.

Most respondents were women (83%), reflecting the gender pattern of social work students worldwide (Brauns & Kramer, 1991). Ages range from 21 to 40 with a mean score of 26.66 (SD = 5.77). There were statistically significant inter-country differences in these two variables. The proportion of men varied from 7% in the Israeli cohort, 10% in the British, 12% in the American, 16% in the Hungarian, 19% in the Australian, 17% in the Hong Kong to 32% in the German cohort. These differences were statistically significant (χ^2 = 34.36; df = 6; p < .001). The mean ages were 22.9 in the American cohort, 23.3 in the Hong Kong cohort, 25.6 in the Israeli, 27.1 in the Hungarian, 27.5 in the German, 28.8 in the British, and 31.7 in the Australian cohort. The differences were statistically significant (F(6, 587) = 21.36; p < .001). Scheffe paired comparisons showed significant differences between the Australian cohort and the American, German, Hong Kong, Hungarian and the Israeli cohorts, with the Australian cohort being older. Significant differences were also found between the British cohort and the American, Hong Kong and Israeli cohorts, with the British cohort again being older. Similarly, the Hungarian students were found to be significantly older than the students from the United States and Hong Kong.

Instrument

Participants were presented with a list of four sectors in which social workers may be employed: government, non-profit or voluntary, for-profit, and private practice. They were asked to indicate how interested they were in working in each upon graduation, on a five-point Likert-type scale ranging from 1 = very little to 5 = very much.

Procedure and Reservation

The questionnaires were distributed to researchers in all the participating countries, all of who were social work educators with previous involvement in cross-national research. The researchers were responsible for translating the questionnaire, adapting it to the country's cultural context, and administering it. All of the questionnaires were completed voluntarily and anonymously in class in all countries other than Australia, where they were filled out by the students outside class. The questionnaires were distributed in 2000 in Israel and in 2001 in the other countries.

A translation problem showed up in the German questionnaire after the answers were submitted. Because the provision of services by the solo social work practitioner is rare in Germany, the researcher translated the "private practice" sector into the German "private praxis/Betrieb," which refers to occupational social work. Nevertheless, Germany was not removed from the analysis because of the large size of the cohort and because of the information it provides about the attitude towards the other sectors. To avoid misleading the reader, the term "occupational social work" is used in the results for the German cohort.

RESULTS

Within-Cohort Differences

ANOVAs with repeated measures were carried out to ascertain differences in the levels of interest in working in the various sectors within each of the national cohorts. Table 1 presents the means and standard deviations of the students' willingness to work in each of the sectors and the ANOVA results and effect sizes.

As can be seen, the non-profit sector was the most favored sector, being first in the order of preferences either alone or along with another sector in five of the seven cohorts (Australia, England, Germany, Hong Kong, Hungary). On the other hand, of all the sectors, the government sector varied most in its

TABLE 1. Willingness to Work in Different Sectors–Within-Cohort Differences: Means, SD, and F values ($N = 594$)

Students from:	Governmental 1 M SD	Non Profit 2 M SD	For Profit 3 M SD	Private Practice 4 M SD	F	Eta^2	SNK
Australia	3.54	3.79	2.11	2.45	26.36***	.31	1,2>4>3
($N = 59$)	1.16	1.07	1.08	1.38			
Britain	3.46	4.01	2.41	3.19	22.69***	.27	2>1,4>3
($N = 62$)	1.12	.94	1.11	1.32			
Germany	2.36	3.55	2.90	3.69[1]	32.31***	.20	2,4>3>1
($N = 127$)	1.30	1.28	1.27	1.18			
Hong Kong	3.88	4.00	2.78	2.50	26.27***	.39	1,2 >3,4
($N = 42$)	1.13	.79	1.07	.99			
Hungary	3.10	4.07	3.71	3.52	9.83***	.10	2>3,4>1
($N = 92$)	1.23	1.01	1.05	1.41			
Israel	3.80	3.81	4.05	3.77	2.06		
($N = 135$)	.98	1.07	.92	1.22			
USA	3.44	3.26	3.33	3.55	.92		
($N = 77$)	1.28	1.20	1.08	1.14			

*$p < .05$ **$p < .01$ ***$p < .001$

[1]Due to a translation problem, "private practice" was translated into "occupational social work."

place in the within-cohort hierarchy, appearing first in the Australian and Hong Kong cohorts, second in the British cohort, and the least preferred in the German and Hungarian cohorts.

More specifically, significant within-cohort differences were found in all the cohorts except the American and Israeli. The greatest within-cohort difference, as indicated by effect size, was found in the Hong Kong cohort and the smallest in the Hungarian cohort. Student-Newman-Keuls (SNK) paired comparison tests conducted to determine the sources of the differences show different national patterns in the interest in working in the various sectors. The Australian and Hong Kong, cohorts favored the government and non-profit sectors over the for-profit and private practice sectors; though the Australian cohort also favored private practice over the for-profit sector while the Hong Kong, cohort did not. The British cohort favored the non-profit sector above all the others and the for-profit sector less than the others, but showed no difference in interest in government work and private practice. The German cohort preferred the non-profit sector and occupational social work to the for-profit and government sectors, and the for-profit sector over the government sector, which they favored least. The Hungarian cohort, like the British, rated the non-profit sector above all the others; and, like the German cohort, rated the government sector lower than all the others; they showed no differences in their interest in the for profit and private practice sectors.

Between-Cohort Differences

A one-way MANOVA was performed to examine the differences in the willingness of the students in the seven countries to work in the various sectors. The analysis showed significant between cohort differences, $F(24,2348) = 15.99; p < .001$. Univariate ANOVAs were performed to examine the sources of the differences. Table 2 presents the Univariate ANOVA and the effect sizes results.

As can be seen, significant between cohort differences were found in willingness to work in all four sectors. However, the effect size was small in all except the for-profit sector, where it was moderate. Scheffe paired comparison tests were conducted to identify the sources of the differences. With regard to the government sector, the findings revealed a difference between the German cohort and all the others, with the German cohort being less interested in working in this sector. With regard to the non-profit sector, the test revealed a significant difference between the American cohort, on the one hand, and the British, Hong Kong, and Hungarian cohorts, on the other, with the American cohort being less interested in working in this sector. With regard to private practice, the findings showed significant differences between the Australian and Hong Kong cohorts, which were less interested in working in this sector, and the Hungarian, Israeli, and American cohorts, which were more interested. With regard to the for-profit sector, several significant differences were found. The Israeli cohort was significantly more interested in employment in this sector than all the other cohorts except the Hungarian. The Hungarian cohort was more interested in working in this sector than the cohorts from Australia, Britain, Hong Kong, and Germany. The American cohort, which was as interested as the Hungarian in working in this sector, was more interested in working in it than the Australian and British cohorts. The German cohort was more interested in working in this sector than the Australian.

Our next step was to examine whether the interest in working in the various sectors was related to the respondents' gender and age and whether the inter-group differences were related to the statistically significant inter-group differences in these two socio-demographic variables. The 7×2 (nation $\times$ gender) MANOVA that was carried out to this end showed no significant difference in males' and females' interest in working in the various sectors:

TABLE 2. Willingness to Work with Different Age Groups–Between Cohorts Differences: Means, SD and F Values, and Results of Sheffe Tests (N = 594)

Students from	Governmental M SD	Non Profit M SD	For Profit M SD	Private Practice M SD
Australia (N = 59)	3.54 1.16	3.79 1.07	2.11 1.08	2.45 1.38
Britain (N = 62)	3.46 1.12	4.01 .94	2.41 1.11	3.19 1.32
Germany (N = 127)	2.36 1.30	3.55 1.28	2.90 1.27	3.69[1] 1.18
Hong Kong (N = 42)	3.88 1.13	4.00 .79	2.78 1.07	2.50 .99
Hungary (N = 92)	3.10 1.23	4.07 1.01	3.71 1.05	3.52 1.41
Israel (N = 135)	3.80 .98	3.81 1.07	4.05 .92	3.77 1.22
USA (N = 77)	3.44 1.28	3.26 1.20	3.33 1.08	3.55 1.14
F	20.16***	5.60***	34.81***	12.97***
Scheffe [2]	G<A,B,HK, H, I, U	U<B, HK, H	A,B,HK,G,U<I A,B,HK,G<H A,B<U; A<G	A,HK<H, I,G,U,
Eta^2 (Effect size)	.17	.05	.26	.12

*p < .05 **p < .01 ***p < .001

[1]Due to a translation problem, "private practice" was translated into "occupational social work."

[2] A = Australia, B = Britain, G = Germany, HK = Hong Kong, H = Hungary, I = Israel, U = USA

$F(4,577) = 1.17$; $p > .05$. Nor was any significant interaction found between national cohort and gender: $F(24,2320) = 1.22$; $p > .05$. The inter-cohort difference remained significant, though was somewhat narrowed: $F(24,2320) = 9.72$; $p < .001$.

To examine whether the differences in the cohorts' willingness to work in the various sectors stemmed from the age differences of the cohorts a MANCOVA with age as the covariate was performed. The analysis showed very similar between-cohort differences ($F(24,2344) = 15.40$; $p < .001$) to those found in the MANOVA without the age covariate.

DISCUSSION

The major finding of this study was that the voluntary non-profit sector was first in the order of preferences either alone or alone with another sector in five of the countries, regardless of the structuring of their welfare economy. In the United States and Israel, where there were no within-cohort differences in interest, this sector was on par with all the others. Conversely in none of the countries did either of the for-profit sectors, firms or private practice, stand at the pinnacle of the hierarchy. The only exception to this was the German cohort that preferred occupational social work in firms.

The large degree of support for employment in the non-profit sector on the part of social work graduates is, at first sight, quite remarkable particularly given the fact that it holds true both for countries in which this sector plays a dominant role in the welfare economy and for those (Britain and Australia) identified as "state-dominant type" countries. Nevertheless, this finding does not necessarily contradict the assumption that employment prospects of social work graduates have a major impact on their preferences. While this is clearly the case for nations identified as "non-profit type" or "transitional type" countries (Germany, Hong Kong, and Hungary), it may also have a certain degree of resonance for the "state-dominant type" countries. Though most social workers in Australia and Britain are indeed employed in the state sector, non-profits are playing an increasingly important role in the provision, though not necessarily, management of social services (Franklin & Eu, 1996; Kendall & Knapp, 1996). Thus while graduates in these countries still view the state sector as a preferred employment sector, they may see the non-profit sector as offering growing job opportunities in the future.

However, the allure of the non-profit sector may also be linked to the values and aspirations of the graduates. One explanation for the well-documented increase in the role of non-profits in welfare across the globe in recent decades (Salamon, Anheier, & Associates, 1999) is that they are commonly associated with notions of a civil society or the "public space" and are seen to provide a more enlightened alternative to the dominance of the state or the market (Evers, 1995). Seemingly untainted by the bureaucratic alienation and inefficiency of state services or by the uncaring profit making orientation of the firm, the non-profit sector is seen as offering a third option, one characterized by voluntarism (Billis & Glennerster, 1998). Non-profits are often assumed to be motivated by a social vision that does not maintain the unjust social order or that is seconded to an overwhelming desire to increase the profits of service providers, but rather one that is committed to achieving social change that will serve the needs of the marginalized within the community (Najam, 1996). Clearly these sentiments sit well with the traditional values of the social work profession.

An expressed preference for employment in the voluntary non-profit sector may then be construed as representing more than just a realistic assessment of employment possibilities but also reflect graduates' quest for work that will enable them to serve the interests of clients and engage in social action in a dynamic and more prestigious setting while releasing them from the hamstrings of low status employment in a rigid, unrewarding, state bureaucracy (Alcock & Christensen, 1995; Jordan & Jones, 1995; Korazim-Korosy, 2000). Thus this sector may be seen to offer the students the type of intrinsic rewards that have been found to influence both job recruitment and job satisfaction among human service workers (Blankertz & Robinson, 1997; Haj-Yahia, Bargal, & Guterman, 2000; Jayaratne & Chess, 1984). This is particularly the case in countries in which there is no major role or legitimacy for private practice employment in a for-profit sector that is commonly associated with an undermining of social work's crucial commitment to the needy and thus is not perceived as a viable option for most graduates. In such cases, the only conceivable alternative to state employment is the non-profit agency.

These two explanations can also help to make sense of the lack of any clear-cut preference on the part of graduates in the "multiple-sector type" welfare economies of the United States and Israel. While non-profits do play an important role in the welfare economies of these countries and are indeed perceived as a potential employment possibility by students, these nations are unique in the major role played by for-profit firms engaged in welfare provision, in the proliferation of social workers providing therapy in the framework of private practice, and in the legitimacy that they enjoy within the social work profession. Thus non-profits are only one of a number of conceivable options for employment, and they do not necessarily have intrinsic advantages over other employment possibilities. As a result, it is not particularly surprising that the findings in these two countries diverge from the dominant trend identified in this study.

Any conclusions drawn from these research findings and attempts to generalize from them must be treated with caution. The data are based on surveys of students in a single university in each country (with the exception of Hungary in which three universities were included). Thus, the study cannot claim that the students included in this study are necessarily representative of the entire social work student population in the various countries. Nevertheless, the findings are intriguing in that they both provide some support for claims as to the impact of specific institutional settings on cultural divergences with social work and the perceptions of graduates of the profession's education process while, at the same time, they also underscore the attraction of the non-profit voluntary sector for social work graduates regardless of national institutional setting. Clearly, a better understanding of the factors that lead to a preference for the non-profit sector requires further studies that will focus specifically on this issue. Recent years have witnessed not only an upsurge in the role of non-profits across the globe but also a concomitant growth in scholarly efforts to understand its causes and implications. Though social welfare is a major sector of non-profit activity, the implications of this for the social work profession have not received adequate attention. The findings of this study clearly indicate that this issue should be on the profession's agenda.

NOTE

1. The study originally included ten countries, but two were removed because there were fewer than 40 participants in each, and one, Brazil, was removed because of a mistranslation of a key variable.

REFERENCES

Abell, N., & McDonell, J.R. (1990). Preparing for practice: Motivations, expectations and aspirations of the MSW class of 1990. *Journal of Social Work Education, 26*, 57-64.

Alcock, P., & Christensen, L. (1995). In and against the state: Community-based organizations in Britain and Denmark in the 1990s. *Community Development Journal, 3:2*, 110-120.

Aviram, U., & Katan, J. (1991). Professional preferences of social workers: Prestige scales of populations, services and methods in social work. *International Social Work, 34*, 37-55.

Billis, D., & Glennerster, H. (1998). Human services and the voluntary sector: Towards a theory of comparative advantage. *Journal of Social Policy, 27:1*, 79-98.

Blankertz, L.E., & Robinson, S.E. (1997). Recruitment and retention of psychosocial rehabilitation workers. *Administration and Policy in Mental Health, 24:3*, 221-234.

Bogo, M., Raphael, D., & Roberts, R. (1993). Interests, activities, and self-identification among social work students: Towards a definition of social work identity. *Journal of Social Work Education, 29*, 279-292.

Bogo, M., Michalski, J.H., Raphael, D., & Roberts R. (1995). Practice interests and self-identification among social work students: Changes over the course of graduate social work education. *Journal of Social Work Education, 31*, 228-246.

Brauns, H.J., & Kramer, D. (1986). *Social work education in Europe: A comprehensive description of social work education in 21 European countries.* Frankfurt-am-Main: Eigenverlag des Deutschen Vereins fur offentliche und private Fursorge.

Burke, A.C., & Rafferty, J.A. (1994). Ownership differences in the provision of outpatient substance abuse services. *Administration in Social Work, 18:3*, 59-91.

Butler, A.C. (1990). A reevaluation of social work students' career interests. *Journal of Social Work Education, 26*, 45-56.

Butler, A.C. (1992). The attractions of private practice. *Journal of Social Work Education, 28,* 47-60.

Chung, W.S., Fitzpatrick, S., & Pardeck, J.T. (1995). Private and nonprofit practitioners: An exploratory study. *Social Work & Social Sciences Review, 6*(2), 98-106.

Darvas, A., & Hegyesi, G. (in press). Hungary. In Weiss, I., Gal, J., & Dixon, J. (Eds.). *Professional ideologies and preferences in social work: A global study.* Westport, CT: Auburn House.

Dixon, J., & Hyde, M. (2002). Globalization, poverty, ideology and the privatization of social protection in western Europe: Welfare retrenchment or social citizenship? *New Global Development, 18,* 1-2, 3-19.

Evers, A. (1995). Part of the welfare mix: The third sector as an intermediate area. *Voluntas, 6:2,* 159-182.

Franklin, J.A., & Eu, K. Comparative employment opportunities for social workers. *Australian Social Work, 49:1,* 11-18.

Haj-Yahia, M., Bargal, D., & Guterman, N.B. (2000). Perception of job satisfaction, service effectiveness and burnout among Arab social workers in Israel. *International Journal of Social Welfare, 9,* 201-210.

Hasenfeld, Y. (2000). Social services and Welfare-to-Work: Prospects for the Social Work Profession. *Administration in Social Work, 23*(3/4), 185-199.

Ife, J. (1997). Australia. In N.S. Mayadas, T.D. Watts, & D. Elliott (Eds.). *International handbook on social work theory and practice* (pp. 383-410). Westport, Connecticut: Greenwood.

Jayarante, S., & Chess, W.A. (1984). Job satisfaction, burnout, and turnover: A national study. *Social Work, 31,* 53-59.

Jordan, B., & Jones, M. (1995). Association and exclusion in the organization of social care. *Social Work and Social Sciences Review, 6:1,* 5-18.

Kendall, J., & Knapp, M. (1996). *The voluntary sector in the United Kingdom.* Manchester: Manchester University Press.

Klug, W. (2001). Social work the Third Sector: The example of the German welfare state. In A.Adams, P. Erath, & S.M. Shardlow (eds.), *Key themes in European Social Work* (69-76). Lyme Regis: Russell House.

Korazim-Korosy, Y. (2000). Towards a new balance between governmental and non-governmental community work. *Community Development Journal, 35:3,* 276-289.

Kramer, D., Landwehr, R., & Kolleck, B. (in press). Germany. In Weiss, I., Gal, J., & Dixon, J. (Eds.). *Professional ideologies and preferences in social work: A global study.* Westport, CT: Auburn House.

Krashinsky, M. (1998). Does auspice matter? The case of day care for children in Canada. In W.W. Powell, & E.S. Clemens (eds.), *Private action and public good* (114-123). New Haven: Yale University Press.

Kuti, É. (1997). Hungary. In L.M. Salamon, & H.K. Anheier (eds.), *Defining the Nonprofit Sector* (471-492). Manchester: Manchester University Press.

Lam, C.W., & Chan, C.L.W. (in press). Hong Kong. In Weiss, I., Gal, J., & Dixon, J. (eds.), *Professional ideologies and preferences in social work: A global study.* Westport: Auburn House.

Lee, P.C. (1992). Social work in Hong-Kong, Singapore, South Korea, and Taiwan: Asia's four little dragons. In M.C. Hokenstad, S.K. Khinduka, & J. Midgley, (Eds.) *Profiles in international social work* (pp. 99-114). Washington, DC: NASW.

Leighninger, L., & Midgley, J. (1997). United State of America. In N.S. Mayadas, T.D. Watts, & D. Elliott (Eds.). *International handbook on social work theory and practice* (pp. 9-28). Westport, Connecticut: Greenwood.

Lymbery, M. (2001). Social work at the crossroads. *British Journal of Social Work, 31:3*, 369-384.

Martin, E.W. (1996). An update on census data: Good news for social work. *Australian Social Work, 49:2*, 29-36.

Masi, A.D. (1992). Should social workers work for for-profit firms? Yes. In E. Gambrill, & R. Pruger, (Eds.) *Controversial issues in social work* (pp. 28-30). Boston: Allyn and Bacon.

McDonald, C., Harris, J., & Wintersteen, R. (2003). Contingent on context? Social work and the state in Australia, Britain and the USA. *British Journal of Social Work, 33*, 191-208.

Najam, A. (1996). Understanding the third sector: Revisiting the prince, the merchant, and the citizen. *Nonprofit Management & Leadership, 7:2*, 203-219.

Payne, M. (1997). United Kingdom. In N.S. Mayadas, T.D. Watts, & D. Elliott (Eds.). *International handbook on social work theory and practice* (pp. 161-183). Westport, Connecticut: Greenwood.

Perry, R. (2001). The classification, intercorrelation and dynamic nature of MSW student practice preferences. *Journal of Social Work Education, 37*, 523-542.

Prince, J., & Austin, M.J. (2001). Innovative programs and practices emerging from the implementation of welfare reform: A cross-case analysis. *Journal of Community Practice, 9:3*, 1-14.

Reisch, M. (1992). Should social workers work for for-profit firms? No. In E. Gambrill, & R. Pruger (Eds.) *Controversial issues in social work* (pp. 30-37). Boston: Allyn and Bacon.

Richey, C., & Stevens, G. (1992). Is private practice a proper form of social work?–No. In E. Gambrill, & R. Pruger (Eds.) *Controversial issues in social work* (pp. 231-238). Boston: Allyn and Bacon.

Rubin, A., & Johnson, P.J. (1984). Direct practice interests of entering MSW students. *Journal of Education for Social Work, 20(1)*, 5-16.

Rubin, A., Johnson, P.J., & DeWeaver, K.L. (1986). Direct practice interests of MSW students: Changes from entry to graduation. *Journal of Social Work Education, 22(2)*, 98-108.

Salamon, L.M., Anheier, H.K., & Associates. (1999). Comparative overview. In L.M. Salamon, H.K. Anheier, R. List, S. Toepler, S.W. Sokolowski, & Associates, *Global civil society* (pp. 1-40). Baltimore, MD: The Johns Hopkins Center for Civil Society Studies.

Schmid, H. (1993). Non-profit and for-profit organizations in home care services: A comparative analysis. *Home Health Care Services Quarterly, 14:1*, 93-112.

Specht, H., & Courtney, M. (1994). *Unfaithful angels: How social work has abandoned its mission.* New York: Free Press.

Spiro, S., Sherer, M., Korin-Langer, N., & Weiss, I. (1997). Israel. In N.S. Mayadas, T.D. Watts, & D. Elliott (Eds.). *International handbook on social work theory and practice* (pp. 223-244). Westport, Connecticut: Greenwood.

Wakefield, J.C. (1992). Is private practice a proper form of social work? Yes. In E. Gambrill, & R. Pruger (Eds.) *Controversial issues in social work* (pp. 222-230). Boston: Allyn and Bacon.

Weisbrod, B.A. (1997). The future of the nonprofit sector: It entwining with private enterprise and government. *Journal of Policy Analysis and Management, 6:4*, 541-555.

Weiss, I., Gal, J., & Cnaan, R.A. (in press). Social work education as professional socialization: A study of the impact of social work education upon students' professional preferences. *Journal of Social Service Research.*

Weiss, I., Gal, J., & Dixon, J. (Eds.). *Professional ideologies and preferences in social work: A global study.* Westport, CT: Auburn House.

Index

Workforce Boards, 93,117
Workplace philanthropy, 31
WorldCom, 142
World Trade Center, 149

Yale University, 8
Youth Services, 54